CU00916935

Meister Eckhart: Master of Mystics

For the members of the Eckhart Society

In memory of Ursula Fleming, Dom Sylvester Houédard, Peter Talbot Willcox, and Yvonne Young

Meister Eckhart:
Master of Mystics

Richard J. Woods, O.P.

continuum

Continuum International Publishing Group
The Tower Building, 11 York Road, London SE1 7NX
80 Maiden Lane, Suite 704, New York NY 10038

www.continuumbooks.com

© Richard Woods, 2011

All rights reserved. No part of this publication may be reproduced or transmitted in any form or by any means, electronic or mechanical, including photocopying, recording, or any information storage or retrieval system, without prior permission in writing from the publishers.

First published 2011.

British Library Cataloguing-in-Publication Data
A catalogue record for this book is available from the British Library.

ISBN: 978–1441–13442–4

Designed and typeset by Kenneth Burnley with Caroline Waldron, Wirral, Cheshire
Printed and bound in India by Replika Press Pvt Ltd

Contents

Preface

Richard Woods, my brother and friend, first infected me with his enthusiasm for Meister Eckhart 25 years ago with his first book on Eckhart, *Eckhart's Way*. I am delighted that he is celebrating the 750th anniversary of the Master's birth with this wonderful book of essays. A collection of essays can be rather a rag-bag, but this book has an unusual coherence and brings into clear focus how Eckhart is both rooted in the tradition and yet startlingly original. He is of his time and yet contemporary.

If, like me, you are not an Eckhart scholar, then you might be a little nervous of tackling a book on this 'Master Mystic'. Will I have to struggle with complex theological concepts and an impossibly demanding way of life, suitable only for a spiritual élite? It is true that Eckhart can be difficult and paradoxical. We are invited to let go of all our conceptions of God, to go into the silent wilderness of the Godhead. His down-to-earth expressions shocked and startled his hearers, rather like a Zen Buddhist teacher: 'I pray to God to rid me of God.'[1] This may have been one reason why some of his propositions were condemned towards the end of his life.

Richard Woods, however, shows that Eckhart was anything but élitist. He was highly suspicious of any spiritual techniques to get hold of God. If someone seeks God's will, then 'it is well with him and he need only lead an ordinary Christian life without considering doing anything special'.[2] Any attempt to trap God with our little practices, our pet devotions, is a sort of betrayal: 'If indeed a man thinks he will get more of God by meditation, by devotion, by ecstasies or by special infusion of grace than by the fireside or in the stable – that is nothing but taking God, wrapping a cloak around his head and shoving Him under a bench.'[3] He insists that the demands of charity always override those of prayer. If you are wrapped up in an ecstatic experience and hear that a hungry person is at the door, leave behind your rapture and go and prepare some soup for him! He combines an insistence on the utter unknowability of God, beyond every thought and image, with a sense of God's tenderness and intimacy. He writes: 'God is so besotted in His love for us, it is just as if He had forgotten heaven and earth and all His Blessedness and all his Godhead and had no business except with me alone, to give me everything for my comforting.'[4] He is both a brilliant theologian and God's close friend.

Richard Woods succeeds in showing that Eckhart is unexpectedly, at least for me, helpful in the face of many contemporary issues, such as the equality of women. He has a profound sense of the equality of all human beings. Woods writes, 'Eckhart frequently exalts equality, particularly the identity of all human persons because of their common nature, which was redeemed and divinised by the Incarnation.'

Despite living within a male-dominated Church and society, Eckhart was deeply influenced by many women writers, especially Hildegard of Bingen, Mechthild of Magdeburg and Marguerite of Porete. He seems to have taken a healthy pleasure in the company of women. Responsibility for the formation of contemplative nuns was a large part of his life.

This easy friendship between the sexes is characteristic of the Dominican tradition. Dominic's first community was for women, at Prouilhe in the south of France. When he was dying he confessed to preferring to talk to young women rather than being talked at by old women! There is the beautiful friendship between Jordan of Saxony and Diana, between Eckhart's disciple Henry Suso and Elsbet Stagel, and between St Catherine of Siena and Raymond of Capua. Thomas said that grace perfects nature, and God's grace blessed these natural friendships with people of the opposite sex.

Another major contemporary concern is with ecology. Has Eckhart anything to say on this? Some people have seen Eckhart as being so wrapped up in God that he had little interest in creation. As a man deeply influenced by Neoplatonism, he was unconcerned with the diversity and multiplicity of creatures, but Woods shows that Eckhart did have a sense of God's presence in everything. Again, there is that typical Dominican insistence on the goodness of creation: 'Someone who knows nothing but creatures would never need to attend to any sermons, for every creature is full of God and is a book.'[5] God is close to everything that exists, otherwise it would not exist. God is present 'in a stone or a log of wood only they do not know it'.[6] What is extraordinary about human beings is not that we are closer to God, but because we may be aware of God at the core of our being.

For me, the most moving chapter is the one in which Woods looks at Eckhart's treatment of suffering, always the hardest topic of all. How we cope with pain and suffering is influenced by how they are understood in a particular society. Some medieval Christians appear to have had an almost masochistic obsession with pain. This is not true of Eckhart who believed that it should never be deliberately sought, but if it comes our way, then we can live with it as part of a God-given life. Richard acknowledges his debt to our mutual friend Ursula Fleming, who taught so many people how to cope with cancer through what she learnt from Eckhart. She showed us how to refuse 'to allow pain to dominate consciousness but to isolate it, accept it, and thus reduce its impact and monopolization of attention'. Eckhart teaches that God would never let anyone suffer except to save that person from further suffering. This is perhaps harder to believe after the Holocaust, but is still a fruitful way of coping with pain in our own lives, as Ursula showed when she had to face her own death from cancer.

Finally, Eckhart can help us face another of the most urgent challenges of our time – the relationship between different faiths, which is today the source of so much suffering and violence in almost every continent. He exemplifies how we can learn from each other. Fidelity to one's own tradition need not close one off from the riches of another. Woods shows how Eckhart was steeped in Jewish and Muslim writers such as Maimonides, Avicenna, Averroes, Ibn'al-Arabi, al-Farabi and many others. They taught him the utter transcendence of God. This challenges the common idea of the Middle Ages as a time of blind religious bigotry. We see a community in which the followers of different faiths were attentive to what they might learn from each other. This is an encouraging example for us today.

So Master Woods' Meister is not a musty mystic, but a Dominican brother who is touched by the mystery of God but rooted in his skin, at ease with women, intellectually adventurous, startlingly direct, and sometimes even, believe it or not, amusing.

TIMOTHY RADCLIFFE, O.P.

Notes

1. Sermon 52 (Walshe No. 87, Vol. II, p. 274).
2. Sermon 62 (Walshe No. 55, Vol. II, p. 76 RW 6).
3. Sermon 5b (Walshe No. 13b, Vol. I, p. 118).
4. Sermon 79 (Walshe No. 91, Vol. II, p. 307.
5. Sermon 9 (Walshe No. 67, Vol. II, p. 115)
6. Sermon 68 (Walshe No. 69, Vol. II, pp. 165)

Foreword

For some time, at the request of a number of readers, I have wanted to collect and update various articles and lectures I have given on Meister Eckhart into a single volume as a follow-up to my older introductory work, *Eckhart's Way* (1986), which was published in a revised edition by Veritas Publications, Dublin, in 2009.

The year 2010 marks the 750th anniversary of the birth of Meister Eckhart as generally accepted by modern scholars. The exact date and place of both his birth and death remain unknown, although it is now thought by a number of historians that he died on 28 January 1328, following a tradition observed in some German priories of the Dominican Order a century later.[1] I 'discovered' Meister Eckhart 656 years later.

Eckhart and I

Although I had a keen interest in the great Christian mystics from my college days, particularly St Teresa of Ávila and St John of the Cross, Raymond Blakney's 1941 volume on Meister Eckhart[2] occupied a niche on my 'Dominican' shelf for many years before I began a serious exploration of the teachings of the great German mystic, philosopher and theologian. I occasionally peered into it the way a small boy might look down a deep well, but my principal concern had turned by then to the fourteenth-century English mystics, especially the teachings of the *Cloud* author and the *Revelations* of Julian of Norwich.

In 1974 I included a controversial article by Matthew Fox, 'Meister Eckhart and Karl Marx', in a special issue of the journal *Listening* which I had edited.[3] But it was not until 1984, when I was invited by Michael Glazier to contribute a volume on Eckhart to a series he had in mind on 'The Way of the Mystics', that Eckhart's life and teaching began to occupy a central focus in my own life and work. At first I tried to put Michael off, suggesting other names; but the charming Irishman was insistent, and so I turned not to Blakney, but to the superb new translation of the German works by Maurice O'Connell Walshe then coming out of England. Happily, the Paulist Press had recently published a selection of Eckhart's sermons and treatises edited by Bernard McGinn and Edmund Colledge.[4] Most of the still-incomplete but critical Kohlhammer edition of the German and Latin works was also available to me at the libraries at Loyola University, Chicago, and Blackfriars, Oxford. I also began reading widely in critical articles, discovering among them the deep and insightful works of Alois Haas, Alain de Libera, Reiner Schürmann and, above all, Bernard McGinn.

But it was Eckhart's own teaching that began to enchant me. Although warned by traditional Thomists that the Meister had suspicious Neo-platonic leanings, I was intrigued by the charm and complexity of his sermons in particular. Philosophical and theological content is certainly not absent from them, but it is less prominent than his spiritual doctrine. However, the problem of distilling a manageable compendium of his mystical teaching was compounded by the fact that Eckhart left no general, much less systematic, overview of his understanding of the spiritual life. Nor was there even much scholarly consensus regarding the chronology of many of his most important works.

So, aided by a fairly sophisticated word processor for the period, I began the long process of identifying themes in each sermon and every other written source I could find, according to the frequency with which Eckhart (and Eckhart scholars) mentioned them, and painstakingly entering the pericopes containing them into a database. By the time I had gone through the German and Latin works and Walshe's new English translation, I was holding the Chair of Philosophy and Theology at the College of St Thomas in St Paul, Minnesota; it was 1985 and the deadline for the manuscript was threateningly close.

Everything came together one early spring evening when I pasted the last citation in the database and entered the command for my trusty (but long since extinct) Dictaphone System 6000 to arrange them into an order determined by topic. It took over six hours just to process the data. I began reading around 11 p.m., and continued, spellbound, for over four hours. I had begun to see at least the thematic rudiments of Eckhart's spiritual doctrine, if not the shape of the man's mind itself. It was coherent and incredibly beautiful. My classes the next morning surely were not, but the structure of my book, *Eckhart's Way*, had found its outline and content.[5]

Since those days, my interest in Eckhart has not diminished, but it has developed in ways I had not foreseen. My research and teaching at Oxford brought me into contact with Mrs Ursula Fleming, one of the most unforgettable women I have ever met. Herself a follower of Eckhart's way for many years, Ursula spearheaded the effort of the Dominican Order to petition the Holy See for an exoneration of the Meister, whose condemnation in a papal bull of 1329 had long since been seriously questioned by reputable scholars. Her work bore fruit with the study initially approved by the Chapter of Walberberg in 1980, commissioned by the Master of the Order in 1986, and the subsequent submission of appeal to the Congregation for the Doctrine of the Faith in 1992.

While Eckhart's formal exoneration has not yet occurred, that may be moot at this point. In an audience of September 1985 (quoted in *L'Osservatore Romano*, 28 October 1985) Pope John Paul II remarked, 'Did not Eckhart teach his disciples: "All that God asks you most pressingly is to go out of yourself . . . and let God be God in you?" One could think that in separating himself from creatures, the mystic leaves his brothers, humanity, behind. The same Eckhart affirms that, on the contrary, the mystic is marvellously present to them on the only level where he can truly reach them, that is, in God.' Such public papal recognition presumes doctrinal orthodoxy.[6]

Hardly content to wait around for commissions to report, Ursula went on to found the Eckhart Society in 1987. As the first chairperson of the Society, Ursula invited me to become a trustee and I willingly accepted. After her sadly premature death in March 1992, just as the Master of the Order was submitting the petition for Eckhart's exoneration, the Society continued to flourish and grow under the care of my good friend Peter Talbot Willcox and, following Peter's sudden death in 2000, that of Fr John Orme Mills, O.P. Eventually and surprisingly, in 2005 the mantle fell on my shoulders, a cloak of responsibility I all too happily shared with Ashley Young, for many years the patient shepherd and resourceful general secretary of the Society.

The following essays on Eckhart have been edited into book form from a number of articles, talks and conferences I have given on Eckhart over the last fifteen years. As presented here, they are not overly technical, but they go beyond (and I hope supplement) the basic outline of his thought given in *Eckhart's Way*. For anyone interested in a very useful introductory guide to the Meister, let me also recommend the recent volume by my colleague, confrère and friend, Michael Demkovich, O.P., *Introducing Meister*

Eckhart.[7] For those looking for a technically precise presentation and penetrating analysis of Eckhart's doctrine, none finer can be found at present than Bernard McGinn's *The Mystical Thought of Meister Eckhart.*[8]

After an introductory chapter on Eckhart's life and then rudiments of his doctrine, I have organized the material into chapters based on important aspects of Eckhart's spiritual teaching: his debt to the great women mystics of the preceding period, his intellectual resources, the 'Wayless Way' he promoted, his notion of 'detachment for commitment', prayer and the art of contemplation, suffering and healing, Eckhart's 'wider ecumenism', and essays about Eckhart's approach to the natural world and the world of art. I have also included a chapter on Eckhart's Christology, an element of his theological doctrine often overlooked.

It is my fond hope that the present ruminations will increase interest and appreciation of one of the greatest spiritual masters of Western history, 'the man from whom God hid nothing', as it was early said of him.[9]

RICHARD WOODS, O.P.

Abbreviations

DW   *Deutschen Werke*, the Kohlhammer edition of Eckhart's German works.

LW   *Lateinischen Werke*, the Kohlhammer edition of Eckhart's Latin works.

DP   *Deutschen Predigten*, Quint's 1955 modern German edition of authentic sermons and treatises.

Pf   The Pfeiffer edition of Eckhart's works (1857).

Unless otherwise noted, English translations of Eckhart's works will be taken from the three-volume edition by Maurice O'C. Walshe (*Meister Eckhart: Sermons and Treatises*, 3 vols, London/Shaftesbury: Watkins/Element Books, 1979, 1981 and 1985), from which I was graciously granted permission to quote. However, individual sermons will be cited according to their numbers in the critical German edition, *Meister Eckhart: Die deutschen und lateinischen Werke*, Stuttgart and Berlin: Verlag W. Kohlhammer (1936) as well as their 'Walshe Number'. Sermons included in the modern German translation by Josef Quint, *Meister Eck-ehart: Deutsche Predigten und Traktate,* Munich: Carl Hanser (1955), will be indicated by 'DP'. For additional references, see the bibliography.

In 2009, a new and revised single-volume edition of Eckhart's German sermons and treatises was published by Crossroad, but my copy came too late for me to be able to benefit from the excellent work of Dr McGinn in updating and sometimes correcting the previous edition.[10]

Notes

1. See Bernard McGinn, *The Mystical Thought of Meister Eckhart: The Man from Whom God Hid Nothing* (New York: Crossroad, 2001), p. 33, note 102; Walter Senner, 'Meister Eckhart in Köln', in Klaus Jacobi, ed., *Meister Eckhart. Lebensstationen – Redesituationen* (Quellen und Forschungen zur Geschichte des Dominikanerordens, Neue Folge, Bd. 7), (Berlin: Akademie-Verlag, 1997), p. 233, citing Friedrich Steill, O.P., *Ephemerides Dominicano-Sacrae* of 1691.
2. Raymond Bernard Blakney, *Meister Eckhart: A Modern Translation* (New York: Harper and Row, 1941).
3. Matthew Fox, O.P., 'Meister Eckhart and Karl Marx', in 'Heterodoxy', *Listening,* 1974.
4. Edmund Colledge, O.S.A. and Bernard McGinn, trans. and eds, *Meister Eckhart: The Essential Sermons, Commentaries, Treatises and Defense* (New York: Paulist Press, 1981).
5. Wilmington, DE: Michael Glazier, Inc. (London: Darton, Longman & Todd, 1987). Published by Liturgical Press, Collegeville, MN, after 1990, revised and published in 2009 by Veritas Publications, Dublin.
6. Cited by Ursula Fleming in *Meister Eckhart: The Man from Whom God Hid Nothing* (London: Collins Fount, 1988), p. xix. See also Édouard-Henri Wéber, O.P., 'À propos de Maître Eckhart et de son procès', *Mémoire Dominicaine,* N. 2 (Printemps 1993), pp. 135–7.
7. Ottawa: Novalis, 2005 and Ligouri, MO: Triumph/Ligouri, 2006.
8. See also Bernard McGinn, *The Harvest of Mysticism in Medieval Germany* (Volume 4 of *The Presence of God*), (New York: Crossroad Publishing Company, 2005).
9. '. . . *Meister Eckehart, dem got nie niht verbarc*'. From the title of the still critically unedited 'Sayings', a collection of aphorisms attributed to Eckhart. See Franz Pfeiffer, ed., *Meister Eckhart* (Göttingen: Vandenhoeck and Ruprecht, 1924 edn), p. 597.
10. *The Complete Mystical Works of Meister Eckhart,* trans. by Maurice O'C. Walshe, intro. by Bernard McGinn (New York: Crossroad Publishing Company, 2009).

Chapter 1

A Mystic Under Fire:
The Life and Legacy of Meister Eckhart[1]

The Chronicles of the Dominican Order omit the scandalous events between 1326 and 1329 that ended the career of one of the most illustrious friars of the late thirteenth century and one of the great masters of Christian spirituality. A veil of official silence appears to have descended over the whole episode, although in fact it was hardly ignored or forgotten.

On 27 March 1329, fifteen propositions cited (inexactly) from the sermons and writings of Eckhart von Hochheim were condemned by the papal bull *In agro Dominico*.[2] Two more propositions were similarly condemned, but were said (incorrectly, as it happens) not to be Eckhart's. Eleven others were denounced as 'evil-sounding, rash, and suspect of heresy'. Eckhart was censured, moreover, for having led 'the uneducated crowd' into error by his preaching and teaching. The bull of Pope John XXII acknowledged, however, that Eckhart had retracted any statements that could generate heretical opinions in the minds of the faithful, and likewise indicated that the old friar had already died. What the bull glides over is the fact that Eckhart consistently denied ever having taught heresy, a judgement sustained today by scores of theologians and historians.

How, one cannot help but wonder, could a pre-eminent theologian and philosopher, twice regent master at the University of Paris, and one of the most trusted members of the Dominican Order, having been assigned several times to reform houses of the Order throughout Europe to provide spiritual guidance for thousands of Dominican nuns and beguines, and to preside over one of the great teaching houses of his Order, be brought to ruin in his old age for promoting heresy? We may never know all the reasons, but over the past hundred years researchers have pieced together elements of the story that point to a number of factors that led to the disaster.

A Friar's Life

Eckhart von Hochheim was born in about 1260 in a Thuringian village, possibly Tambach, in north-eastern Germany in the vicinity of Erfurt. Little is known of his family, birth or childhood, although it is now accepted by a number of scholars that he was the son of a knight of the region, also known as Eckhart of Hochheim, whose death was recorded in 1305.[3] The Dominican historian William Hinnebusch maintained that Eckhart studied as a youth in Paris under Siger of Brabant, although support for his thesis is scant.[4] Some time after he was fifteen, young Eckhart entered the Dominican novitiate at Erfurt. Having completed his preliminary studies, the promising young friar was sent, in 1280, to the famed Dominican House of Study in Cologne for further study. There he would have met its aged and saintly founder, Albert the Great. 'Bishop Albrecht' died in the autumn of that year, but Eckhart was surely taught by some of his disciples, who included later scholars and preachers such as Ulrich of Strassburg, Dietrich of Freiburg, the brothers Gerard and Johann Korngin of Sterngassen, and Berthold of Moosburg.

At that time, the Dominican *studium generale*, the precursor of the University of Cologne, was a major nodal intersection in the growing network of Rhineland mysticism, which could not have failed to impress the young friar.[5] At Cologne, Eckhart also became an ardent, if selective, follower of Thomas Aquinas, the most famous of Albert's students, who had died six years earlier. But he absorbed even more readily the ancient mystical tradition of Christian Neoplatonism favoured by several of Albert's students, particularly Dietrich of Freiburg.[6]

After finishing his studies at Cologne, Eckhart was ordained to the priesthood, probably in 1293. That year he was sent to Paris as a lecturer and to begin studies for the coveted title 'Master of Theology'. Even so, he was soon elected to a number of important positions in the Dominican Order. In 1294, he became prior of Erfurt. About the same time, he was also appointed vicar of Thuringia. Four years later, after the terms of those offices expired, Eckhart was finally able to finish his studies. In 1302, nine years after his departure for Paris, he was granted the title of '*Magister in theologia*', the highest academic honour of the age and the reason he became known as 'Meister' (Master) Eckhart – the only medieval figure still known by that title.

Eckhart was now 43, and no longer a young man even by today's standards. After a year as Regent Master for Externs at St Jacques, the

Dominican house of studies in Paris, he was elected to be the first provincial of the new Province of Saxony, which included Erfurt. Eckhart was also charged with the spiritual guidance of the Dominican nuns of the region.

Four years later, in 1307, the Provincial Chapter of Strassburg appointed Eckhart vicar of Bohemia and commissioned him to reform the houses there. Between 1309 and 1310 he founded three new communities. He was then elected provincial of the Teutonian Province. But this election was overturned by the General Chapter meeting at Naples the following year. The Meister was needed again in Paris, where once more he occupied the Chair for Externs. There, in addition to teaching, Eckhart began his great *Opus Tripartitum* ('The Three Part Work') which he intended to be his crowning academic achievement.

Eckhart was not destined to finish his projected masterwork, however. In 1313 he was recalled to Germany, where he became professor of theology, spiritual director and preacher in the exciting city of Strassburg. In 1314, he was elected prior of the Dominican house there and soon afterwards was named vicar by the Master of the Order, who once more placed Eckhart in charge of the Dominican nuns of the region.

For some time, large numbers of beguines had been entering Dominican convents. Both Dominican and Franciscan friars had also been charged with responsibility for the spiritual direction of other beguine houses which were not formally related to either order. Whole convents of other religious orders had also changed their affiliation to the Dominicans, and several new foundations were made. The friars were faced with an explosion of vocations and extensive responsibilities.

What attracted large numbers of devout, well-educated women to the Dominicans in the late thirteenth and early fourteenth centuries was, it appears, the emphasis placed on study in the order together with the mystical character of its spirituality at this time. The encounter between dynamic preachers and these God-centred women produced one of the most spectacular upsurges of mystical spirituality in the history of Europe. Eckhart, of course, was not the only Dominican, nor the only preacher influential in the formation of the mystical revolution of the fourteenth century; but he was undoubtedly the greatest.

Many of Eckhart's sermons were memorized by the nuns and later committed to writing. Despite being seized by the Archbishop's inquisitors as evidence, or perhaps even because of it, over 100 authentic German sermons and four treatises on the spiritual life have survived to the present. Several volumes of his Latin writings, mainly theological works and scriptural commentaries, have also been discovered since the mid-nineteenth century.

After several years of preaching and teaching in Strassburg and its environs, Eckhart was recalled to Cologne in 1322. But three years later, at the age of 66, he was summoned before the Inquisition of the Archbishop of Cologne, the formidable Henry of Virneburg, accused of preaching heresy. Even in an age of often violent and repressive measures, this was a shocking event. For over a year Eckhart vigorously defended himself, claiming that the charges were lodged out of jealousy by two rogue Dominicans and pursued out of ignorance. But the verdict went against him. Outraged, Eckhart reaffirmed his innocence, denounced the decision and, with the support of his superior and fellow friars, appealed to the pope. Thus, at the age of 67 or 68, Eckhart and several companions began the 500-mile walk to the papal court at Avignon to plead his case.

Once again, the process lasted for more than a year. Pope John XXII appointed a commission to adjudicate the charges of the Cologne tribunal. It was headed by Cardinal Jacques Fournier, the Cistercian abbot and future Pope Benedict XII, and included at least one Dominican cardinal, William Peter of Godin, whose mitigating hand almost surely shaped the final document. Before the end of the process, however, Eckhart died, some believe on the feast of St Thomas Aquinas, 28 January 1328, having first retracted anything that could be proved heretical in his teachings.

At the insistence of Henry of Virneburg, the Pope issued a bull of condemnation on 27 March 1329, and ordered it to be promulgated in the ecclesiastical province subject to Cologne. But its impact was far more widespread. Not only had Eckhart been the most famous preacher of his day, but he was also the first member of the Dominican order to be tried for heresy. His teachings were suppressed, his memory tainted. Many of his writings were subsequently lost or destroyed. Not even his gravesite has ever been discovered.

Why was Eckhart Condemned?

At least four factors contributed to the trials in Cologne and Avignon and the eventual issue of the bull of condemnation.[7] First, new ideas and movements had proliferated in Europe since the end of the twelfth century – philosophical innovations, dissident theological interpretations and radical political theories created an unstable and turbulent social climate. Insurrection was not uncommon. Princes such as the Archbishop of Cologne (who was an Elector of the Holy Roman Emperor as well as a bishop and prince) were keen to ferret out and destroy corrupting influences from their realms. Eckhart's daring expressions, designed to provoke his hearers into attending both to the divine presence within and to the world outside by often outrageous comparisons, puns and comic examples, seem to have particularly irritated the guardians of pious sobriety. Not only the uncompromising Archbishop of Cologne, but Cardinal Jacques Fournier who led the theological commission in Avignon, and the English Franciscan philosopher, William of Ockham, dismissed Eckhart's playful but profound assaults on conventional God-talk as mad and dangerous.

Second, the beguine movement, with which the Dominicans were intimately involved and Eckhart especially so, had fallen into ecclesiastical disfavour. In 1310, the beguine Marguerite Porete had been burned to death in Paris for heresy and disobedience, and at the Council of Vienne the following year, Pope Clement V succeeded in enacting suppressive legislation. Eckhart's apparently continuing support of the beguines would have earned him the suspicion and enmity of both the state and many bishops.

Third, envy and jealousy may well have played a role in Eckhart's misfortunes. He was a reformer within the Order and, in addition, a famous and respected preacher; in short, a prime target for disaffected friars bent on revenge. The two key witnesses against him in Cologne and Avignon, Hermann of Summo and William of Nidecken, were malcontents who were later seized and imprisoned for disobedience and treachery.[8]

Finally, inter-order rivalry between Dominicans and the Spiritual Franciscans over the issue of evangelical poverty was probably an element in Eckhart's initial prosecution. Henry of Virneburg's inquisitors were Franciscans, although the Archbishop was not. Eckhart's angry defense suggests that a more professional rather than doctrinal conflict was at stake.

For whatever reasons, a fraction (only about ten per cent) of the propositions condemned at Cologne were also reprobated in the Pope's bull, possibly as a sop to the irritable Archbishop in whose province the condemnation was promulgated. The impact, of course, had a chilling effect far beyond the reaches of the Province of Cologne. Even so, Eckhart's memory was cherished and his writings preserved, sometimes secretly, by both Dominican friars and sisters.

Nearly 600 excerpts from his commentary on St John's Gospel copied by the friars at Cologne were discovered as late as 1960 by Thomas Kaepelli.

Several Dominicans who had been Eckhart's students at Strassburg and Cologne incorporated his doctrine into their preaching and writing, principally among them Bl. Henry Seuse (Suso) and John Tauler. Thirty-two of Eckhart's sermons, fully half the total, were incorporated anonymously into a volume circulated by Dominican friars some time after Eckhart's death under the title *Paradisus animae intelligentis* (*The Paradise of the Intellectual Soul*).[9] Eckhart was also remembered with special affection by the nuns of the southern Rhineland, who had committed his sermons to memory and then to writing. His teaching likewise remained alive in the circle of spiritual associates who became known as The Friends of God, including the secular priest Henry of Nördlingen and the Strassburg merchant Rulman Merwsin. Towards the end of the century, Eckhart's doctrine appeared once more in the anonymous *Book of Spiritual Poverty* (*Das Buch von geistlicher Armuth*), for a while attributed to Tauler.[10] Within a generation, the spirit of Dominican Rhineland mysticism had even penetrated the Franciscan order and reached England, where it influenced the author of *The Cloud of Unknowing*.[11] For as the Meister had taught, 'For you to know God in God's way, your knowing must become a pure unknowing, and a forgetting of yourself and all creatures.'[12]

'The Man from Whom God Hid Nothing'[13]

There were undoubtedly many other reasons why fifteen propositions from Eckhart's sermons and treatises were condemned by papal decree, some of them political, some historical, some personal. We may never know the whole story. But whatever the force of the combined reasons for the condemnation, what has become increasingly clear over the past century is that the condemnation was unjust.

The panel of experts commissioned by the Dominican General Chapter of Walberberg agreed with most modern scholars that Eckhart was no heretic. But they also felt that a declaration made in Eckhart's favour would be appropriate and, considering the world-wide quest for authentic mystical spirituality, timely. In any case, the Meister's position as the preeminent preacher of his time and fountainhead of fourteenth-century German mysticism will remain secure. His world-wide recognition as a spiritual master as well as a philosopher and theologian of note may even be expected to grow as the final volumes of the great critical edition begun 70 years ago near completion. In the meantime, new and accurate English translations by Maurice Walshe, Bernard McGinn, Edmund Colledge,

Oliver Davies and Frank Tobin have added scholarly lustre to the popular appeal given to Eckhart in recent times.

Eckhart, even though recognized undeniably as a devout and holy man, nevertheless remains an elusive and often difficult teacher, not only because his doctrine is deep and dense. It is that, but centuries of controversy have obscured even the order in which his works were composed. Further, many of his writings were lost or destroyed. One other thing is clear, however: the difficulty Eckhart's judges had understanding his teaching contributed to his condemnation. That difficulty, in turn, rests in some measure on the fact that, as Gregory Baum once said to me, as a Dominican he had no business being the greatest dialectician of the Middle Ages. For all that, it is safe to say that Eckhart will continue to influence God-seekers today and, no doubt, for ever. Whether or not Vatican authorities 'rehabilitate' him, as happened recently in the case of Galileo Galilei, Eckhart remains *the* Meister.

Notes

1. Sections of this chapter are based on a paper originally delivered at the Conference on Christian Mysticism, held at Notre Dame University, Beirut, Lebanon, 16 May 2003 and subsequently published as 'Meister Eckhart: Preacher and Teacher', *God in Multicultural Society: Religion, Politics, and Globalization*, ed. by Edward Alam (Louaize, Lebanon: Notre Dame University Press, 2006), pp. 99–110; and 'The Condemnation of Meister Eckhart', *Spirituality*, 33, 6 (November–December 2000): 342–7.
2. The bull is contained among other important writings and sermons of Eckhart edited by Edmund Colledge and Bernard McGinn in *Meister Eckhart: The Essential Sermons, Commentaries, Treatises and Defense* (New York and London: Paulist Press/SPCK, 1981).
3. See Bernard McGinn, *The Mystical Thought of Meister Eckhart: The Man from Whom God Hid Nothing* (New York: Crossroad, 2001), p. 2, n. 8.
4. Hinnebusch mentions that Eckhart studied at Paris before entering the Dominicans, which is possible but without additional support remains conjectural. See William A. Hinnebusch, O.P., *The History of the Dominican Order*, Vol. II (Staten Island, NY: Alba House, 1973), p. 304. If true, Eckhart may have been in Paris when Bishop Stephen Tempier's condemnation of theses of both Siger and Thomas Aquinas was promulgated in 1277. Cf. Joseph Koch, *Kleine Schriften*, Vol. II (Roma: Edizioni di Storia e Letteratura, 1973), p. 254 and *The Essential Sermons*, ed. cit., p. 6.
5. Such is the general argument of Alain de Libera in his important study, *Introduction a la mystique rhénane d'Albert le Grand à Maître Eckhart* (Paris: O.E.I.L., 1984).
6. See Loris Sturlese, 'Mysticism and Theology in Meister Eckhart's Theory of the Image', *Eckhart Review* (August 1992): 18–31.

7. In addition to the articles and commentary of Bernard McGinn, see Oliver Davies, 'Why Were Eckhart's Propositions Condemned?', *New Blackfriars* 71 (1990): 433–44; and Richard Woods, 'The Condemnation of Meister Eckhart', *Spirituality*, 33, 6 (November–December 2000): 342–7.

8. See Bernard McGinn, 'Meister Eckhart's Condemnation Reconsidered', *The Thomist* 44 (1980): 392.

9. *Paradisus animae intelligentis*, Philip Strauch, ed. (Deutsche Texte des Mittelalters 30, from Oxford MS Laud Misc. 479) (Berlin: Weidmann, 1919). See McGinn, *The Harvest of Mysticism in Medieval Germany* (New York: Crossroad, 2005), pp. 97, 321–6, 613, n. 107.

10. *Das Buch von geistlicher Armuth*, H. Denifle, ed., (Munich, 1877). An English translation by J. R. Morell was published under the title *The Following of Christ* (London, 1886), and a new translation by C. F. Kelley, *The Book of the Poor in Spirit by a Friend of God*, was published in New York in 1954 by Harper.

11. On the influence of Rhineland mysticism on the *Cloud* author, see Dom David Knowles, O.S.B., *The English Mystical Tradition* (New York: Harper and Bros., 1961), p. 38.

12. Sermon 103 (Walshe No. 4, Vol. I, p. 40f; DP 59). Josef Quint doubted this sermon's authenticity (*Meister Eckehart: Deutsche Predigten und Traktate* [Munich: Carl Hanser, 1955], p. 525). But it is now generally accepted as authentic and is numbered in the critical edition edited by Georg Steer, DW IV as Predigt 103.

13. This phrase, which has become emblematic of Eckhart, was used as a title for the first of a number of 'sayings' (*Spruche*) attributed to Eckhart and are still being critically evaluated for authenticity. A number can be found in *Meister Eckhart*, ed. by Raymond Blakney (New York: Harper and Row, 1941). The collection can also be found online at http://members.wwisp.com/~srshanks/Meister_Eckhart/Sayings.html.

Chapter 2

Meister Eckhart and the Women Mystics of the Middle Ages[1]

Despite the rise and fall of modernity, many of the deeper psychological and spiritual issues underlying contemporary battles between the sexes, at least in the industrialized northern hemisphere, are largely medieval in provenance, whether matters of clerical misogyny, marital bondage or 'traditional' gender roles as a whole. The similarities between our times and that 'distant mirror', as Barbara Tuchman insightfully described it,[2] are particularly noteworthy in regard to women's issues and spirituality, particularly during the early fourteenth century.[3]

Although his sermons and treatises are remarkably lacking in contemporary references, it is clear from Eckhart's assignments and travels that as an able and trusted administrator as well as a popular preacher, spiritual director and teacher, he was keenly aware of the pressing concerns of his world, among them the rising spiritual aspirations of women, especially the congregations of devout women known as *beguines*.[4] During the late thirteenth and early fourteenth centuries, the spiritual guidance of many beguine houses was assigned to the mendicant orders, particularly the Franciscans and Dominicans.

Tantalizing similarities between aspects of Eckhart's thought and the writings of women mystics of the previous century were also noted, first in the nineteenth century by Wilhelm Preger and Heinrich Denifle, and more thoroughly investigated decades later by Herbert Grundmann and Josef Koch. Even so, the likelihood that influence, whether direct or indirect, might have been at work seems to have dawned slowly on the wider scholarly world. Only in recent times has the true extent to which Eckhart was indebted to the women mystics of the preceding generation begun to be revealed to a new generation of scholars by critical textual comparison. This is particularly the case with Hildegard of Bingen, Hadewijch of Antwerp, Mechthild of Magdeburg and, most significantly, the French beguine and martyr, Marguerite Porete.

Matters of Influence

Establishing the actual influence of these writers on Eckhart presents complex and difficult problems of textual interpretation; but a number of scholars have been intensively investigating the likelihood of such influence for over two decades now.[5] Many of their conclusions are still necessarily tentative, but several points seem to be generally accepted: it remains evident, for instance, that despite the likelihood of Eckhart's awareness of the teachings of the women mystics, his doctrine differs from theirs in important respects, as Frank Tobin has shown clearly in relation to Mechthild of Magdeburg.[6] Nevertheless, some points of similarity are too significant to be ignored or trivialized.

Among the problematic areas that emerge from a comparison of texts, one of the most glaring pertains to the diverse approaches of Eckhart and the women mystics of the earlier period with regard to the place of the body, and especially bodily penance, in the spiritual life.

Redefining embodiment and bodily ways of knowing was a crucial element in beguine spirituality and, as such, constituted metaphysical as well as practical grounds for tension with their male instructors, antagonists, counterparts and biographers. In his important study, *Hadewijch and Her Sisters: Other Ways of Loving and Knowing*,[7] John Giles Milhaven explored the ethical and epistemological implications of this theme. Milhaven identified 'bodily knowing' and 'loving mutuality' as joint themes characteristic of, but not limited to, Hadewijch and her circle. However, the employment of language rich in bodily metaphors for knowing has also provided ample matter for critics who remain committed to more 'traditional' interpretative criteria for evaluating the relationships among males and females with regard to knowing and loving, 'male' representing reason, disembodied knowledge and sufficiency; whereas 'female' stands for emotion, feeling, impulsiveness, eros and, of course, deficiency – echoes of which are present even in Porete as well as Eckhart.

Eckhart's attitude towards the body thus presents an important area of exploration in regard to the complex relationship of his teaching with beguine spirituality before his time, as well as during and after it.

The Problem of Embodiment

It is beyond cavil that Eckhart consistently taught that one of the three obstacles to union with God was human corporeality. In Sermon 12, he typically proclaimed,

There are three things that prevent us from hearing the eternal Word. The first is corporeality, the second is multiplicity, the third is temporality. If a man had transcended these three things, he would dwell in eternity, he would dwell in the spirit, he would dwell in unity and in the desert and there he would hear the eternal Word.[8]

While Amy Hollywood accurately assessed the spirit of both Eckhart's and Marguerite Porete's effort 'to subvert the association of women with the body, suffering, and Christ's suffering humanity' by means of mystical *apophasis*, she overstated the case in claiming that the Meister simply rejected bodily and ecstatic forms of spirituality. As Frank Tobin has observed, unlike Porete, Eckhart nowhere vilifies or disparages the body as wretched or corrupt.[9] Rather Eckhart recognizes the moral neutrality of the body, just as he accepts the inescapable reality of suffering without either denouncing it or endorsing it. Eckhart's goal is to direct our attention *beyond* the limits of the body, time, suffering and the ecstatic imagination.

Hollywood does not exaggerate, however, in claiming that by 'undercutting the place of asceticism, paramystical phenomena and visionary experience in the religious life, Porete and Eckhart effectively subverted the main avenues of religious authority and expression open to women in their culture'.[10] This is especially true in the case of seeking pain as a means of attaining sanctification, a view which Eckhart at least tacitly repudiated.[11]

The Quest for Parity

The effort to achieve equality among women and men featured prominently in many of the new religious movements of the Middle Ages, and not merely those of the radical sectarians. In her analysis of the letters between the fourteenth-century Dominican nuns and their spiritual advisers, Debra Stoudt cited 'insights into the divergent attempts religious women made at asserting their own spiritual identity and offering the male confessors some advice and guidance of their own'.[12] Similar examples can be cited from the lives of Mechthild of Magdeburg and Eckhart's disciple Henry Seuse (Suso), whose spiritual friendship with Elsbet Stagel created some of the finest epistolary literature of the Middle Ages.[13]

The extent to which Eckhart himself contributed to the sense of mutuality and equality among women and men, and especially in this regard the beguines and Dominican nuns with their Dominican and other spiritual advisers, is difficult to assess. In his sermons, Eckhart frequently exalts equality, particularly the identity of all human persons because of their common nature, which was redeemed and divinized by the Incarnation.[14] On the other hand, Eckhart was a man of his own era and it would be unrealistic to expect him to manifest the inclusive attitude of a twenty-first-century preacher and writer. As Grace Jantzen has pointed out, he was prone, for instance, to resort to medieval gender stereotypes when attempting to expound his admittedly metaphorical description of human spiritual abilities and activity:

. . . he matter-of-factly adopts the ubiquitous patristic and medieval identification of woman with sensuality and man with reason. At the same time, he links sensuality with sinful desire, with original sin, and with female bodiliness again, an all too familiar linkage, but all the more oppressive to women for its very familiarity.[15]

Even so, Eckhart also manifests a characteristically positive regard for women in much of the imagery used in his homilies, sidestepping many of the misogynistic minefields that disfigure the landscape of medieval literature.[16] From contemporary references, it is also clear that Eckhart and his younger confreres, Henry Seuse and John Tauler, were highly esteemed by these women. It can be reasonably argued that even the apocryphal literature associated with Eckhart, especially 'Meister Eckhart's Daughter'[17] and 'Swester Katrei',[18] indicate that Eckhart was perceived, most likely within his lifetime, as an advocate and practitioner of gender parity and reciprocity.

Hildegard and Eckhart: God and the Greenness of Creation

Of the German women mystics whose influence on Eckhart has been under study, pride of place belongs in the first instance to the Benedictine abbess Hildegard of Bingen (1098–1178), one of the most influential if often controversial figures of her age. A visionary from the age of three, she grew to maturity in the Benedictine abbey at Bermersheim, where she mastered the arts of pharmacy and music. She later demonstrated an extraordinary interest in scientific observation as well as ascending the heights of mystical contemplation. During her lifetime her counsel was sought by bishops, priests, monks, nuns and a variety of lay persons of both sexes, including princes and the Emperor Frederick

Barbarossa himself. Her replies to over 300 letters are extant, and she left for posterity a stunningly illuminated manuscript (destroyed in World War II), the *Scivias*, containing her visions and revelations. In addition, she wrote scriptural commentaries and composed hymns for the liturgical office.[19]

Hildegard's influence would extend over centuries, finding its first resonance in the major women mystics and saints of the next century, especially Mechthild of Magdeburg, Mechthild of Hackeborn and Gertrude the Great. Her influence on Eckhart may have been indirect, but it also seems at some points to be palpable. This is especially true with respect to the idea of Creation and Hildegard's favourite expression for the presence of God as life-giving spirit.

Greenness

Hildegard speaks of the Holy Spirit as having 'poured out this green freshness of life into the hearts of men and women so that they might bear good fruit'.[20] Elsewhere she said, '. . . there is nothing in creation that does not have some radiance – either greenness or seeds or flowers, or beauty – otherwise it would not be part of creation. For if God were not able to make all things, where would be his power?'[21] She continues,

> And when fulfilling the precepts of God's commandments, man, too, is the sweet and dazzling robe of Wisdom. He serves as her green garment through his good intentions and the green vigour of works adorned with virtues of many kinds. He is an ornament to her ears when he turns away from hearing evil whispers; a protection for her breast, when he rejects forbidden desires. His bravery gives glory to her arms, too, when he defends himself against sin. For all these things arise from the purity of faith . . .[22]

Eckhart may have had Hildegard's image in mind when he preached

> So Our Lord promised to feed his sheep on the mountain on green grass. All creatures are green in God. [. . .] As Augustine says: 'What God creates has a channel through the angels.' In the height all things are green: on the 'mountain-top' all things are green and new: when they descend into time they grow pale and fade. In the new 'greenness' of all creatures Our Lord will 'feed his sheep'. All creatures that are in that green and on that

height, as they exist in the angels, are more pleasing to the soul than anything in this world. As the sun is different from night, so different is the
least of creatures, as it is there from the whole world.[23]

Elsewhere he said,

> . . . not fully satisfied with this light, [the Spirit] presses right through
> the firmament and drives through heaven till it reaches that spirit that
> revolves the heavens, and from the revolution of the heavens all things
> in the world grow and green. Still the mind is not satisfied till it pierces
> to the apex, to the primal source where spirit has its origin.[24]

Oliver Davies has argued that, in citing Hildegard's characteristic use
of 'greenness' (*viriditas*) as a spiritual metaphor, Eckhart intentionally
altered its meaning, a twist which would have been obvious to anyone
familiar with her writings. This likely interpretation provides a useful
model for looking at some of the images found in Eckhart and Mechthild,
Hadewijch and Marguerite Porete.[25]

The reversal of valence with regard to *viriditas* in Eckhart's development
of desert imagery is also conveyed by Hildegard's use of *ariditas*
('dryness'), which characterizes the desert as a place of chaos and drought
deprived of beauty and blessing, rather than one of peace and stillness.
But for Eckhart the desert represents the final stage of the spiritual
journey – union with God. In Sermon 48 he describes the soul's desire to
'go into the simple ground, into the quiet desert in which distinction
never gazed, not the Father, nor the Son, nor the Holy Spirit . . .' True
blessedness is thus found 'in the soul's return to its divine ground'.[26]

Eckhart's doctrine of creation differs radically from that of Hildegard in
other respects, as it does from the teaching of Thomas Aquinas. Eckhart,
for instance, did not attribute to the act of existence any inherence in
created things, but stressed only how it flows from God towards creatures.
Thus, creatures for Eckhart have no intrinsic meaning in themselves and
lack the sacramental function Hildegard and Thomas emphasized.
According to the German *Meister*, '. . . in God there is light and being, and
in creatures there is darkness and nothingness, since what is in God is
light and being, in creatures is darkness and nothingness'.[27] For Eckhart,
consequently, 'All creatures are too base to be able to reveal God, they are
all nothing compared to God. Therefore no creature can utter a word
about God in his works.'[28]

Eckhart's most striking statement of this theme became the occasion for condemnation in Article 26 of the papal bull: 'All creatures are pure nothing. I do not say they are a trifle or they are anything: they are pure nothing. What has no being, is not.'[29]

Hadewijch and Eckhart: Dis-Covering God

In many circles today, the visionary poet Hadewijch of Antwerp is perhaps the best known of the beguines, although little information about her life can be found in her poems, letters and prose works, which are some of the first works in the Dutch vernacular.[30] Contemporary scholarship in fact points to two poets of that name who were confused for centuries. The 'first' Hadewijch lived in the middle of the thirteenth century in that part of the Netherlands still called Holland. Her writings featured in later German mysticism and especially the Flemish spirituality of Jan van Ruysbroeck and Gerard Groote. But after the fifteenth century they were not referred to until rediscovery of a number of manuscripts at the Royal Library in Brussels in 1838.[31] The 'second' Hadewijch, whose poems were added to those of the earlier figure, seems to have lived about a century later. Only fairly recent scholarship has detected the work of a hand different from that of earlier works.

The theme of ecstatic love prominent in the writings of St Bernard permeates the works of Hadewijch I and II, and through them, *Brautmystik* – the 'bridal mysticism' of loving union with God – became a major element in beguine spirituality and later forms. Oliver Davies has drawn attention to important textual parallels between Eckhart and Hildegard of Bingen as well as Mechthild and Marguerite Porete, but he has also questioned whether the Saxon Eckhart would have been able to understand Hadewijch's Netherlands dialect.[32] Saskia Murk-Jansen's linguistic analysis seems to have overcome that objection, but also raised the possibility that reciprocal influence might have been at work with respect to poems attributed to Hadewijch but most likely emanated from a later period.[33] As both Murk-Jansen and Paul Dietrich have shown, the poems of the 'later' Hadewijch resonate with some of Eckhart's most distinctive themes.

Among these are mutual love, *minne*, which means 'friendship' but also points to the erotic love favoured in the romantic literature of the time. With Hadewijch (and Eckhart), it also has theological significance: 'For with nothing the mind says can one put into words the theme of Love, which I desire and want for you. I say no more; here we are obliged to speak with our soul. Our theme is boundless; for this theme – Love – which we take, is God himself by nature.'[34]

And Eckhart said,

> We see indeed that in God there is neither wrath nor grief, but only love and joy. Even if sometimes he seems to be wrathful, against the sinner, this is not wrath but love, for it proceeds from a great divine love. Those whom he loves, he punishes, for he is love itself, which is the Holy Spirit.[35]

Nor is this an exception, as passages extolling love can be found scattered throughout Eckhart's sermons. In one of them he said with characteristic excess, 'God is so besotted in His love for us, it is just as if He had forgotten heaven and earth and all His blessedness and all his Godhead and had no business except with me alone, to give me everything for my comforting.'[36] And elsewhere, 'Nothing brings you closer to God or makes God so much your own as the sweet bond of love. A man who has found this way need seek no other. He who hangs on this hook is caught so fast that foot and hand, mouth, eyes and heart, and all that is man's, belongs only to God.'[37]

Other themes appear in the writings of Hadewijch and Eckhart which cannot prove influence one way or another, but nevertheless demonstrate a confluence of ideas and often of treatment – the abyss of God, the Birth of God within our souls, spiritual growth through stages of advancement towards union, the importance of detachment, divine–human similarity, spiritual nakedness, not-knowing (or unknowing), and the metaphor of flow and overflowing love – a motif also found in another extraordinary figure of the period, Mechthild of Magdeburg, whose Low German was much closer to Eckhart's native tongue and posed little problem of understanding.

The Divine Wilderness: Mechthild and Eckhart

Whether or not she is considered a beguine, Mechthild of Magdeburg (c. 1210–82), one of the most impressive of the thirteenth-century women mystics, was for most of her life a lay woman. She was strongly influenced by Dominican spirituality, as the first editor testifies in the preface to her remarkable book *The Flowing Light of the Godhead*, and Mechthild herself describes in some detail.[38]

Towards the end of her life, ill and growing blind, Mechthild sought refuge in the Cistercian abbey at Helfta, where she may have taken simple vows. It was at Helfta that she finished her great book of prophecies, poetry, visions, parables and letters, one so critical of the spiritual laxity she often perceived in the world around her that threats were made to burn it.

The convent at Helfta had been relocated from Rodersdorf in 1258 by its abbess, St Gertrude of Hackeborn (1232–92). Intent on promoting the contemplative life, Gertrude had made the abbey a recognized centre of mystical spirituality, attracting to it holy women such as her sister, St Mechthild of Hackeborn (1241–99) and St Gertrude the Great (1256–1302), themselves both poets and scholars.[39] The influence of Mechthild of Magdeburg on these extraordinary women was at least as profound as their effect on her. Possibly the first mystic to have experienced a vision of the heart of Jesus as the focus of divine love and human compassion, Mechthild's devotion to the Sacred Heart became especially characteristic of the Helfta nuns.

Helfta at this period was under the spiritual influence of Dominican Friars. Henry of Halle, a disciple of Albert the Great, arranged and edited Mechthild's manuscript and translated the first six parts into Latin. (It was later translated into Middle High German by the secular priest Henry of Nördlingen for Bl. Margareta Ebner and the Dominican nuns at Maria Medigen.) Mechthild's younger brother Baldwin was also a Dominican and lived in the same priory as Henry. Unfortunately, nothing has yet surfaced of Henry's own writings, nor do we possess any other information about him.

Oliver Davies has suggested a plausible connection between Mechthild of Magdeburg and Eckhart in the person of another Dominican, Dietrich of Apolda, a friar of Erfurt whose writings cite the Latin version of the *Flowing Light of the Godhead*:

Dietrich, who was born around the year 1228 and died circa 1298, was a member of Eckhart's own Dominican community at Erfurt. Moreover, his vita of Dominic is dated to the last decade of his life (1287–98), which substantially overlaps with the period during which Eckhart was Prior of the convent at Erfurt (1294–1302). It seems inconceivable that Meister Eckhart should not have known of the work of Mechthild of Magdeburg . . .[40]

Both Henry of Halle and Baldwin, who became sub-prior at Halle, would have been some years older than Eckhart, who probably entered the order at Erfurt about 1275. But if it is true that Eckhart was in Cologne by 1280, the likelihood that he would have known or at least met both older friars is considerable, and through them would have come into contact with the doctrine of the formidable old beguine, Mechthild.

In many respects the doctrine of Eckhart and Mechthild could scarcely be more dissimilar. Both their teaching and their modes of expression differ significantly. Mechthild's book is a mélange of allegory, legend, dialogue, poetry, prayers, visions and other revelations, commentary and letters. Eckhart's German and Latin works include sermons, treatises, commentaries on scripture and fragments of technical scholastic discussion. Mechthild fills her book with concrete, sometimes even erotic imagery. Fascinated with eschatology as well as the protocols of courtly love, she provides descriptive maps of purgatory, hell, along with demons and angels, suffering souls, Christ, Mary, angels and a variety of saints – all rare or absent in Eckhart. Her references to the Heart of Jesus and the near-divinity of Mary are unique.[41]

By comparison, Eckhart's doctrine and style are as spare and apophatic as Mechthild's are rich and kataphatic. Mechthild's book is also virtually devoid of the Meister's characteristic themes: the birth of the Word in the soul, detachment, the reciprocal nothingness of God and creatures, essential identity with the Son, the equality of justice, the simplicity and purity of God and the soul, the obstacles to union with God, 'breaking through', and the return of all things to God.

Some areas of overlap are detectable – themes and images, even matters of verbal similarity between the two mystical writers which are sufficiently close to suggest influence.[42] One of these is the image of the desert. For Mechthild, unlike Hildegard, the desert is a stark place of freedom and possibility, the realm of testing and proof. She writes,

> *The desert has twelve things*
> You should love nothingness.
> You should flee somethingness.
> You should stand alone
> And should go to no one.
> Seeking help from none,
> You should not be excessively busy,
> And be free from all things.

You should release captives
And subdue the free.
You should restore the sick
And yet should have nothing yourself.
You should drink the water of suffering
And ignite the fire of love with the kindling of virtue:
Then you are living in the true desert.[43]

As with the difference between Hildegard's and Eckhart's use of 'greenness' and dryness, Eckhart alters the sense and reference of the metaphor. The difference lies largely in Eckhart's understanding of the mutual groundedness of God and the soul in the divine wilderness, the trackless void wherein lies no distinction of person or ontological differentiation between Creator and creature. For Eckhart, that desert is not the origin or the proving ground, nor even the soul, but the ultimate destination of all spiritual encounter, the divine ground itself:

There are three things that prevent us from hearing the eternal Word. The first is corporeality, the second is multiplicity, the third is temporality. If a man had transcended these three things, he would dwell in eternity, he would dwell in the spirit, he would dwell in unity and in the desert and there he would hear the eternal Word.[44]

Elsewhere, he said that the human spirit 'must transcend number and break through multiplicity, and God will break through him: and just as He breaks through into me, so I break through in turn into Him. God leads this spirit into the desert and into the unity of Himself, where He is simply One and welling up in Himself. This spirit is in unity and freedom.'[45] For Eckhart, the passage to ultimate simplicity and unity lies in and through what he called the desert of the Godhead, 'the silent desert into which no distinction ever peeped, of Father, Son and Holy Ghost'.[46] Citing or alluding to one of his favourite biblical passages (Hosea 2:14: 'I will lead her into the wilderness and speak to her heart'), elsewhere Eckhart said, characteristically, 'God leads His bride right out of all the virtues and nobility of creaturehood into a desert place in Himself, and speaks Himself in her heart, that is, He makes her like Himself in grace.'[47]

Also of significance are certain themes which apparently occasioned sporadic opposition to Mechthild's teaching and were formally attacked in Eckhart's work as heretical. Paramount among them is the acceptance of sinfulness as the condition for receiving God's mercy. Mechthild writes, 'I would rather be clothed with hell and crowned by all the devils if this could happen through no fault of mine.'[48] Similarly, in the *Book of Divine Consolation*, Eckhart explains,

> . . . because in some way or other it is God's will that I should have sinned, I should not want not to have done so, for in this way God's will is done 'on earth', that is, in misdeeds, 'as it is in heaven', that is, in good deeds. Thus a man wishes to be deprived of God for God's own sake and for God's own sake to be separated from God, and that alone is true repentance for my sins.[49]

Eckhart reasons that someone should be 'so much of one will with God that he wills everything that God wills, and in the fashion in which God wills it'. Similarly, in his earlier *Talks of Instruction*, Eckhart had said,

> . . . that man would indeed be established in God's will who would not wish that the sin into which he had fallen had never been committed, not because it was against God, but since, through that, you are obliged to greater love, and, through that, brought low and humbled. He should only wish that he had not acted against God.[50]

Both mystics seem to be alluding to the '*felix culpa*' motif in the ancient Easter liturgy (among other places), the 'happy sin' of Adam that invoked the redemption of the human race. Since God has brought an immeasurably greater good out of evil, in this case, personal sins, to wish not to have sinned would be to will the cancellation of an aspect of overwhelming sovereign goodness. But this is not to be construed, both are quick to add, as a licence to sin or entitlement to easy forgiveness. As Mechthild writes,

> . . . there is no sin so small
> That it does not leave its eternal mark on the soul.
> Why is this so?
> Never was a sin repented so completely
> That it were not have been better left undone.[51]

Another example of the difference between the teaching of the two mystics is found in their description of the pre-existence of the ideas of creatures in the mind of God. Mechthild asks,

Where was God before he created anything? He was in himself and all things were as present and as manifest to him as they are today. What form did our Lord God have then? Exactly like that of a sphere, and all things were enclosed in God with no lock and no door. The lowest part of the sphere is a bottomless foundation beneath all abysses. The highest part of the sphere is a top above which there is nothing. The circumference of the sphere is an immeasurable circle. At this point God had not yet become Creator. But when he created all things, did the sphere open? No, it has remained whole and it shall remain whole for ever. When God became Creator, all creatures became manifest in themselves; man in order to love God, to enjoy and know him, and to remain obedient; birds and animals to live according to their nature . . .[52]

Eckhart seems to reflect the last sentence in particular:

God *becomes* when all creatures say 'God' then God comes to be.
   When I subsisted in the ground, in the bottom, in the river and font of Godhead, no one asked me where I was going or what I was doing: there was no one to ask me. When I flowed forth, all creatures said 'God'. If anyone asked me, 'Brother Eckhart, when did you leave your house?', then I was in there. That is how all creatures speak of God.'[53]

Elsewhere Eckhart said, similarly,

While I yet stood in my first cause, I *had* no God and was my own cause . . . I was free of God and all things. But when I left my free will behind and received my created being, *then* I had a God. For before there were creatures, God was not 'God': He was That which He was. But when creatures came into existence and received their *created* being, then God was not 'God' in Himself. He was 'God' in creatures.[54]

But here too the imagery has been subtly shifted from the sense of brooding confinement, first to a surging spring rising irresistibly to the surface of the ground, then to that of an ordinary house. Eckhart also expands the notion that before creation creatures were unmanifest to arrive at the the startling and paradoxical view that before creation, God was not God. Here his teacher perhaps more closely resembles the mystical 'a-theism' of yet another female writer of the period, the doomed beguine Marguerite Porete.

Blessing the Poor in Spirit

The possible influence of Beatrice of Nazareth and other beguines on Eckhart has yet to be fully assessed. But the impact of Marguerite Porete's teaching on Eckhart has received increasing recognition since Romana Guarnieri established, in 1946, that she was the 'anonymous' author of *The Mirror of Simple Souls*. Following this revelation, in the mid-1980s Kurt Ruh, Edmund Colledge, J. C. Marler and other scholars began to argue that Eckhart composed his sermon '*Beati pauperes spiritu*' specifically with Porete's teachings in mind.[55]

It is highly likely that Porete's execution in 1310, the year before Eckhart returned to Paris, and the condemnation of Eckhart's propositions in 1329, were both related to the strenuous competition between the popes and the French King, Philip IV; a struggle in which the condemnation and destruction of the Templars figure prominently.[56] Porete's execution was undoubtedly part of a larger struggle on the part of women to be accepted on equal terms with men, a struggle that resulted in an occasional 'victory' over male church authorities by nuns such as Bl. Margaret Ebner, Christine Ebner and their Dominican sisters a generation later, as well as Catherine of Siena and other Italian tertiaries and nuns later in the fourteenth century.

A number of scholars have supported the likelihood that Eckhart not only knew Porete's story and had access to her doctrine, but even sympathized with her teaching in many respects. This is particularly apparent in Sermon 52, '*Beati pauperes spiritu*', which exalts spiritual poverty in terms clearly evocative of Porete's language and emphasis. But as Michael Sells has cautioned, 'This affinity is not dependent upon any direct textual influence or upon any personal relationship between the two writers. The resonances between the two sets of writings would be just as profound in the unlikely event that Eckhart had never read or heard any of Porete's ideas.'[57] Still, similarities between Eckhart and Porete with respect to spiritual poverty cannot be dismissed in view of the problem that embodiment posed for both mystics, and the struggle towards 'gender-parity' which affected not only them, but other mystical aspirants of the period.

For both Eckhart and Porete, the 'annihilation' of self-will, as well as the evacuation or emptying of the mind of all concepts and images of God, are the necessary preconditions for the inrush of the Spirit of God, 'the Birth of the Word in the soul of the just', in Eckhart's words. For both mystics, this awakening to God's presence in the depths of the soul is the point and purpose of poverty of spirit, which is to say radical detachment (*abgescheidenheit*). If Sermon 52 is to be dated after 1310, which is very likely, then it offers testimony that, in Eckhart's words, Marguerite Porete's voice lived on.

Widening the Circle

Even such a brief excursion into the rich and troubled arena encompassing the struggle of medieval women for place and voice cannot avoid leading to a number of conclusions, however tentative they may be, considering the involvement of the Dominican friars who supported them, not least of whom was Meister Eckhart.

First, as Michael Sells has argued persuasively, both Porete and Eckhart sought to 'undo' gender disparity by a linguistic destabilization of gender distinctions in regard to God. This is also the case, I believe, with his 'borrowings' from the other women mystics of the previous period. Whether this was Eckhart's explicit intention may be debated and, as Grace Jantzen has argued, the Meister wavers occasionally in his political correctness. But the evident fact that Eckhart deliberately reduced the erotic aspect of the beguines' portrayals of union with God can be cited in favour of an effort to 'degender' the image of God.

Second, while Jantzen reluctantly concludes that Eckhart's reversion to the 'sexist' linguistic patterns of the age disqualifies him as a particularly liberating guide for women today, she concedes that for his time, Eckhart's attitude was fundamentally egalitarian:

> Eckhart himself, as we have seen, preached – and preached *this* – to congregations of women. His own view must have been egalitarian, at least to the extent that he believed the women capable of just as much as men in spiritual and intellectual terms. Perhaps at some considerable cost to himself, he offered them everything he had as resources for their own spiritual breakthrough. If, from our perspective, we do not find the resources of the system liberating, the example of his practice, at least, is one that we should not fail to honor.[58]

Third, Eckhart's adoption and transformation of themes and expressions current in the spiritual milieu of the beguines illustrate how a master preacher, theologian and poet deepened and grounded them in the older and larger tradition of Christian mysticism. That Eckhart

ultimately failed to persuade the ecclesiastical establishment that many of
the suspect doctrines of mystics such as Hadewijch of Antwerp,
Mechthild of Magdeburg, and the tragic Marguerite Porete were consonant with the ancient teachings of Christian apophatic theology and spirituality, says more about the confusion of the times and the
preoccupations of the Academy and the Chancery than it does of
Eckhart's diminishing powers.

Fourth, it is now clear that it is no longer possible fully to understand or
appreciate the mystical doctrine of Meister Eckhart without reference to
the great women mystics who preceded him and to whose ideas he was
directly or indirectly indebted – most notably Hildegard of Bingen,
Hadewijch of Antwerp, Mechthild of Magdeburg and Marguerite Porete.

Finally, thus enlarging the circle of resources from which Eckhart drew
to create his sermons in no way detracts from his originality. If anything,
it elevates the stature of his creativity, disclosing a sensitivity to crucial
spiritual and, indeed, theological issues which prophetic women writers
had already raised to new levels of conceptualization and expression. It
further reveals Eckhart's mastery in integrating these themes into the
fabric of his own teaching, often transforming them in order better to
expose their consonance with the mystical tradition he sought to recover
and interpret for his own times.

Notes

1. Sections of this chapter are based on 'Meister Eckhart and the Women Mystics of
   the Rhineland', conferences given at the Ammerdown Centre, Bath (England),
   27–29 May 1994 and 'Women and Men in the Development of Late Medieval
   Mysticism', in Bernard McGinn, ed., *Meister Eckhart and the Beguine Mystics*
   (New York: Continuum, 1994), pp. 147–64.
2. Barbara Tuchman, *A Distant Mirror: The Calamitous Fourteenth Century* (New
   York: Alfred Knopf, 1978).
3. Among many works, Robert Johnson's study, *The Fisher King and the Handless
   Maiden* (San Francisco: Harper, 1993), explores the persistent influence of
   medieval romance on the contemporary literary and therapeutic imagination.
   Social themes are examined in works such as Georges Duby, *The Knight, the Lady
   and the Priest: The Making of Modern Marriage in Medieval France*, trans. by
   Barbara Bray (New York: Pantheon, 1983); William H. McNeill, *Plagues and
   Peoples* (Garden City, NY: Doubleday, 1976); and perhaps especially Caroline
   Walker Bynum, *Fragmentation and Redemption: Essays on Gender and the Human
   Body in Medieval Religion* (Brooklyn: Zone Books, 1992).
4. Following the research of Herbert Grundmann, it seems evident that as first
   applied to religiously inclined women who did not want to be nuns, the term had

negative, even dangerous connotations. Grundmann maintained that 'religious women in Belgium and the bishopric of Liege were actually suspected of Catharism when they were called beguines. The probable though not absolutely certain conclusion is that the word "beguine" is identical with "Albigensian".' See *Religious Movements in the Middle Ages*, trans. by Steven Rowan, intro. by Robert E. Lerner (Notre Dame and London: University of Notre Dame Press, 1995), p. 304, n. 26. Gradually, however, the designation lost its heretical aura and came to be accepted throughout northern Europe as a convenient way to refer to what was in fact a highly variegated movement. Grundmann remarks, 'The transformation of the word "beguine" shows how much the perception of the religious character of the new feminine piety had clarified in the course of the first decades of the thirteenth century. In 1215, it still raised suspicion of heresy for a woman to be called a "beguine", since that was the name of the heretics of Southern France, but as early as 1223 the Cologne town council records speak without hesitation of religious women as beguines.' Ibid., pp. 81–2.

5. See, for instance, *Meister Eckhart and the Beguines*, ed. cit.; Amy Hollywood, *The Soul as Virgin Wife: Mechthild of Magdeburg, Marguerite Porete, and Meister Eckhart* (Notre Dame and London: University of Notre Dame Press, 1996); Maria Lichtmann, 'Marguerite Porete and Meister Eckhart: *The Mirror for Simple Souls* Mirrored', *Meister Eckhart and the Beguine Mystics*, ed. cit., pp. 65–86; Emilie Zum Brunn and Georgette Epiney-Burgard, *Women Mystics in Medieval Europe* (New York: Paragon House, 1989); Derek Baker and Rosalind Hill, eds, *Medieval Women* (Oxford: Basil Blackwell, 1981); and especially Caroline Walker Bynum, 'Religious Women in the Middle Ages', in Jill Raitt, ed., *Christian Spirituality: High Middle Ages and Reformation* (New York: Crossroad, 1987), pp. 121–39.

6. See Frank Tobin, 'Mechthild and Meister Eckhart: Points of Comparison', in *Meister Eckhart and the Beguine Mystics*, ed. cit, pp. 44–61.

7. Albany: State University of New York Press, 1993.

8. Walshe trans., No. 57, Vol. II, p. 83. For the same list in reverse order, see Sermon 11 (Walshe No. 68, Vol. I, pp. 157ff.). For the same list in a different order (2, 3, 1), see Sermon 85 (Walshe No. 85, Vol. II, p. 264). For 'time, place, and corporality', cf. 'The Nobleman' (*Von dem Edeln Menchen*), Walshe ed., Vol. III, p. 111.

9. Tobin, op. cit., p. 3: 'Eckhart nowhere condemns visions and ecstasies; rather, he pays them scant attention while, at the same time, emphasizing the astonishing union with God possible to souls based simply on their nature as his creatures.'

10. Hollywood, art. cit., p. 29.

11. See below, Chapter 11, 'Eckhart, Suffering and Healing'.

12. Debra L. Stoudt, 'The Production and Preservation of Letters by Fourteenth-Century Dominican Nuns', *Medieval Studies* 53 (1991): 325.

13. In regard to Mechthild's doctrine, Frances Beer pointed out that 'Contemporary heterosexual models [of union with God] tended to be unequal; in marriage, the husband was dominant; in the courtly relationship the knight became the vassal, bowing down before his often aloof lady. But the lovers in Mechthild's experience are equal because they are of the same nature, and their longing for one another is fully mutual. With this affirmation of her essential participation, by nature, in the divine, Mechthild transcended the medieval misogynist view of women as "naturally" corrupt, and found the confidence to speak out – insisting on the legitimacy of her own voice and experience.' Frances Beer, *Women and Religious*

Experience in the Middle Ages (Woodbridge, Suffolk and Rochester, NY: The Boydell Press, 1992), p. 159, n. 39.

14. For an exploration of the development of this Christian Neoplatonic theme in Eckhart, see Chapter 3 below.

15. Grace Jantzen, 'Eckhart and Women', *Eckhart Review* 3 (Spring 1994): 37. She explains, 'More frequently, Eckhart connects women, not quite with sensuality as such, but with inferior reason, and men with superior reason, though the distinction between sensuality and inferior reason is not always easy to discern. Whatever precisely it is, it is clear that the superior reason, which is metaphorically male, is that by virtue of which human beings can be said to be the image of God, while the inferior reason, linked with sensuality, is metaphorically female. At its best this "female" inferior reason is a servant of the "male" superior reason; at its worst, it is that which tempts "him" into sin.'

16. See in this regard especially Frances Beer, op. cit.; Carolyn Walker Bynum, *Fragmentation and Redemption*, op. cit.; Janet Soskice, *After Eve: Women, Theology, and the Christian Tradition*, (London: Collins-Marshall Pickering, 1990); and Marty Williams and Anne Echols, *Between Pit and Pedestal: Women in the Middle Ages* (Princeton, NJ: Markus Wiener Publications, 1994).

17. Walshe, Vol. III, pp. 138–9.

18. 'The "Sister Catherine" Treatise', trans. by Elvira Borgstädt, in *Meister Eckhart: Teacher and Preacher*, ed. and trans. by Bernard McGinn with Frank Tobin and Elvira Borgstädt, preface by Kenneth Northcott (New York: Paulist Press/ London: SPCK, 1987), pp. 347–87.

19. On Hildegard, see Sabina Flanagan, *Hildegard of Bingen: A Visionary Life* (London and New York: Routledge, 1989); and 'The German Visionary: Hildegard of Bingen', by Kent Kraft in *Medieval Women Writers*, ed. by Katharina Wilson, pp. 109–30. Recent editions of Hildegard's works include *Holistic Healing*, Manfred Pawlik et al., eds, (Collegeville, MN: Liturgical Press, 1994); *Secrets of God: Writings of Hildegard of Bingen*, ed. by Sabina Flanagan (Boston and London: Shambala Press, 1996); *Scivias*, trans. by Mother Columba Hart and Jane Bishop (New York: Paulist Press, 1990); and *Saint Hildegard of Bingen, Symphonia: A Critical Edition of the Symphonia armonie celestium revelationum*, ed. and intro. by Barbara Newman (Ithaca and London: Cornell University Press, 1988).

20. *The Book of Divine Works*, 10, 2. Cited by Oliver Davies, *Meister Eckhart: Mystical Theologian* (London: SPCK, 1991), p. 56.

21. *Hildegard of Bingen. An Anthology*, Fiona Bowie and Oliver Davies eds, trans. by Robert Carver (London: SPCK, 1990), p. 96.

22. Ibid.

23. Sermon 72 (Walshe No. 95, Vol. II, pp. 327–8).

24. Sermon 29 (Walshe No. 16, Vol. I, pp. 135–6).

25. Davies, *Meister Eckhart*, op. cit., pp. 57–9.

26. *Essential Sermons*, ed. cit., p. 198.

27. Sermon 84 (Walshe No. 84, Vol. II, p. 258).

28. Sermon 20b (Walshe No. 32b, Vol. I, p. 243).

29. Sermon 4 (Walshe No. 40, Vol. I, p. 284). The examiners failed, however, to consider Eckhart's qualification, which accords well enough with Thomas' view on

the preservation of Creation: 'All creatures have no being, for their being consists in the presence of God. If God turned away for an instant from all creatures, they would perish.'

30. See *Hadewijch: The Complete Works*, trans. by Mother Columba Hart (New York: Paulist Press, 1980) and Ria Vanderauwera, 'The Brabant Mystic: Hadewijch', in Katharina Wilson, *Medieval Women Writers* (Athens: The University of Georgia Press, 1984), pp. 186–203.
31. Milhaven, op. cit., p. 4.
32. Oliver Davies, *Meister Eckhart*, op. cit., p. 79, n. 1.
33. Saskia Murk-Jansen, 'Hadewijch and Eckhart: *Amor intelligere est*', in *Meister Eckhart and the Beguines*, ed. cit., pp. 17–30. See also Paul A. Dietrich, 'The Wilderness of God in Hadewijch II and Meister Eckhart and His Circle', ibid., pp. 31–43.
34. Hadewijch of Antwerp, 'Letter 19'.
35. Sermon 76 (Walshe No. 7, Vol. I, pp. 67–8).
36. Sermon 79 (Walshe No. 91, Vol. II, p. 307, DP 41).
37. Sermon 103 (Walshe No. 4, Vol. I, p. 47).
38. See *Mechthild of Magdeburg: The Flowing Light of the Godhead*, Frank Tobin, ed. (New York: Paulist Press, 1997), pp. 35–6, 163–7. An older English translation also exists: *The Revelations of Mechthild of Magdeburg (1210–1297), or The Flowing Light of the Godhead*, trans. by Lucy Menzies (London: Longmans Greens, 1953). See also John Howard, 'The German Mystic: Mechthild of Magdeburg', in Katharina Wilson, *Medieval Women Writers*, ed. cit., pp. 153–85.
39. See Gertrud the Great of Helfta, *Spiritual Exercises*, trans. and ed. by Gertrud Jaron Lewis and Jack Lewis (Kalamazoo: Cistercian Publications, 1989); St Gertrude the Great, *The Life and Revelations* (Westminster, MD: Christian Classics, 1986); and Theresa A. Halligan, *The Booke of Gostlye Grace of Mechthild of Hackeborn* (Toronto: Pontifical Institute of Medieval Studies, 1979).
40. Oliver Davies, *Meister Eckhart: Mystical Theologian*, op. cit., p. 60. See note 44 below.
41. For examples of the latter, see *The Revelations of Mechthild of Magdeburg*, ed. cit., pp. 203–4, 246–7, 251–2, 265 and 287.
42. For likely influence on Eckhart, see Dom Gall Morel, ed., *Das fliessende Licht der Gottheit* (Einsiedeln MS 277), (Regensburg, 1869), cited by Menzies, ed. cit., p. xxvi and p. 17, n. 1.
43. *The Flowing Light of the Godhead*, ed. cit., Book I, 35, pp. 55–6. Compare Menzies' translation:

> Thou shalt love the naughting,
> And flee the self.
> You shall stand alone
> Seeking help from none,
> That thy being may be quiet,
> Free from the bondage of all things.
> You shall loose those who are bound,
> And exhort the free
> You shall care for the sick

Yet dwell alone.
You shall drink the waters of sorrow,
And kindle the fire of love
With the faggot of virtue –
Thus shall you dwell in the desert. (Menzies, ed. cit., pp. 17–18.)

44. Sermon 12 (Walshe No. 57, Vol. II, p. 83). See also Sermon 11 (Walshe No. 68, Vol. II, p. 157ff.).
45. Sermon 29 (Walshe No. 16, Vol. I, p. 136).
46. Sermon 48 (Walshe No. 60, Vol. II, p. 105).
47. Sermon 81 (Walshe No. 64, Vol. II, p. 126).
48. *The Flowing Light of the Godhead*, ed. cit., Book VI, 1, p. 227.
49. DW V, 22, 58. 10, in *The Essential Sermons, Commentaries, Treatises and Defense*, ed. and trans. by Bernard McGinn and Edmund Colledge (New York: Paulist Press, 1981), pp. 216–17.
50. *Talks of Instruction* (Counsels of Discernment), c. 12, ibid., pp. 261–2.
51. *The Flowing Light of the Godhead*, ed. cit., Book VII, 27, p. 297.
52. Ibid., Book VI, 31, p. 257.
53. Sermon 26 (Walshe No. 56, Vol. II, p. 81).
54. Sermon 52 (Walshe No. 87, Vol. II, p. 271).
55. Additional references and discussion regarding these developments can be found in Ellen Babinsky's introduction to her translation of *The Mirror of Simple Souls* (New York: Paulist Press, 1993), pp. 5 and 49f. See also the articles by Maria Lichtmann, Amy Hollywood and Michael Sells in *Meister Eckhart and the Beguine Mystics*, ed. cit.
56. The involvement of William de Nogaret, Philip's adviser and champion, during the proceedings against both the Templars and Marguerite Porete is especially significant in light of his role in the arrest and ultimate death, in 1303, of Boniface VIII, the second-to-last Italian Pope before the Avignese 'captivity' of the papacy from 1309 to 1377. Nogaret's role in the process against the Templars and Marguerite Porete is discussed with pertinent references by Ellen Babinsky in her introduction to her translation of *The Mirror of Simple Souls*, ed. cit., pp. 17–20.
57. Michael Sells, 'The Pseudo-Woman and the Meister: "Unsaying" and Essentialism', in McGinn, ed., *Meister Eckhart and the Beguine Mystics*, op. cit., p. 146, note 74.
58. Jantzen, art. cit., p. 46.

Chapter 3

The Thinker's Way to God: Meister Eckhart and the Neoplatonic Heritage[1]

In his life and preaching, Meister Eckhart's 'way' was pre-eminently a spirituality of the mind, although he can hardly be said to have disregarded the works of mercy, as revealed in one of his more famous aphorisms: 'As I have often said, even if someone were in a rapture like St Paul, and knew a sick person who needed some soup, I should think it far better you left the rapture for love and would serve the needy man in greater love.'[2] And if the speculative inquiries and probings that animate his scholarly works often pervade his sermons and treatises, it is no less true that a homiletic, even pastoral, intention reciprocally permeates Eckhart's scholarly works, particularly in regard to his fascination with the Word.

It is therefore not surprising, perhaps, that Heinrich Denifle, the Dominican scholar who discovered and first commented upon Eckhart's Latin writings in the 1880s, concluded that the Meister lacked the clarity of conception and precision of expression characteristic of the great scholastic figures who preceded him, particularly Albert the Great and Thomas Aquinas.[3] But later Eckhart scholars convincingly argued that Denifle's concern to refute uncritically inflated characterizations of Eckhart's philosophical genius, notably that of Wilhelm Preger, led him to undervalue and, in fact, misrepresent the Meister's real goal and true achievement. To the modern critical eye, aided by more than a century of further discoveries and study, 'the scholastic Eckhart is an original and speculative thinker, and not only a great mystic.'[4] Far from being considered Denifle's 'unclear thinker', in more recent times Eckhart has been favourably compared with Thomas Aquinas, Fichte, Hegel, Husserl, Heidegger and Sartre.[5]

While recognizing Eckhart's speculative brilliance as well as his spiritual gifts and eloquence, other early commentators, including Dominicans such as Gabriel Théry and Gundolf Gieraths, nevertheless found the Meister's reliance on Neoplatonic themes philosophically and

29

theologically disconcerting, as did Denifle. Moved perhaps by defensive sentiment in face of the charges of unorthodoxy laid against Eckhart's doctrine and its subsequent condemnation in 1329, some commentators have claimed that Eckhart ultimately disavowed Neoplatonism.[6] More cautious scholars have contended that Eckhart was not only a profound exponent of Christian Neoplatonism, but was the outstanding representative of the Dominican School of Cologne, founded by his mentor Albert the Great, whose explicit agenda was a sweeping synthesis of Platonic, Aristotelian and Neoplatonic philosophy with Christian, Islamic and Jewish theology.[7]

The issue is not whether Eckhart was an out-and-out Neoplatonist, for, like most medieval theologians, he was eclectic, but to what extent his teaching, both speculative and spiritual, was indebted to the Christian Neoplatonic tradition and what that means for understanding Eckhart today.

Eckhart's Sources

Only a more intensive textual analysis of Eckhart's works than any so far published can possibly reveal the full scope of the sources on which he drew to develop and support his philosophical and theological doctrine.[8] Often he only alludes to them. Sometimes he transforms them. But only rarely does he bother to dispute, remaining content to acknowledge some 'master', taking from any quarter what furthers his argument, leaving objections and contentions to others.

Eckhart's erudition was undeniably comprehensive. Like both Albert and Thomas, he drew from the wisdom of ancient pagan thinkers, Jewish and Muslim scholars, the long history of eastern and western Christianity and, of course, the Bible. Even a cursory tabulation of the hundreds of references in the Meister's German and Latin works reveals a close similarity regarding both the authorities he cites and the frequency with which he calls upon them.

Significantly among his ancient sources, pride of place belongs to Aristotle, who is cited more than four times more frequently than any other source. Other authors he mentions are, in decreasing order of frequency, Plato, Proclus, Porphyry, Macrobius, Cicero, Seneca, Horace, and even Aesop, among many others.[9] Nevertheless, as Alain de Libera, Bernard McGinn and other scholars have shown, it is the philosophical mysticism of Plotinus that provides much of the structure and sometimes the content of Eckhart's teaching, which is philosophically more Neoplatonic than Aristotelian in its fundamental intent and achievement.[10] However, Eckhart does not cite Plotinus directly in any of his works.

The Jewish and Islamic sources Eckhart drew on for both philosophical and theological doctrine were also indebted to the Neoplatonic tradition. These include Solomon Ibn Gabirol (known to the Latin West as Avicebron), Moshe ben Maimon (Moses Maimonides), Al-Kindi, Ibn Sina (Avicenna), Ibn Rushd (Averroes) and, perhaps above all, *The Book of Causes*. (Tradition had assigned this work to Aristotle, but Thomas Aquinas correctly identified it as an Arabic paraphrase of the Neoplatonist Proclus' *Elements of Theology* written some time in the twelfth century.)[11]

Among ancient Christian authorities, Augustine was Eckhart's favourite, being cited five times more frequently than Thomas Aquinas. Aquinas and Dionysius the Areopagite are next, followed by Gregory the Great, Eckhart's old teacher Albert the Great, Bernard, Jerome, Origen, John Damascene, Boethius, Peter Lombard, John Chrysostom, the Ordinary Gloss on Scripture and, less frequently, the Lives of the Fathers, Ambrose, Bede, John Scottus Eriugena, Anselm, Hugh of St Victor, Alan of Lille, and others, most of whom Eckhart also cited in his Cologne defence.[12] But Eckhart's biblical sources outnumber all others combined, as might be expected of a preacher and theologian. Of the Jewish Scriptures, Eckhart relies (in descending order) on Genesis (having written two commentaries on it), Wisdom and Exodus (having composed commentaries on each), the Psalms, Sirach (of which only a fragment of his commentary survives), Isaiah, the Song of Songs, Proverbs, Jeremiah and Hosea. Less frequently cited are Job, Zechariah, Qoheleth, 1 and 2 Samuel, Lamentations, Ezekiel, Daniel, Tobit, Esther and Maccabees. Eckhart's fondness for the Wisdom literature is important in light of his indebtedness to the Christian Platonism of Alexandria for his mystical exegesis and doctrine.

Eckhart's preferences among Christian scriptures are no less indicative of his mystical leanings. Most frequently cited is the Gospel of John, Eckhart's commentary on it being perhaps his greatest single work.[13] The Johannine writings figure pre-eminently in other works as well, followed in frequency by the writings of Paul (including the Pastoral Epistles and Hebrews), the Gospel of Matthew, the Gospel of Luke, the First Epistle of John, the Gospel of Mark, the Book of Revelation, the Acts of the Apostles and the Epistles of James and Peter.

The location and frequency of citations from common sources provides only a sketch of the intellectual provenance of Eckhart's thought, however. More important for an understanding of the character of his philosophical and theological 'system' are his masters, primarily those of the Dominican order who were responsible for his education and development.

Eckhart, Albert and Thomas

A powerful spiritual and intellectual bond, as well as a fraternal one, connected the three most famous second-generation Friars Preachers. But differences as well as similarities among them are significant. Albert and Eckhart were German, from Bavaria and Thuringia respectively. Although Thomas had Germanic ancestors and relatives, he was born at Roccasecca near Naples in south central Italy, then part of the kingdom of Sicily. As a Dominican student, Thomas was nonetheless closely associated with Albert at Cologne and even before that at Paris. Eckhart, too, spent many years in both places as both student and professor.

All three incepted at the University of Paris. There Eckhart had also received his baccalaureate. All three occupied the so-called chair of theology for externs, Albert being the first German to do so, Thomas the first Italian. All three espoused the newly introduced and controversial Aristotelian philosophy, although varying in their interpretation and extent of dependence. Similarly, each variously incorporated Neoplatonic elements reintroduced into Western spiritual theology with the appearance of new translations of the *Corpus Areopagiticum* and the *Liber de Causis*.[14] All three were renowned for their philosophy, theology and preaching, although it is Albert who is best remembered for the first and Thomas for the second, while Eckhart was considered the greatest German preacher of his day.

The Master of Cologne

Albert's influence on Eckhart cannot be measured in terms of whatever living contact may have existed between them, and this is all the more true in the case of Thomas. Of the two older Dominicans, Albert evidently exercised the greater intellectual influence, as seen especially in the prominent Dionysian strand in his and Eckhart's teaching; in both cases this is far more extensive in depth and scope than in that of Aquinas.[15]

Eckhart would have met the old bishop on coming to Cologne in 1280, when he began his studies at the *studium generale*, built, as was the Dominican church, by Albert himself 30 years earlier. But Albert died only a few months later, giving Eckhart at most a very brief opportunity to hear the old doctor speak and to join the other students in order to hear his colloquies. However, Eckhart would certainly have been taught by some of Albert's students who had formed, with their great master, a 'school' of thought and mystical spirituality which would have lasting influence throughout the Rhineland, paramount among them Dietrich of Freiburg and Ulrich of Strassburg.[16] Elsewhere, however, this important tradition was almost completely eclipsed by the school of Albert's great student, Thomas Aquinas.[17]

The Sun of Naples

Next to Albert, Thomas Aquinas undeniably exercised the greatest intellectual influence on Eckhart. The Angelic Doctor himself died three or four years before his younger contemporary entered the order. But Eckhart may well have been a student in the faculty of arts at Paris in 1277, when several of Thomas's propositions were condemned along with those of Siger of Brabant.[18] Shortly thereafter, according to traditional accounts, Albert gathered the brethren in the *studium generale* to eulogize his late student and commend his doctrine in the strongest terms to the safe keeping of the order.[19]

Despite his Dionysian and Augustinian enthusiasms, there can be no doubt about Eckhart's pronounced loyalty to the memory and doctrine of Thomas, even apart from the adherence to the basic tenets which had been enjoined upon members of the order at the Chapters of Montpellier and Paris in 1278 and 1279.[20] Thus, Eckhart's occasional departures from Thomas are especially significant. In his reliance on the Platonic–Neoplatonic Christian tradition, Eckhart was in some respects actually closer to Bonaventure and Duns Scotus than to Thomas, with the all-important exception of promoting the intellect and knowledge over the will and love in the spiritual hierarchy of human powers and acts. But even here, Eckhart on occasion ranked them equally or even reversed his position, granting superiority to the will and love even as had Thomas Aquinas in a limited frame of reference:

Nothing brings you closer to God or makes God so much your own as the sweet bond of love. A man who has found this way need seek no other. He who hangs on this hook is caught so fast that foot and hand, mouth, eyes and heart, and all that is man's, belongs only to God.[21]

Elsewhere he said, 'The perfection of blessedness lies in both, knowledge and love.'[22] Again, 'God and I are one. Through knowledge I take God into myself, through love I enter into God.'[23] Ultimately, however, in a splendid example of Eckhart's dialectical synthesis of opposing viewpoints, he preached that 'Some teachers hold that the spirit finds its beatitude in love. Some make him find it in beholding God. But I say he does not find it in love, or in gnosis or in vision.'[24] Rather, as he clarifies elsewhere, 'I say that above these two, understanding and love, there is mercy: there God works mercy in the highest and purest acts that God is capable of.'[25]

It is likewise noteworthy that while Eckhart explicitly 'corrects' Aquinas on a number of points, he rarely – if ever – disagrees with either Augustine or Aristotle. In the light of such differences, the trust and respect with which Eckhart was uniformly regarded in the order by his confrères, his provincials, even the Master and his vicars, illustrates the latitude with which the injunctions to support Thomas were applied.

Ironically, propositions taken from the works of both Thomas and Eckhart, and very nearly Albert as well, were condemned, surely without cause in the case of Thomas and most likely so in that of Eckhart. Thomas, however, was exonerated; Eckhart was not. Moreover, both Thomas and Albert were canonized, the former in 1323, his master in 1931. Both were also declared doctors of the Church. Eckhart, whose integrity and holiness of life were never impugned, even by his Dominican antagonist Hermann of Summo, was consigned to oblivion, but one that could not hold him.

Eckhart and the Christian Neoplatonism of the Middle Ages

It is evident that, in addition to his reliance on the doctrine of Thomas, and at least to some extent that of Albert, Eckhart's own teaching drew heavily upon the spiritual and dogmatic resources of the Christian mystical tradition from its origins in third-century Alexandria until well into the Middle Ages. In his extant works there are only a few citations from Plato and virtually no direct references to either Philo or Plotinus. Yet the Christian Platonism (i.e., Neoplatonism) developed by the Alexandrian theologians and Augustine exercised an influence on his thought that can be truthfully characterized as formative. As noted above, he was especially and profoundly influenced, as were his Dominican contemporaries and most spiritual writers of the period, by the manifestly Neoplatonic doctrine of the anonymous fifth-century Syrian writer who styled himself 'Dionysius the Areopagite'.[26]

Dom David Knowles concluded that it is impossible to decide whether Eckhart's mystical temperament led him to adopt (and adapt) a 'Dionysian' framework, or whether his exposure to Christian Neoplatonism under Albert the Great led him to a mystical spirituality.[27] Without doubt, however, Eckhart embraced the Neoplatonic tradition in a general sense as he continued the revival inaugurated by Albert and his immediate followers, including to some extent Aquinas himself. The continuing and pervasive influence of that tradition warrants a closer if brief exploration of its origins and development as an aid to understanding both the goal and the accomplishment of Eckhart as a Christian Neoplatonist.[28]

The Alexandrian Inheritance

The contribution of the ancient Church of Alexandria to the spiritual theology of both Eastern and Western Christianity has often been overlooked in historical accounts, possibly because of the pervasive anti-Hellenic bias that dominated late nineteenth-century German scholarship and still lingers among many Catholic and Protestant spiritual writers. It is impossible, however, to continue to ignore or dismiss it in view of the deep indebtedness of Albert, Dietrich, Eckhart and other important medieval and Renaissance writers to this ancient tradition, a bond which connects Eckhart with the earliest developmental stages of mystical theology and spirituality. It is also one which provides an ecumenical basis for spiritual as well as theological dialogue between Eastern and Western Christians as well as between Roman Catholics, with their now largely tacit Aristotelian bias, and Anglicans, for whom Platonism and Neoplatonism exercised enduring attraction.[29]

Partly Jewish, partly Homeric and Stoic, the symbolic or 'mystical' exegeses characteristic of the Alexandrian approach, developed in large measure by Philo Judaeus before the advent of Christianity, was believed to provide access to the hidden, true meaning of obscure passages in scripture. By the time of Paul at the latest, it was deeply established in Christian attitudes and came to influence scriptural study until the Reformation.[30] Out of this 'Wisdom tradition' of Alexandrian Judaism, both hermeneutical and doctrinal elements passed into Christian thought and praxis and would eventually appear in Eckhart's writings: the pre-eminence of the Word; the pre-existence of the Ideas of all things in the eternal mind of God; the unknowability of God's essence; the effulgence or brightness of God; the primacy of the soul over the body; and the doctrine of the human person as the image of God.[31] It also contributed substantially to its mystical vision.

Among other themes favoured by Eckhart, the first traces of the doctrine of the 'spark of the soul' can be found in a purely Christian context in the writings of Clement of Alexandria early in the third century. Detachment and moderation were also prominent in the Alexandrian catechesis. Eckhart does not cite Clement, whose writings were not rediscovered until fairly recent times. But certain works of his disciple and successor Origen were known to and cited by Eckhart.[32] In terms of influence, however, no figure in antiquity (with the exception of Augustine) exercised so powerful a sway over the Meister as the Egyptian savant some twenty years Origen's junior, the last great philosopher of the ancient world and the fountain-head of what later came to be known as Neoplatonism – the great Plotinus.[33]

Although a vastly misunderstood figure in the centuries after his death (and even today), Plotinus's doctrine was highly fluid, just as his vision of reality was dynamic yet unified. Like that of Plato, it was also essentially theocentric, one reason why it was appealing to Christian theologians of the fourth and fifth centuries.[34] Deeply spiritual, Plotinus sought unity with God ('The One') through the contemplation of truth, goodness and beauty. Like Philo, he held that the intimate life of God remained unknown and incomprehensible. Even so, all reality emanated from God, Himself utterly simple and self-sufficient, by a process he described as 'seething' or 'boiling', a bubbling up of being, life, and intelligence that broke forth into the world in successive stages.[35]

During the fourth century, the religiously irenic movement begun by Philo and continued by Clement and Origen rose to new prominence in the work of St Basil the Great, his brother St Gregory of Nyssa, and their friend, St Gregory Nazianzus – 'the Cappadocian Fathers'. Far more mystical in their approach than churchmen such as St Athanasius, the Cappadocians developed the major themes of Alexandrian spirituality in a profound and even somewhat systematic fashion. Among these themes, particularly as found in the writings of Gregory of Nyssa, is the biblically funded notion of the birth of the Word of God in the soul of the just, the keystone of Eckhart's spiritual edifice.[36] But even here the philosophical context was almost palpably Plotinian.

Another important theme of the mystical theology of the Alexandrian tradition that would reappear in Eckhart's teaching is *aphairesis*, a Neoplatonic term for 'the progressive stripping away of every concept that the mind can form about God in the certainty that every one will be inadequate'.[37] With deep roots in scripture and the teachings of Philo, then adapted and developed by the Cappadocian Fathers, such 'negative knowledge' formed the core of Christian apophatic theology. It would appear in even greater sharpness in the late sixth-century writings of the enigmatic figure who called himself 'Dionysius the Areopagite', whose approach to God, alongside that of Augustine, would determine the content of mystical theology for the next thousand years, including that of Eckhart.

Dionysius's writings were first successfully brought to the attention of the West by the translations of the ninth-century scholar John of Ireland.[38] Further translations were made in the twelfth century by John Sarracenus, and in the following century a series of paraphrases was written by Thomas Gallus, the Abbot of Vercelli. These Dionysian writings had an enormous impact on Eckhart who, like Albert the Great and Thomas Aquinas, would have composed a commentary on several of the small books of the Areopagite as part of his scholastic training.[39] John of Ireland also translated some of the writings of St Gregory of Nyssa and St Maximus the Confessor, whose teachings were also known to Eckhart. All were Neoplatonic in their thinking, as was Eckhart's other great theological and spiritual source, St Augustine of Hippo.[40]

The Medieval Revival

A century before Albert the Great's influential revival of Neoplatonism, elements of the ancient teaching had surfaced in the writings of several Christian scholars, among them Gilbert of Poitiers (1080–1154) and Amaury of Béne, who died in 1207. Reaction at the time, occasioned especially by the perceived pantheistic implications of the doctrine of Gilbert and Amaury, was strongly negative. Gilbert was summoned to defend himself before the Council of Rheims in 1148; it is not certain that an official condemnation resulted. But in 1215, Gilbert's attempts to formulate a diversity within God between the Trinity and the Godhead were condemned by the Fourth Lateran Council in 1215. For good measure, Amaury's teachings were also condemned at the Council. Several related doctrines attributed to Origen and John of Ireland were similarly condemned. To the mind of the Western ecclesiastics, unused to the speculative language of the less turbulent Eastern Church, such teachings seemed to lead to pantheistic or subordinationist tendencies, that is, identifying God with creation or ranking the persons of the Trinity in a descending order.

Despite the condemnations of the previous period, Albert and his disciples, now equipped with new and better translations from the Greek, included the main sources of Christian Neoplatonism in their plan to unify the major intellectual and spiritual currents of the West. It succeeded in some respects but also occasioned an intense reaction on the part of the secular Averroist (notably Siger of Brabant) and the conservative (i.e., Augustinian) theological schools of both the Franciscan and Dominican orders.

Most prominent among the first generation of students who continued Albert's effort to synthesize the major currents of Hellenic, Christian, Islamic and Jewish thinking were Ulrich of Strassburg – Albert's favourite student and the most ardent proponent of Albert's 'Neoplatonic revival' in the later thirteenth century – and the remarkable Dietrich (Theodoric) of Freiburg, whom Eckhart would certainly have known at Cologne and Paris.

Other notable Dominicans of Albert's school were the brothers Johann and Gerhard Korngin of Sterngassen, Johannes Picardi of Lichtenberg, Heinrich of Lübeck, Nicholas of Strasburg and Johannes of Freiburg, at least some of whom were personally known to Eckhart. After his death, noteworthy members of this school included the Dominican Berthold of Moosburg and Heimerich of Kampen, who died in 1460. Nicholas of Strasburg, who would play a very important role in Eckhart's trials in Cologne and Avignon, and especially the brothers Korngin, were less indebted to Albert's Neoplatonic revival than were Ulrich, Dietrich and, especially, Eckhart and Berthold. But the completion of the Cologne school's metaphysical synthesis of Aristotelian and Neoplatonic thought was in fact more successfully realized in Eckhart's teaching and preaching than in the works of any of Albert's earlier students. His accomplishment seems to have had disastrous consequences, however, leading in several instances to the condemned propositions of 1329.[41]

Eckhart's Neoplatonism

As a philosophical attitude or sensibility, Christian Platonism (and Neoplatonism) manifests certain characteristic features, most if not all of which are evident in Eckhart's teaching: his insistence on the intelligibility of experience and the reality of ideal forms, interpreted as eternal ideas in the mind of God; a notion of participation in being on a universal scale; a conviction of the pre-eminence and interdependence of unity, truth, beauty and goodness; and a commitment to the sovereign power of love. To these may be added a tendency towards psychophysical dualism, a yearning for otherworldliness, and an ontological view of the degrees or levels of reality.

For the Christian Platonist (and Neoplatonist), the human individual is primarily spirit, although involved in earthly existence as a harmoniously functioning whole of body, mind and spirit. Our spiritual and therefore true home is not of the earth, however, but lies in a suprasensory dimension beyond time, space and matter. Humankind has no abiding city on earth. In this respect, Eckhart's philosophical ancestry is part of an ancient tradition, a vital component of classical Christian theology and spirituality. More specifically, the influence of Plotinus upon Eckhart's doctrine, whether direct or mediated through the ancient tradition of Christian mysticism, is manifold: from the 'boiling' metaphor for the inner life of God, to the vision of the created universe as an expanding and contracting emanation from the Godhead, to the image of the soul's journey back to God through the obstacles of time, space and multiplicity or corporality.[42]

Similarly, the ancient Alexandrian ideal of 'dispassionate equanimity' (*apatheia* and *ataraxia*) became a cornerstone of the psychological asceticism Eckhart promoted in his sermons: 'When a man's heart grieves for nothing: then a man has the essence and the nature and the substance and the wisdom and the joy and all that God has. Then the very being of the son of God is ours and in us and we attain to the very essence of God.'[43]

Here, Eckhart's emotional *abgescheidenheit* or detachment, so akin to the ancient Christian *apatheia*, is not an attempt to smother sensibility or feeling, but rather to achieve inner harmony: 'You may think that as long as words can move you to joy or sorrow you are imperfect. That is not so. Christ was not so [. . .] Therefore I declare that no saint ever lived or ever will attain to the state where pain cannot hurt him or pleasure please.'[44]

To the programme of his Dominican Neoplatonic predecessors, which built upon the Augustinian theme of divine descent and return culminating in the intellectual vision of God, Eckhart further added the thematic of the birth of the Word in the soul of the just and the dynamic vision of successive 'breakthroughs' as the soul ascends ever higher levels of awareness and immediacy in her return to God. By thus 'internalizing' the Albertine synthesis in a spiritual doctrine of immense scope and power, Eckhart attempted to bring the work of the Cologne school to completion, although he never finished his articulation of that vision.

Eckhart's Divergence from Neoplatonism

As noted earlier, to regard Eckhart simply as a medieval Neoplatonist would be an oversimplification. Like his great confreres Albert the Great and Thomas Aquinas, he was academically eclectic. The Neoplatonic strand in his teaching is only one among many elements in a complex, multiform and admittedly unfinished system. It is undeniably a major component, both structurally and substantially, but one already modified when he received it by centuries of Christian interpretation (and misinterpretation). Eckhart transformed it even more.

Despite the similarity of Plotinus's teaching to early Christian spirituality, and its influence on its development, especially perhaps in regard to Eckhart, there are many important differences. One of the most significant concerns the place of action. For Plotinus, any kind of involvement in the world served to weaken contemplation, which he regarded as the highest form of human activity. For the great Christian spiritual writers without exception, however, the true test of authentic contemplation was charitable service to those in need. This was no less true for Eckhart, as we have already had occasion to note.[45] But it is not to the realms of pure speculation sought by Platonist and Middle-Platonist mystics, much less the ecstatic union of the later Neoplatonists, that Eckhart summons us. Rather, he beckons towards the desert of unknowing dear to the Greek mystical tradition of Alexandria, whose pioneer was Philo the Jew and whose most eloquent cartographer was St Gregory of Nyssa.

Another major divergence concerns the role of grace. At least insofar as Plotinus was capable of articulating his own experience, contemplation of the One was achieved by means of human effort, the unaided work of the soul. In authentic Christian spirituality, while the achievement of contemplation by self-direction is not only possible but in some degree necessary, the completion of the soul's journey to God is possible only by the gift of grace, when human consciousness, having exhausted its own capacities and now passive and still, is filled with the inrush (or, in Eckhart's word, the 'upsurge') of that Presence. Here too, despite all his concurrence with Neoplatonic thought, Eckhart is solidly one with the orthodox Christian tradition:

> The grace which the Holy Ghost brings to the soul is received without distinction, provided the soul is collected into the single power that knows God. This grace springs up in the heart of the Father and flows into the Son, and in the union of both it flows out of the wisdom of the Son and pours into the goodness of the Holy Ghost, and is sent with the Holy Ghost into the soul. And this grace is a face of God and is impressed without co-operation in the soul with the Holy Ghost, and forms the soul like God. This work God performs alone, without co-operation.[46]

Given the jostling for dominance among philosophical systems in the Middle Ages as well as in more recent times, it is difficult to resist concluding that no philosophy can claim privileged status as the framework best suited to articulate the Christian faith in a reasonable manner. For radically differing systems of thought have in fact functioned in that capacity, some more, some less satisfactorily according to the particular exigencies of the day. Neither Platonism nor Aristotelianism, Kantianism nor Marxism, nor any other way of thinking can be disqualified as a potential 'handmaid of theology' so long as it adequately meets the challenge of interpreting human experience in its time.

Even so, in much of the West a certain *odium theologicum* still clings to Eastern Christian thought, including its Neoplatonic heritage. Yet this ancient tradition is clearly replete with wisdom and depths of truth. And it should therefore give us pause when, for instance, R. T. Wallis observes that 'the dominant trend of Christian theology, in both its Platonic and Aristotelian forms, has always been Neoplatonic'.[47] Moreover, it is surely worth noting that when the great mystics of the Church attempted to lay out their teaching, they characteristically gravitated towards the Platonic–Neoplatonic co-ordinates on the philosophical chart. Perhaps not the greatest, but hardly the least among them was Meister Eckhart.

Christian Platonic and Neoplatonic influence survived its condemnation in Gilbert's, Amaury's, and Eckhart's teachings, appearing both in its Dionysian spiritual expression in *The Cloud of Unknowing*, and in similar works up to the masterful theology and poetry of St John of the Cross. It also endured in philosophical form in the writings of Nicholas of Cusa, Marsilio Ficino, Pico della Mirandola, Giordano Bruno, the Cambridge

Platonists, Descartes, Spinoza, Schelling and Bergson, among others.[48] Only recently, however, has the immense treasury of this ancient Christian tradition once more begun to find wider appreciation among Western scholars and spiritual writers.[49]

Today, recovering this overlooked strand of Christian thought and life may help to advance our understanding of the place and meaning of Eckhart's theology and spirituality, as well as the teaching and great plan of Albert the Great and his immediate disciples. Perhaps Eckhart's profound and pervasive emphasis on the unity and intelligibility of God, the 'boiling' metaphors for the inner life of God, the dialectical dynamics of emanation and return, and his characteristic interpretations of analogical attribution and participation can be truly understood *only* in the light of ancient Christian Alexandria. Reciprocally, as Vladimir Lossky perceived, a thorough appropriation of Eckhart's theological openness to the East may well be able to assist in advancing the ecumenical dialogue with Orthodox Christians, much as the dissemination of his works in East Asia has fostered Buddhist–Christian dialogue in Japan and elsewhere.

One way or another, it can no longer be seriously doubted that Eckhart adopted and adapted a fundamentally Neoplatonic structure for his interpretation of the theological and spiritual mysticism. Even so, it is important to remember that Eckhart was far more than a medieval Neoplatonist. Through the ages the temptation to fit him into some constricting system of thought has been powerful and pervasive. Still, the authority and richness of his teaching have overcome all efforts to confine and use him, breaking through to awaken and enlighten yet another generation.

Notes

1. Portions of this chapter have been adapted from 'Meister Eckhart and the Neoplatonic Heritage: The Thinker's Way to God', *The Thomist* (October 1990): 609–39.
2. 'Talks of Instruction', trans. Hilda Graef, Jeanne Ancelet-Hustache, *Master Eckhart and the Rhineland Mystics* (New York and London: Harper and Row/Longmans, 1957, p. 79.)
3. 'Eckhart ein unklarer Denker war, der sich der Consequenzen seiner Lehrer resp. seiner ausdruckweise nicht bewusst war.' 'Meister Eckharts lateinische Schriften, and die Grundanschauung seiner Lehre', in *Archiv für Literatur und Kirchengeschichte des Mittelalters*, H. Denifle and Franz Ehrle, eds (Graz: Akademische Druck u. Verlagsanstalt, 1956), vol. 2, pp. 482, 521.
4. John Caputo, 'The Nothingness of the Intellect in Meister Eckhart's Parisian

Questions', *The Thomist* 39 (1975) : 87. Cf. also Karl Kertz, 'Meister Eckhart's Teaching on the Birth of the Divine Word in the Soul', *Traditio* 15 (1959): 327.

5. On Aquinas, Fichte, Hegel, Husserl and Sartre, cf. Caputo, art. cit., p. 88. On Heidegger, cf. John Caputo, *The Mystical Element in Heidegger's Thought* (Athens, Ohio: Ohio University Press, 1978), pp. 140–217 and passim; Reiner Schürmann, *Meister Eckhart, Mystic and Philosopher* (Bloomington, Ind.: Indiana University Press, 1978), pp. 192–210; and John Macquarrie, 'Eckhart and Heidegger', *Eckhart Review* (Spring 1992). On Eckhart and Fichte, see Ernst von Bracken, *Meister Eckhart und Fichte* (Würzburg: verlag Konrad Triltsch, 1943). I am indebted to Fr Philip McShane, O.P., for this reference).

6. Cf. Matthew Fox, O.P., *Breakthrough: Meister Eckhart's Creation Spirituality in New Translation* (Garden City, NY: Doubleday Image Books, 1980), pp. 27–8, 40–2. But also see p. 41.

7. Such is the underlying thematic, for instance, of Alain de Libera's study, *Introduction à la Mystique Rhénane d'Albert le Grand à Maître Eckhart* (Paris: O.E.I.L., 1984). Cf. also John Macquarrie, *The Search for Deity* (New York: Crossroad, 1985). For specific references to Eckhart's Neoplatonism, see notes 10 and 41 below.

8. The most comprehensive account in English to date can be found in 'Eckhart's Sources', the Appendix to Bernard McGinn's important work, *The Mystical Thought of Meister Eckhart* (2001), op. cit., pp. 162–82.

9. Cf. Josef Koch, 'Meister Eckhart: Versuch eines Gesamtbildes', *Kleine Schriften* (Roma: Edizioni di Storia a Letteratura, 1973), 1: 212–13. These are generally the same authorities Eckhart cited in his defense at Cologne. Cf. Bernard McGinn, 'Meister Eckhart's Condemnation Reconsidered', *The Thomist* 44 (1980): 406. On the importance of Aristotle in Eckhart's thought, cf. Bernard Welte, 'Meister Eckhart als Aristoteliker', in *Auf der Spur des Ewigen* (Frieburg, 1965). Cited by Schürmann, op. cit., p. 265.

10. On Eckhart as a Christian Neoplatonist, see (among other sources) Ancelet-Hustache, op. cit., pp. 7ff.; Benedict Ashley, O.P., "Three Strands in the Thought of Eckhart, the Scholastic Theologian," *The Thomist* 42 (1978):, p. 232; Caputo, art. cit., p. 198; James M. Clark, *Meister Eckhart: An Introduction to the Study of His Works with an Anthology of His Sermons* (London; Nelson, 1957), p. 71; *Meister Eckhart, The Essential Sermons, Commentaries, Treatises and Defense*, ed. and trans. by Bernard McGinn and Edmund Colledge (New York: Paulist Press, 1981), pp. 27, 34, 40-44; Gundolph Gieraths, *Life in Abundance, Spirituality Today* 38 Supplement (Autumn, 1986), pp. 163-65, 314, 322, William Hinnebusch, O.P., *The History of the Dominican Order*, Vol. II (Staten Island, NY: Alba House, 1973, p. 306; Kertz, art. cit., p. 330 n. 10; de Libera, pp. 242-50, 256, 265, 278-79, 290-92; Vladimir Lossky, *Théologie négative et connaissance de Dieu chez Maître Eckhart* (Paris: Vrin, 1960), pp. 22-26 et passim; Andrew Louth, *The Origins of the Christian Mystical Tradition* (Oxford: Clarendon Press, 1981), pp. 110f.; Koch, art. cit., p. 214; *Pseudo-Dionysius: The Complete Works*, trans. by Colm Luibheid and Paul Rorem (New York: Paulist Press, 1987), p. 30; Bernard McGinn, "Meister Eckhart on God as Absolute Unity," *Neoplatonism and Christian Thought*, ed. by Dominic J. O'Meara (Albany: State University of New York Press, 1982), pp. 137-39; Kurt Ruh, *Meister Eckhart: Theologe, Prediger, Mystiker* (München: Beck, 1985), pp. 55-58, 87-89; Schürmann, op. cit., pp. 140-43 and

passim, and Frank Tobin, *Meister Eckhart: Thought and Language* (Philadelphia: University of Pennsylvania Press, 1986), p. 62, 210, n. 81. Cf. also Evelyn Underhill, *The Mystics of the Church* (London: James Clarke, n.d.), p. 134.

11. Cf. Koch, art. cit., pp. 212–13. For Thomas's identification of the Neoplatonic origin of the *Liber de Causis*, see *Thomas Aquinas: Commentary on the Book of Causes*, trans. by Vincent A. Guagliardo, O.P., Charles R. Hess, O.P. and Richard C. Taylor (Washington: Catholic University of America Press, 1996) and the earlier edition by H. D. Saffrey (Fribourg/Louvain, 1954), p. 3.

12. Cf. Koch, art. cit., pp. 211–12. For a brief survey of some of Eckhart's major sources, see Bernard McGinn, *The Harvest of Mysticism in Medieval Germany* (New York: Crossroad, 2005), pp. 108–12.

13. From a biblical perspective, Eckhart's mysticism was essentially Johannine. In the 592 Latin excerpts made by Eckhart's brethren at Cologne and rediscovered by Kaepelli in 1960, 270 were from his commentary on John's gospel. Of the remainder, 97 were from the commentary on Wisdom, 74 were from the first commentary on Genesis, 69 from the commentary on Exodus, 46 from the second commentary on Genesis, 21 from the commentary on Sirach, and 15 from other sources. For a discussion of Eckhart's exegetical approach, see Bernard McGinn, *The Mystical Thought of Meister Eckhart*, op. cit., pp. 25–31 and 162–4. An index of biblical citations is appended to Colledge and McGinn, eds, *Meister Eckhart: The Essential Sermons, Commentaries, Treatises and Defense*, and McGinn, ed. cit., *Meister Eckhart: Teacher and Preacher*. A more extensive biblical index to the German works is appended to Vol. III of Maurice O'C. Walshe's edition of the *Sermons and Treatises* (Longmead, Shaftesbury, Dorset: Element Books, 1987) and especially the recently revised edition, *The Complete Mystical Works of Meister Eckhart*, revised with Foreword by Bernard McGinn (New York and London: Crossroad Books, 2009).

14. Cf. Simon Tugwell, O.P., ed. and trans., *Albert and Thomas: Selected Writings* (New York: Paulist Press, 1988), pp. 10, 258.

15. For an interpretation of Aquinas which is open to a greater Neoplatonic influence, see W. Hankey, *God in Himself: Aquinas' Doctrine of God as Expounded in the Summa theologiae* (Oxford University Press, 1987).

16. See above, Chapter 1. On Albert's revival of Neoplatonism and its influence on Eckhart, see Tugwell, ed. cit., pp. 10–11, 55–92; Alain de Libera, op. cit., pp. 25–58; Gundolph Gieraths, *Life in Abundance, Spirituality Today* 38 Supplement (Autumn, 1986): 3–5; Bernard McGinn, 'Meister Eckhart: An Introduction', *An Introduction to the Medieval Mystics of Europe*, ed. by Paul E. Szarmach (Albany: State University of New York Press, 1984), p. 244 (hereafter: 'Introduction'); and Francis Catania, 'Albert the Great', *Encyclopedia of Philosophy* 1: 66.

17. On Albert and the 'Cologne School', see de Libera, op. cit., pp. 10–13, 31–41. On Eckhart and Albert, see B. Geyer, 'Albertus Magnus and Meister Eckhart', *Festschrift Josef Quint anlässliche seines 65 Geburtstages überreicht* (Bonn: 1964), pp. 253–4. On Eckhart's part in the Neoplatonic revival inaugurated by Albert the Great and his disciples, see de Libera, pp. 29–58; McGinn, 'Introduction', art. cit., p. 214; Hinnebusch, op. cit., Vol. II, p. 156; and James M. Clark, *Meister Eckhart: An Introduction to the Study of His Works with an Anthology of His Sermons* (London: Nelson, 1957), pp. 71, 97–8; and Clark, op. cit., pp. 71, 97–8.

18. According to William Hinnebusch, a premier historian of the Dominican Order, '. . . Eckhart began his training at the University of Paris, where he studied philosophy under Siger of Brabant about 1277.' Op. cit., p. 303. See above, p. 2.

19. The story was related during canonization proceedings in Naples in 1319 by Bartholomew of Capua, who had heard it from Hugo of Lucca. For a full account, see James A. Weisheipl, O.P., *Thomas d'Aquino and Albert His Teacher*, Gilson Lecture No. 2 (Toronto: Pontifical Institute of Medieval Studies, 1980), pp. 19–20. Cf. Kenelm Foster, *The Life of St Thomas Aquinas: Biographical Documents* (London: Longmans, 1959), pp. 112–13; and Sr. M. Albert, O.P., *Albert the Great* (Oxford: Blackfriars, 1948), p. 79. Tugwell supplies a critical corrective and plausible explanation of the story, ed. cit., pp. 26–7.

20. The general chapter of 1309, and that at Metz in 1313, similarly legislated that Dominicans must conform to Thomas' doctrine. See Hinnebusch, op. cit., 2: 156f.; Jeanne Ancelet-Hustache, *Master Eckhart and the Rhineland Mystics*, op. cit., pp. 36f.; and Ashley, art. cit., p. 227, n. 3. Dom David Knowles writes, 'In 1880 Denifle discovered at Erfurt a string of Latin works which, when examined and analyzed, showed Eckhart as holding and using all the metaphysical framework that Aquinas had created out of Aristotelian materials, and using exactly the same authorities as the schoolmen – Augustine, William of Auvergne, Bonaventure and Aquinas.' 'Denifle and Ehrle', *History* 54 (1969): 4.

21. Sermon 103, DP 59 (W 4, Vol. I, pp. 46–7).

22. Sermon 70 (W 41, Vol. II, p. 287).

23. Sermon 6 (W 65 Vol. II, p. 136). Cf. also *Talks of Instruction* (Counsels on Discernment), Colledge-McGinn, ed. cit., pp. 256–7.

24. Sermon 39. (W 59, Vol. II, p. 100).

25. Sermon 7 (Walshe No. 72, Vol. II, p. 189). On Eckhart and Aquinas, cf. Ashley, art. cit., p. 232. On significant differences between the two Dominicans, see Colledge-McGinn, ed. cit., pp. 27, 32 and 36, and McGinn, 'Condemnation', p. 405, nn. 76–7. For Aquinas on relative priority of will: *Summa Theologiae* I, Q. 82 a. 3. On charity and union with God, see II-II, Q. 24 a. 4; Q. 45, a. 4; Q. 172 a. 4; Q. 184 a. 1 ad 2; III, Q. 89, a. 6. On the absolute priority of intellect as highest of faculties, see I, Q. 82 a. 3 and II-II, Q. 83, a. 3 ad 1. On eternal happiness as an act of the speculative intellect (i.e., the beatific vision), see I-II, Q. 3 aa. 3–5, 8. Eckhart seems ultimately to have gone beyond the moderate intellectualism of Aquinas with regard to the nature of human beatitude and also the nature of God as subsisting intelligence. See also Woods (2009), op. cit., pp. 40–7.

26. See *Pseudo-Dionysius: The Complete Works*, ed. cit.; Andrew Louth, *Denys the Areopagite* (London and Wilton, CT: Morehouse-Barlow, 1989); and Louth, *Origins*, esp. pp. 159–78. Cf. I. P. Sheldon-Williams, 'The Greek Christian Platonist Tradition from the Cappadocians to Maximus and Eriugena', *The Cambridge History of Later Greek and Early Medieval Philosophy*, ed. by A. H. Armstrong, (Cambridge University Press, 1970), pp. 425–533; and Henry Chadwick, ed. and intro., *Alexandrian Christianity*, (Philadelphia: The Westminster Press, 1954, General Introductions). For a recent synopsis of the Neoplatonic revivals of the Middle Ages, see Tugwell, ed. cit., pp. 50–7.

27. 'There is still room for debate as to whether Eckhart was a mystic using scholastic terminology or a theologian adopting a Neoplatonist outlook, but of his

radical traditionalism and orthodoxy there is no longer any doubt.' Knowles, art. cit., p. 4.

28. Before its appearance in the German Dominican school, Neoplatonic influence was most clearly present in the West in the dominant Augustinian tradition and in the Celtic-Dionysian tradition of John Scottus Eriugena and Richard of St Victor. Cf. John J. O'Meara, *Eriugena* (Oxford: Clarendon Press, 1988); John J. O'Meara and Ludwig Bieler, eds, *The Mind of Eriugena* (Dublin: Irish University Press, 1973); and G. H. Allard, 'The Primacy of Existence in the Thought of Eriugena', in O'Meara, ed. cit., pp. 89–96.

29. Although a defining emblem of the 'Cambridge Platonists' of the seventeenth century, evocation of the 'Ancient Theology' was no less characteristic of later figures such as Dean William Inge, whose many works contributed significantly to the rediscovery of the English mystical tradition at the turn of the twentieth century.

30. 'There are some cases where the similarities are too clear, both in vocabulary and in ideas, for us to exclude the hypothesis of a direct influence of Philo's writings on the authors of the New Testament.' Marcel Simon, *Jewish Sects at the Time of Jesus*, trans. by James H. Farley (Philadelphia: Fortress Press, 1967), p. 140.

31. Cf. Acts: 12:25; 13:5, 13, 15:37, etc. and 1 Peter 5:13.

32. Cf. John Dillon, 'Origen's Doctrine of the Trinity and Some Later Neoplatonic Theories', in *Neoplatonism and Christian Thought*, ed. cit., pp. 19–23. For the influence of Origen on Eckhart, see Hugo Rahner, 'Die Gottesgeburt: Die Lehre der Kirchenväter von der Geburt Christi im Herzen der Gläubigen', *Zeitschrift für katholische Theologie* 59 (1935): 412ff.

33. For a concise history of this philosophical tradition, see R. T. Wallis, *Neoplatonism* (London: Duckworth, 1972). On Eckhart, see p. 169.

34. For an overview, see Louth, *Origins*, pp. 36–51. On Plotinus, see Wallis, op. cit., pp. 37–93; and Rufus Jones, *Some Exponents of Mystical Religion* (London: Epworth, 1930), pp. 44–76. The standard translation of the *Enneads* is that by Stephen MacKenna and revised by B. S. Page (London: 1969). A. H. Armstrong's Loeb Classical Library edition is now complete in seven volumes.

35. Cf. Koch, art. cit., pp. 211–12. The 'boiling' metaphor is found in Enneads VI, 7, 12, where Plotinus says 'There no indigence or impatience can exist but all must be teeming, seething with life.' Cited by Schürmann, op. cit., p. 247, n. 140.

36. For a discussion of this theme in Eckhart, see especially Rahner, art. cit. pp. 333–418. Cf. also Kertz, art. cit.; Robert S. Stoudt, 'Meister Eckhart and the Eternal Birth: The Heart of the Preacher', *The Thomist* 50 (1986): 238–59; and Richard Woods, op. cit, pp. 109–27.

37. I. P. Sheldon-Williams, loc. cit., p. 434.

38. Hence the redundant Latin soubriquet 'Scottus Eriugena', 'the Scot born in Ireland', the ancient name of that country being *Eriu* and the dominant tribe of the area being the Scots. John of Ireland was not the first to undertake translating the Greek texts, but until the twelfth century, his were the most reliable versions.

39. On the Neoplatonism of Dionysius, see Henri Dominique Saffrey, O.P., 'New Objective Links between the Pseudo-Dionysius and Proclus', in O'Meara, ed. cit., pp. 64–74. For John's influence on Eckhart, see Rahner, art. cit., pp. 400–6, 416; and Rudolf Otto, *Mysticism East and West*, trans. by Bertha Bracey and Richenda

Payne (New York: The Macmillan Co., 1960), pp. 273–4.

40. Cf. John J. O'Meara, 'The Neoplatonism of Saint Augustine', in O'Meara, ed. cit., pp. 34–41. For Augustine's influence on Eckhart, see especially Rahner, art. cit., p. 416. Abundant additional references will be found in the articles and books by Colledge, Kertz, Lossky and McGinn.

41. 'Along with John the Scot and Nicholas of Cusa, Eckhart is arguably the most systematic of the Latin Neoplatonic dialecticians, and he is the one who suffered the most for it. The majority of the twenty-eight propositions from his works condemned by Pope John XXII in the bull "In Agro Dominico" of March 27, 1329, involve or imply aspects of his appropriation of Neoplatonism. Three of them (articles 23, 24 and 26) relate directly to his doctrine of God . . .' McGinn, 'God as Absolute Unity', p. 129.

42. See Woods (2009), op. cit., pp. 97, 114–25. For the influence of Proclus on Eckhart, see Schürmann, op. cit., p. 248 n. 6 and p. 265 (under Schrimpf).

43. Sermon 76 (W 7, Vol. I, p. 67).

44. Sermon 86 (W 9, Vol. I, p. 87).

45. Rudolf Otto observed that Eckhart's concept of love was not that of the emotional love-mystics. 'Nor has his agápe anything in common with the Platonic or Plotinian eros, but . . . is the pure Christian emotion in its elemental chastity and simplicity without exaggeration or admixture.' See *Mysticism East and West*, op. cit., p. 232. Cf. p. 231.

46. Sermon 81 (W 64, Vol. II, p. 125). For discussion see Woods (2009), op. cit., pp. 79–89, 119–22.

47. Wallis, op. cit., p. 160.

48. Cf. D. P. Walker, *The Ancient Theology, Studies in Christian Platonism from the Fifteenth to the Eighteenth Centuries* (London: Duckworth, 1972). Cf. also Louth, *Origins*, pp. 179–204 and Macquarrie, op. cit., passim.

49. For an eloquent argument for reappropriating the original philosophical tradition of Christian mystical spirituality and dogma, see Andrew Louth, *Discerning the Mystery* (Oxford: Clarendon Press, 1983).

Chapter 4

On Creation: Did Eckhart Love the World?[1]

The death in September 2002 of Peter Talbot Willcox, my friend of many years and second chairman of the Eckhart Society, impoverished us all. I remember back in 1992 browbeating him into taking on that task, among the many others he shouldered, despite his professed lack of expertise in matters Eckhartian, academic and, indeed, Roman Catholic, not to mention Dominican. Among his many interests and, in fact, passions, if I may so describe them, was a profound concern with the environment. On several occasions I had participated in conferences Peter organized on the subject, especially in league with the late Teddy Goldsmith, editor of *The Ecologist*, one of Peter's vast number of friends. While teaching in Oxford I was privileged to be included among the core group of the Friends of the Centre, which Peter organized and out of which there developed another of his brainchildren, the Religious Education and Environment Programme, a project to introduce environmental studies into the British religious education curriculum.

There was much more to Peter's passions, not least his work for the World Congress of Faiths. But as I came to know and work with Peter, what impressed me most personally about his insatiable quest to get at the heart of things in a theoretical, and especially a practical way, was his struggle to bring Eckhart and environmental concern together. As we strolled around his lovely gardens at Thanescroft one evening, he confided to me his suspicion that the Meister might find his ecological pursuits somewhat questionable. Peter was a man of many 'whys'. In any event, he struggled to integrate these two poles of interest – and not without cause.

What follows is more an investigation of themes rather than an exposition of a thesis. Like Peter, I harbour a few suspicions about how comfortably Eckhart's way and the ecologist's way interconnect. I certainly cannot promise that I have resolved what Peter recognized, correctly,

I think, as real spiritual tension in the spirituality of Meister Eckhart. But there are at least hints of a resolution of the perceived tension.

In regard to the environmental situation itself, I must presume rather than argue that the crisis facing the present and next generations is real, that it is grave, and that it is global. Even ten years ago, debating whether climate change, habitat deterioration and widespread species destruction were real might still be possible, but not today. The volume of evidence, both scientific and personal, is unmistakably clear. We may choose to ignore the facts at our peril, but it is no longer possible to deny them except by dint of wilful ignorance.

Having followed the progress of environmental research and action for over 30 years, my own view is that the situation is far more advanced and far-reaching than is generally acknowledged today. Even should the world's governments respond more effectively than they have at Kyoto and Copenhagen to curb the emission of greenhouse gases, reverse the pollution and despoliation of the seas, rivers and fresh-water lakes, halt the destruction of rainforests and the eradication of habitat, I am convinced that within the next twenty years not only will the delicately balanced biological systems of this planet reach a point of lethal stress, but that hundreds of millions of people will have to contend with ecological catastrophe.

Almost twenty years ago, in November 1990, I attended an inaugural lecture at Oxford University by Sir Crispin Tickell, later the president of Green College, who predicted that the principal social problem confronting the world of the early twenty-first century would be the dislocation and suffering of environmental refugees rather than political refugees. His prediction has become alarmingly true as the world watched in horror the human catastrophes that followed in the wake of Hurricane Katrina and the Boxing Day tsunami of 2004. It goes without saying that, as always, the greatest burden of suffering will fall upon the poor, particularly children, the elderly, women, and the infirm. We are already beginning to see that prediction come true as tropical storms increase in intensity in southeast Asia and vast numbers of people, especially the poorest, are driven from their flooded villages and towns. Simultaneously, millions of people in Africa alone have been dislocated by drought and famine, much of it caused by the violent civil wars engulfing the continent.

Spirituality, it seems to me, offers individuals, and the human race as a whole, two routes out of the messy situation we are in – one forward and one backward. Many Christians, I am sure, find those spiritualities most congenial which turn away from the present and the future, back to a supposedly simpler and presumably more wholesome way of living. Other people, impatient with ancient formulas and procedures, are willing and ready to start off in wholly new directions.

The fact is that any spirituality which cannot aid people in facing the challenges of the present and the future in a responsible and constructive manner is hardly worth the name 'Christian'. But it is not likely that any spirituality which simply ignores or rejects past wisdom and experience will have the capacity to guide or inspire those with the motivation and ability to recognize the problem and act.

Thus I believe that our task today is to address the future out of the most resourceful heritage of the past. The question I would like to place before you is not how Eckhart would respond to the ecological crisis were he here, for any answer would be necessarily conjectural and probably beside the point. The present situation is so remote from anything Eckhart could have experienced in his time and circumstances as to be all but meaningless. The question is, rather, how can *we* respond to the situation confronting us, and especially whether Eckhart's way provides resources for responsibly and constructively addressing the major issues certain to challenge us in the immediate future, and for decades to come.

The Ecological Challenge to Eckhart

In the week before I travelled over from Ireland for the 2001 Eckhart Society Conference, two events sharpened my ruminations about Eckhart and ecology. The first was a report on the disappearance of eels from Irish coastal waters. For a decade now, the number of eels returning to Ireland to spawn has been diminishing steadily, like those of salmon. Now while that is of immediate concern to fishermen, whose incomes depend on plucking unlucky eels from the rivers and selling them abroad, since the Irish, unlike their continental counterparts, do not particularly dote on fried eel, the reason for the disappearance of the eels, again like that of the salmon, is of deeper significance. Ten years of study have persuaded marine ecologists that two factors may be at work: intestinal parasites acquired in the waters off Japan and, more ominously, the withdrawal of the Gulf Stream away from the Irish coast as a consequence of climate change. The first factor points to the planetary character of marine pollution, like the Mediterranean Zebra mollusks suffocating the coastal areas of the Great Lakes or the more recent advent of Asian carp into the same area. The second factor points not only to the local economic and gastronomic disruptions caused by changes in the sea, but the planetary shifts that will increasingly alter global weather patterns, the level of the seas, and the pattern of life of whole populations. In both instances, let me add, the events that led to these changes are considered by many to be the result of human activity.

The second event occurred as I was walking with an English friend along the beaches of Brittas Bay, just north of Arklow, a couple of years later. As we walked and talked and admired the breathtaking scenery, I noticed something curious on the sand. It turned out to be a tiny starfish, a little smaller than a 50-pence coin, probably cast up by the tide earlier that day and stranded. I picked it up with the thought of giving it to one of the children playing on the beach, or adding it to interesting bits and pieces of my window-shelf collection. But as my friend Michael quickly noticed, when I touched one of its legs, the little creature moved. It was still alive.

I was preparing to return it to the sea when I noticed two little boys playing nearby, both of them about five years old. I showed it to them and told them it was still alive but needed to be taken into the sea or it would die. They were delighted and certainly thought seriously about putting it into a jar or just taking it home in a pocket. But when I explained that it was a baby starfish that needed to go back to its home, they immediately agreed to take it into the sea. That was more than an educable moment, as my teacher friends call them. It was a sign of hope. We can be stewards of creation.

But is this consonant with *abgescheidenheit*? Did Eckhart really love the world?

Three areas present themselves for consideration as we begin to explore Eckhart and ecology: first, Eckhart's doctrine of Creation, or at least aspects of it, the holiness of creation as he understood that from the biblical and early Christian spiritual tradition as opposed, in many respects, to the Neoplatonic tradition he inherited with its well-known allergy to space, time and matter. Second, I wish to look at some of the ethical implications of Eckhart's ascetical teaching, particularly detachment as renunciation, versus detachment for the sake of action. Finally, I will take a brief look at Eckhart's teaching on suffering.

Eckhart on Creation

The tension in Eckhart's teaching springs partly from the difference between the ancient Hebrew, and later Christian, tradition regarding creation and the Neoplatonic animadversions regarding matter that Eckhart inherited from his Alexandrian sources. He was certainly aware of the great biblical teaching about the goodness and dignity of creation, as is evident from his commentaries on Genesis. There is no Manichaean strain there or elsewhere in his sermons and treatises. He knew the Book of Isaiah well and was surely knowledgeable about the vision of the Peaceable Kingdom found there and in Hosea. Eckhart was also familiar with the Book of Wisdom, that very late and beautiful work of Alexandrian Judaism in which the whole creation-tradition is so wonderfully epitomized:

> For you [God] love all things that exist,
>   and loathe none of the things you have made,
> for you would not have made anything
>   if you had hated it.
> How would anything have endured
>   if you had not willed it?
> Or how would anything not called forth by you
>   have been preserved?
> You spare all things, for they are yours,
>   O Lord who loves the living.
> For your immortal spirit is in all things.
> (Wisdom 11:24–12:1)

The positive evaluation of the natural world found in Hebrew tradition and the New Testament was preserved and amplified by the Latin Christian tradition in its early period, eloquently enough in the exhortations of Pope St Leo I, who preached, much as would Eckhart a millennium later:

> For every one of us Christians, nature [*ipsas rerum natura*] is full of instruction that we should worship God. The heavens and the earth, the sea and all within them, proclaim the goodness and the almighty power of their maker. The wonderful beauty of these inferior elements of nature demands that we, intelligent beings, should give thanks to God.[2]

Elsewhere, the saintly Pope expounds the ethical imperatives of this vision in terms that are not without relevance today as we ponder the religious foundations of an ecological ethic:

> Use creatures as they should be used: the earth, the sea, the sky, the air, the springs and the rivers. Give praise and glory to their Creator for all that you find beautiful and wonderful in them. See with your bodily eyes the light that shines on earth, but embrace with your whole soul and all your affections *the true light which enlightens every man who comes into this world* . . .
>
> Our words and exhortations are not intended to make you disdain God's works or think there is anything contrary to your faith in creation, for the good God has himself made all things good. What we do ask is that you use reasonably and with moderation all the marvellous creatures, which adorn this world . . .[3]

The Greek tradition was more likely to see the natural world as an allegory of the heavenly kingdom, as in this Easter homily of St Gregory of Nyssa:

> On this day, as the prophet says, God makes a new heaven and a new earth [Cf. Rev. 21:1]. What is this new heaven? you may ask. It is the firmament of our faith in Christ. What is this new earth? A good heart, a heart like the earth, which drinks up the rain that falls on it and yields a rich harvest.
>
> In this new creation, purity of life is the sun, the virtues are the stars, transparent goodness is the air . . .[4]

There is, of course, an alternative tradition, a largely eschatologically driven vision that emphasized the evanescence and transience of the natural world, coupled with exhortations to use it as if not using it, to be in the world but not of it. But above all is the common view that whether helpful or hurtful, the natural world, Creation, was meant for and subject to humankind. Although there were biblical exceptions such as the Book of Job, and even the ultimately world-affirming oracles in the Book of Revelation, the biblical code tended, as a whole, to be anthropocentric.[5]

Like St Gregory, Eckhart allegorized, to be sure. But like Thomas Aquinas before him and whom he professed to follow, he did not lose sight of the inherent sanctity of creation, its *sacramental* character as a revelation of God as creator. 'Someone who knew nothing but creatures would never need to attend to any sermons,' he said, 'for every creature is full of God and is a book.'[6] Again, 'All things speak God. What my mouth does in speaking and declaring God, is likewise done by the essence of a stone, and this is understood more by works than by words.'[7]

Like Thomas, moreover, he was not much given to enthusiasm in regard to particulars, in contrast to their great mentor, St Albert the Great, who could spend hours observing the behaviour of the ant-lion, or testing to see if ostriches really liked the taste of iron filings. However creation-centred Eckhart might have been, on the other hand he was certainly no nature mystic. He might have preached to the collection box if no one else had been present,[8] but I doubt very much that it would have occurred to him to take his message to the birds or the fish or marvel at the dietary preferences of ostriches.

Eckhart was not much impressed, if at all, with the 'thinginess of things', their particular matter, colour, texture or shape. In one sermon he says,

> I look at the lilies in the field, their brightness, their colour and all their petals, but I do not see their fragrance. Why not? Because the scent is in me. But on the other hand, what I say is in me and I speak it forth from me. All creatures have the flavour of creatures only for my outer self, like wine, bread and meat. But for my inner self nothing has the flavour of a creatures but rather that of a gift from God, though for my innermost self they smack not of a gift from God but of eternity.[9]

The varied hues of a sunset, the intoxicating fragrance of a rose, the melancholy call of the cuckoo, never seem to enter his spiritual compass as marvels in their own right. God knows what he would have made of the 40 shades of green on an Irish hillside or the rapturous vision of Gerard Manley Hopkins:

> For skies of couple-colour as a brinded cow;
>   For rose-moles in all stipple upon trout that swim;
> Fresh-firecoal chestnut-falls; finches wings;
>   Landscape plotted and pierced – fold, fallow, and plough;
>   And all trades, their gear and tackle and trim.
>
>   (*Pied Beauty*)

But Eckhart was also fully capable of paradoxically reversing himself in regard to the revelatory power of creation. 'All creatures are too base to be able to reveal God, they are all nothing compared to God. Therefore no creature can utter a word about God in his works.'[10] True to his Neoplatonic philosophical orientation, he frequently pointed out that it is the physical dimensions of human existence that tend to obstruct our clear perception of the presence of God, especially within. The apophatic tradition was not inclined to love the material Creation of space and time:

> There are three things that prevent us from hearing the eternal Word. The first is corporeality, the second is multiplicity, the third is temporality. If a man had transcended these three things, he would dwell in eternity, he would dwell in the spirit, he would dwell in unity and in the desert – and there he would hear the eternal Word.[11]

These are, of course, the fundamental dimensions of the created universe as such, and thus not only distinct from but in some sense opposed to the spirituality Eckhart recognized in God and all intelligent creatures. He observes, in a characteristic iteration of his thematic, that:

> Three things prevent the soul from uniting with God. The first is that she is too scattered, that she is not unitary for when the soul is inclined towards creatures, she is not unitary. The second is when she is involved with temporal things. The third is when she is turned towards the body, for then she cannot unite with God.
>
> So too there are three things that favour the union of God with the soul. The first is that the soul should be simple and undivided: for if she is to be united with God, she must be simple as God is simple. Secondly, that she should dwell above herself and above all transient things and adhere to God. The third is that she should be detached from all material things and work according to her primal purity.[12]

Eckhart did not shy away from the implication that the material component of human nature itself presented a barrier to complete union with God. In a virtual paraphrase of St Paul's exhortation to the Romans, he preached,

> . . . body and flesh are always opposed to spirit. The body is often too strong for the spirit, and there is a real fight between them, an unceas-

ing struggle. Here in the world the body is bold and strong, for it is at home, the world helps it, the earth is its fatherland, it is helped by all its kin: food, drink, soft living – all is opposed to spirit. The spirit is an alien here, but in heaven are its kin, its whole race, *there* it has good friends, if it strives for there and makes its home there. And so, in order to succour the spirit in this alien realm, and to impede the flesh somewhat in this strife lest it should conquer the spirit, we put on it the bridle of penitential practices, thus curbing it so that the spirit can resist it.[13]

It is perhaps too easy to quote Eckhart against Eckhart. He was, after all, a dialectical thinker, if not just a thinker in the mould of Walt Whitman who said, 'Do I contradict myself? Very well then, I contradict myself, (I am large, I contain multitudes).'[14] Eckhart, too, was large and contained multitudes. In any case, it is less in Eckhart's doctrine of creation that I find reason for ecological hope than in his doctrine of detachment.

Abgescheidenheit: Asceticism for a Possible Future

In times of religious and social crisis, new forms of asceticism tend to appear, most likely as a rejection of the prevailing norms of consumption and the rule of a market economy perceived as hostile to spiritual values. It is clearly present in the mission of John the Baptist and the early followers of Jesus. It reappears in the declining years of the Roman Empire, as the 'new asceticism' favoured by Jerome and Augustine and their contemporaries, including Pelagius, stood in stark opposition to the opulence of late classical antiquity. So also in the Middle Ages, first in the form of Celtic and Benedictine monasticism, then in the revolutionary movement known as the *Vita Apostolica* that animated the great mendicant orders.

Eckhart almost certainly inherited his enthusiasm for apostolic poverty from his training as a Dominican, itself a product of the quest for the true Apostolic Life. But Eckhart's teaching about spiritual poverty is unusual for a number of reasons. While radical, Eckhart's vision of detachment, *abgescheidenheit* in his quite literal Middle High German, was not primarily a rejection of worldly values and possessions predicated on some perceived wrongness in them, but represented a logical consequence of his metaphysics of spirit and matter. Further, his ascetical teaching was not based on works – of devotions and practices such as pilgrimages, the pursuit of relics, or even an intensification of ordinary Christian liturgical life. It was essentially founded on faith in the all-merciful divine presence within.

Not that Eckhart was opposed to religious behaviour. He simply saw it for what it was, a means to an end that could be safely jettisoned when the goal was at hand. And for him, the goal was attained in breaking through the veils of time, multiplicity and matter, in grasping God without a why or a wherefore. And this was achieved not by holding on but by letting go, even, eventually, of God. For, as he said,

> Every attachment to every work deprives one of the freedom to wait upon God in the present and to follow him alone in the light with which he would guide you in what to do and what to leave alone, free and renewed in every present moment, as if this were all that you had ever had or wanted or could do.[15]

That the radical freedom implicated in Eckhart's understanding of detachment has relevance for us today, particularly in regard to the environmental crisis facing the world, may seem obvious, but it is certainly not so to the world at large.

The Groaning of Creation

I would like to put forward another area of spiritual instruction in which Eckhart can be of assistance as the human race faces an uncertain future in the wake of ecological disruption and global environmental deterioration. Eckhart's teaching about suffering and patient endurance is not only surprisingly original but, as Ursula Fleming came to see many years ago, both sound and effective.[16]

Adequately exploring the theme of suffering would require another and probably very long discussion, so I will have to leave it to the side at this point with only a few passing observations. First, Eckhart teaches, like all wise spiritual masters, that there is no route around suffering in this life. Here he confronts one of the most pervasive illusions of the modern world – that suffering is curable by means of the ever-increasing application of technological remedies, from over-the-counter drugs to lavishly expensive medical treatments. As a psychiatric counsellor, I do not mean to disparage the development of effective treatments for physical and mental illness – Jesus himself, after all, was a healer. But what Jesus taught, and Eckhart repeated, is that the way beyond suffering is not around it, but through it.

It hardly needs noting that when it comes to the social and economic cost of avoiding even minor suffering, much less treating calamitous illness and injuries, the major beneficiaries are the rich, whether in affluent North America and Europe or in the vast populations of Asia, Africa and Latin America.

Second, Eckhart explains – and here I think he is most original and compelling – that it is in embracing suffering with a detached heart that we encounter God. For, as he says in a striking phrase in his *Book of Divine Comfort*, God is not only *in* our suffering, but *is* our suffering.

> However great the suffering may be, if it comes through God, then God suffers first from it. Indeed, by the truth that *is* God, there never was so tiny a pang of sorrow that befell a man, not the least little discomfort or inconvenience, but if he placed it in God, then it would pain God incomparably more than that man, and incommode God more than the man himself. But if God endures this for the sake of such benefit as He intends for you thereby, and if *you* will endure that which God endures and which comes to you *through* Him, then it inevitably becomes godlike, so that shame is like honour, bitterness like sweetness and the blackest darkness like the brightest light. It takes all its savour from God and becomes godlike: for whatever comes to such a man conforms to God, because he seeks nothing else and has no taste for anything else. Accordingly, he gets hold of God in all bitterness just as in the greatest sweetness.[17]

It is towards the end of this remarkable work that Eckhart so surprisingly tells us,

> whatever someone good suffers for God's sake, he suffers in God, and God is with him in his suffering. If my suffering is in God and God suffers with me, how then can my suffering be painful when suffering loses its pain, and my pain is in God and my pain *is* God? In truth, as God is truth and wherever I find truth I find my God, the truth – so likewise, neither more nor less, whenever I find pure suffering in God and for God, there I find God, my suffering.[18]

This is not to say that for Eckhart suffering is a good thing or redemptive in itself, much less that it should be pursued as a means to union with God. Such aspects of Christian spirituality must be sought elsewhere.

Eckhart's sanity and sanctity led him in an entirely different direction, one that can be of real value in the years to come. Here I urge you not only to read Eckhart, but also to rediscover Ursula.

What Eckhart is affirming in regard to the suffering, especially of the poor as a consequence of environmental degradation – and not only of the poor, but of everyone else as well as the animals and plants and even the planet itself – is that God is very much present within the suffering. We will not find God, then, by attempting to insulate ourselves more and more from the results of our folly, but, by entering into it, into the suffering of God, find a way through it. For as St Paul himself proclaimed,

> I consider that the sufferings of this present time are not worth comparing with the glory that is to be revealed to us. For Creation waits with eager longing for the revealing of the children of God; for Creation was subjected to futility, not of its own will but by the will of the One who subjected it in hope; because Creation itself will be set free from its bondage to decay and obtain the glorious liberty of the children of God. We know that all of Creation has been groaning in travail together until now; and not only Creation, but we ourselves, who have the first fruits of the Spirit, groan inwardly as we wait for adoption as children, the redemption of our bodies. (Rom. 8:18–23)

Reflecting on Eckhart's reliance on the teachings of Moses Maimonides, the twelfth-century Jewish scholar, the late Rabbi Albert Friedlander called attention to their mutual puzzlement regarding the absence of a blessing after the creation of water in the Genesis story, which sheds some light on Eckhart's attitude toward the place of humankind in the order of Creation.

> . . . the fourth day of creation leads both of them into a fascinating area of speculation concerning the stars. Eckhart follows Maimonides here, who will not accept the meaning and purpose of these heavenly bodies to be their function of illuminating the earth: the lesser should not define the function of the greater! In the *Liber parabolarum* Eckhart also follows Maimonides in viewing Jacob's ladder as the symbol of the cosmos. Where angels pass one another on the same rung, Maimonides and Eckhart both view this as an image of the harmony of the spheres which thus, in their movement, maintain the heavenly constellations. Against existing theologies, they feel that it is not their function within the lower world which justifies their existence: the more perfect does

not become defined through the less perfect; and the movement of the spheres is the harmony of the whole cosmos, not the maintenance of one of its parts.[19]

Friedlander adds, significantly, 'It is here that Maimonides argues against the notion that man is the ultimate and real purpose of the whole cosmos (a view rejected also by Aquinas).' To Eckhart also it seems evident that the world in all its enticing splendour was not simply 'made for man'. It can be argued, I believe, that Eckhart's vision of Creation was not essentially anthropocentric. He did not, however, develop an environmental ethic even as rudimentary as that of Pope Leo the Great. Nevertheless, it would be well to recall that such an enterprise was noticeably lacking from the medieval outlook in general, even in the teachings of St Francis of Assisi.

Did Eckhart love the world? Does he have anything to offer the world as it faces the very serious crises of global environmental deterioration? The obvious answer might seem to be, 'Not very much', but it would be well to bear in mind that in sharp contrast to the world-weary spiritualities of the *Devotio Moderna* which arose out of the natural and social calamities that befell the later fourteenth and fifteenth centuries, and the world-denying approaches of much post-Reformation devotionalism, Eckhart never disparaged the natural world, but recognized it as a sign, if an imperfect one, that effectively revealed the presence of God.

Saving Creation

In concluding, I first take it for granted that the environmental crisis confronting this and the following generations is real, extremely serious, and in large measure the result of human selfishness, greed and short-sightedness. This is particularly so in regard to the industrial exploitation of increasingly rare natural resources, and the resulting contamination of the planetary system upon which life depends both absolutely and in terms of the quality of life – the atmosphere, the oceans, plant life – especially the great forests and animal habitats.

In most respects, resolving the environmental crisis or at least reducing its impact, especially on the poor and powerless, is the most important challenge facing humanity in the twenty-first century. We should not forget that not only in the undeveloped and so-called developing world, but in Britain, Ireland, the United States, Canada, Australia, and other parts of the industrialized world, poor and lower-middle-class families suffer the greatest hardships from pollution, the sometimes criminal mismanagement of hazardous wastes, and bureaucratic foot-dragging. Environmental degradation is thus a major form of social injustice, especially in the developing nations of the world, but in our own as well, as natural and social resources are diverted from their proper objective, which is establishing and maintaining justice for all, to the illusory ends of ever-increasing profits and especially war-making potential.

One way or another, for many years into the future we may expect to experience widespread suffering created by the degradation of earth's interconnected biosystems in the form of climate change, resulting weather disturbances, coastal flooding, drought, population displacement, famine, epidemics and species extinction – to name only the major factors.

Second, I have questioned whether Eckhart's long-silent voice can tell us anything out of the pages of his sermons and treatises that will assist us in confronting and hopefully reducing the impact of environmental degradation. I believe it can, and in three related areas:

1. Eckhart's notion of the holiness of Creation.
2. His articulation of detachment as selfless commitment to contemplative action flowing from unity with God in the depths of being.
3. His vision of the transforming power of suffering.

Eckhart reminds us that even in the midst of struggle, perhaps of defeat, it is possible to continue our efforts to be just, to bring the Word of God to birth within us and in the marketplace and field. One of his most creative breakthroughs was surely Eckhart's insistence that the contemplative-in-action is the true mystic, the follower of Christ, able to act joyfully and effectively, being devoid of self-interest. Did he not tell us that

> Anyone who is established thus in God's will wants nothing but what is God's will and what is God. If he were sick he would not want to be well. To him all pain is pleasure, all multiplicity is bare simplicity, if he is truly established in the will of God. Even though it meant the pains of hell it would be joy and happiness to him. He is free and has left self behind, and must be free of whatever is to come in to him: if my eye is to perceive colour, it must be free of all colour. If I see a blue or white colour, the sight of my eye which sees the colour, the very thing that sees, is the same as that which is seen by the eye. The eye with which I see God is

the same eye with which God sees me: my eye and God's eye are one eye, one seeing, one knowing and one love.[20]

Let us pray, then, as he taught us, that we may follow Christ faithfully in the practice of true virtue, fulfilling our task and destiny as the Stewards of Creation, may God help us. Amen.[21]

Notes

1. Sections of this chapter appeared in 'Ecology, Spirituality, and Eckhart: On Loving the World', *Eckhart Review*, No. 11 (Spring, 2002): 36–47.
2. Sermon 6 on Lent: 1–2 (*Patrologia Latina* 54), 285b.
3. Sermo in Nativitate Domini 7, 2. 6, Ibid., 217–18, 220–1.
4. Oratio 1 in Christi resurrectionem, *Gregorii Nysseni opera*, Werner Jaeger and Herman Langerbeck, eds, Vol. IX (Leiden: Brill, 1992), pp. 277–80, 305.
5. On the Book of Job see Calvin B. DeWitt, 'Behemoth and Batrachians in the Eye of God: Responsibility to Other Kinds in Biblical Perspective', in Dieter T. Hessel and Rosemary R. Ruether, eds, *Christianity and Ecology* (Cambridge: Harvard University Press, 2000), pp. 291–316. On the book of Revelation, see Sarah Hobson and Jane Lubchenko, eds, *Revelation and the Environment AD 95–1995* (Singapore, New Jersey, London: World Scientific Publishing Co., 1997); Barbara R. Rossing, 'River of Life in God's New Jerusalem: An Eschatological Vision for Earth's Future', in Hessel and Ruether, ed. cit., pp. 205–24; and Richard Woods, 'Seven Bowls Of Wrath: The Ecological Relevance of Revelation', *Biblical Theology Bulletin* 38 (2007) 2: 64–75.
6. Sermon 9 (Walshe No. 67, Vol. II, p. 155, DP 10).
7. Sermon 53 (Walshe No. 22, Vol. I, p. 179), also Sermon 5 in Oliver Davies, ed. and trans., *Meister Eckhart: Selected Writings* (London: Penguin, 1994).
8. See Sermon 26 (Walshe No. 56, Vol. II, Sermon 27 in Davies, ed. cit).
9. Ibid. Oliver Davies' trans., p. 234.
10. Sermon 20b (Walshe No. 32b, Vol. I, p. 243).
11. Sermon 12 (Walshe No. 57, Vol. II, DP 13, Sermon 16 in Davies, ed. cit.).
12. Sermon 85 (Walshe No. 85, Vol. II, p. 264, Sermon 26 in Davies, ed. cit.).
13. Sermon 103, (Walshe No. 4, Vol. I, p. 46, DP 59).
14. Walt Whitman, *Song of Myself*, No. 51. A similar and equally pertinent remark is found in the writings of another American philosopher, Ralph Waldo Emerson: 'A foolish consistency is the hobgoblin of little minds, adored by little statesmen and philosophers and divines. With consistency a great soul has simply nothing to do.' *Essays*, Second Series: 'Self-Reliance'.
15. Sermon 2, in *The Essential Sermons, Commentaries, Treatises and Defense*, ed. by Bernard McGinn and Edmund Colledge (New York: Paulist Press, 1981), p. 178.
16. Fleming, who founded the Eckhart Society, made significant contributions in the treatment of intractable pain. Her book, *Grasping the Nettle*, has recently been republished by The Old Forge Press (2002). See Chapter 11 below.

17. *Book of Divine Comfort*, Walshe trans., No. 11, Vol. III, pp. 27–8. Cf. Sermon No. 2 (Walshe No. 8, vol. I, p. 75). For Eckhart's approach toward suffering, also see Chapter 11 below.
18. Ibid., pp. 95–6.
19. Albert Friedlander, 'Meister Eckhart, Maimonides, and Paul Celan', *Eckhart Review* 3 (Spring 1994): 20–1.
20. Sermon 12 (Walshe No. 57, Vol. II, p. 87, slightly adapted, DP 13).
21. See Sermon 86 (Walshe No. 9, Vol. I, p. 89).

Chapter 5

'I am the Son of God': Eckhart and Aquinas on the Incarnation[1]

Today Eckhart's appeal to readers espousing a wide variety of religious beliefs, or even none at all, can overshadow his deep Christian commitment. As a consequence, his teaching about Jesus Christ is one of the less well-known elements of his doctrine. Some commentators have suggested that it is even possible to formulate Eckhart's teaching without any reference to its Christian underpinnings.[2] Others, such as Daizetz Suzuki, looked on Eckhart favourably for his Zen-like doctrine but reckoned his teaching to be at least unorthodox from a Christian perspective.[3] Shizuteru Ueda similarly concluded that Eckhart's doctrine departed considerably from orthodox Christian doctrine.

As with other elements of his teaching, scattered references appear throughout his surviving works regarding Jesus as a divine and human Person, the work of salvation, and especially the great mysteries of the Incarnation and Resurrection, but the extant writings lack a complete and systematic exposition. That is hardly surprising, since one searches in vain in the collected works for any topical theological treatment. That does not mean that Eckhart lacked a bold and comprehensive grasp of the importance and essential role of Jesus Christ in his preaching and teaching, but only that his Christology must be sought throughout his sermons and treatises rather than in a single location.[4]

Neither his views on the relation of the Son of God to the Trinity in the unity of the divine nature (*Gotheit*, the 'Godhead'), nor those concerning our relation to Christ in the mystery of the Incarnation, escaped scrutiny by his inquisitors, or indeed censure. But in statements defending himself in both Cologne and Avignon against charges of preaching heretical doctrine, Eckhart appealed to the authority of Thomas Aquinas with respect to his claim that 'the Son begotten in me is the Son himself, undifferentiated from the Father in nature, himself One, and without distinction or differentiation; nor is he one in me and another in another man'.[5]

Eckhart considered himself to be loyal to Thomas. Yet few topics could better serve to illustrate the significant difference between Eckhart and Thomas than the Incarnation. The divergence between the two Domini- cans concerns, first, the manner in which the Word of God assumed human nature and, second, how the hypostatic union ontologically, theologically and spiritually affects humanity, both as a whole and in regard to each individual.

Seized upon by his prosecutors as an instance of heretical doctrine,[6] Eckhart's teaching on the Incarnation is, in fact, an emphatic elaboration of the Christology of Nicene–Chalcedonian orthodoxy found in the teachings of Irenaeus, Clement of Alexandria, Athanasius, the Cappado- cian Fathers, Cyril of Alexandria, Augustine, and many other orthodox theologians of the Eastern and Western Churches. When viewed in the light of this ancient tradition, despite its Neoplatonic colouring and regardless of the startling inferences Eckhart drew from it, his teaching itself is not only orthodox, but even more conservative than Thomas's formulation, tinged as it was by his strong (and once highly suspect) Aristotelian proclivities.

In this chapter, I will explore the apparent and real elements of conflict between Thomas and Eckhart regarding the redemptive force of the Incarnation, here understood as identification with the Son of God achieved ultimately by means of 'the grace of adoption'. In assessing the disagreements between the two Dominican masters, it would be well to bear in mind that evident areas of fundamental agreement are much more extensive. For despite the crucial differences, Eckhart did largely follow Thomas in his incarnational theology. But he remained a Thomist with a difference.

The Ancient Christology

Differences in interpretation notwithstanding, major figures in the great orthodox tradition of Nicene–Alexandrian theology are as one in affirm- ing that the goal of human destiny and the purpose of divine salvation coincide in *theosis* (or later, *theopoesis*) – deification. Rooted in scripture, developed by Irenaeus and Clement, and perfected by Athanasius, the answer to the question 'Why did God become man?' is uniformly 'So that man could become God.'[7]

According to Gregory Nazianzen, here amplifying Basil the Great's statement that 'man is under a mandate from God to become God',

I am to be buried with Christ and to rise again with him, to become a coheir with him, a son of God, and indeed God himself. This is what the great mystery means for us; this is why God became man and became poor for our sake: it was to raise up our flesh, to recover the divine image, to re-create mankind, so that all of us may become one in Christ who perfectly became in us everything that he is himself.[8]

Cyril of Alexandria, Patriarch of Alexandria and architect of Chalcedonian orthodoxy, comments,

by repudiating, in a sense, our own life, and taking on the supernatural likeness of the Holy Spirit, who is united to us, our nature is transformed so that we are no longer merely men, but also sons of God, spiritual men, by reason of the share we have received in the divine nature.[9]

That such sentiments were not by any account lacking in the Western Church is evident from the following striking but unobjectionable statements, which may be taken as representative. In a third-century sermon on the Baptism of Jesus attributed to Hippolytus of Rome, we read,

To give us a new birth that would make our bodies and souls immortal, [God] breathed into us the spirit of life and armed us with incorruptibility. Now if we become immortal, we shall also be divine; and if we become divine after rebirth in baptism through water and the Holy Spirit, we shall also be coheirs with Christ after the resurrection of the dead. Whoever goes down into these waters of rebirth . . . is raised to filial status. He comes up from baptism resplendent as the sun, radiant in his purity, but above all, he comes as a son of God and a coheir with Christ.[10]

Augustine similarly echoes what might be called the Athanasian thematic:

. . . he who in his divine nature is the equal of the Father assumed the condition of a slave and became like us, and so restored to us our likeness to God. The only Son of God became a son of man to make many men sons of God.[11]

In his commentary on the Gospel of John, he likewise writes,

'A new commandment I give you, that you love one another'; not as men love one another on account of their common humanity, but because they are all gods and sons of the Most High. They love one another as God loves them so that they may be brothers of his only Son.[12]

In his famous Christmas sermon, Pope Leo the Great slightly qualifies but fundamentally reiterates the Athanasian motif: 'For every believer regenerated in Christ is reckoned to be of the stock, not of his earthly father, but of Christ, who became Son of Man precisely that men could become sons of God . . .'[13] Similar statements could be cited from any number of writings both before and after Eckhart's time. Their gist is admirably summarized in a sermon by Blessed Isaac of Stella, the English Cistercian Abbot of Etoile (died 1169):

Just as the head and body of a man form one single man, so the Son of the Virgin and those he has chosen to be his members form a single man and the one Son of Man. 'Christ is whole and entire, head and body', say the Scriptures, since all the members form one body, which with its head is one Son of Man, and he with the Son of God is one Son of God, who himself with God is one God. Therefore the whole body with its head is Son of Man, Son of God and God. This is the explanation of the Lord's words: 'Father, I desire that as you and I are one, so they may be one with us.'[14]

It may be safely concluded that qualified, and sometimes glaringly unqualified, claims of identity with the Son of God are close to the heart of traditional doctrinal and homiletic Christology right up to Eckhart's day. Despite the apparently shocking implications Eckhart drew from it, the condemnation of his use of this motif must therefore be sought on grounds other than heterodox statement, much less intent.

The adoption of the deification theme by radical spiritual enthusiasts of Eckhart's time undoubtedly contributed to the suspicion with which it was greeted in his sermons and treatises. However, the incorporation of an Aristotelian infrastructure into Christian theology, particularly by Thomas Aquinas and his followers, reflected and also effected a paradigm shift which to some extent distanced them from Eckhart, whose Neoplatonic sympathies remained more constant.[15]

Thomas's Departure from the Platonic Tradition

Like all medieval Christology, Thomas's teaching on the Incarnation owes a considerable debt to patristic and early medieval sources.[16] But Thomas was also strongly influenced by the new Aristotelianism promoted by Albert the Great, Siger of Brabant, and other radicals, and assumed a cautious stance with respect to Platonic–Neoplatonic themes such as deification (*theosis/theopoein*), the capstone of the ancient mystical theology.[17] In effect, Thomas applied Aristotelian metaphysical logic to the Nicene–Chalcedonian formulas in order to construct a rigorous and integral Christology, consonant with the realistic tenor of the new approach. His 'moderate realism' precluded recognizing a notion of universal human nature existing apart from individual human beings, contrary to classical Platonic approaches, even when divinized as ideas in the mind of God. Nor could Thomas accept the nominalist position that human nature existed only in concrete individuals, thus lacking universal extension. His typical 'middle way' between idealism and nominalism was to assert the conceptual reality of universal human nature based on formal similarity abstracted from existing individuals.

This allows for Christ's true humanity (and ours), but affirms with John Damascene that the nature assumed by the Word of God was the singular humanity of Jesus Christ, not 'common' human nature nor the collective human nature of all human beings. It also provides the metaphysical foundation for understanding the redemption of the human race by merit of Christ's sacrificial death and resurrection, to which individual human beings are joined sacramentally and morally, not merely by sharing the same human nature assumed by the Word in the Incarnation.

Thomas establishes the philosophical basis of his Christological edifice early in the *Summa*, where he considers the object and modality of human understanding:

> . . . the words 'abstract universal' [*universale abstractum*] imply two things, the nature of a thing and its abstraction or universality. Therefore the nature itself to which it occurs to be understood, abstracted, or considered as universal is only in individuals; but that it is understood, abstracted or considered as universal is in the intellect. We see something similar in the senses . . . In like manner, 'humanity' is understood only in this or that man; but that humanity be apprehended, that is, that

it be abstracted and consequently considered as universal, occurs to humanity inasmuch as it is brought under the consideration of the intellect, in which there is a likeness of the specific nature, but not of the principles of individuality.[18]

Thomas's Christological departure from, and argument with, the Platonic tradition primarily concerns the modality of the assumption of human nature by the Eternal Word. Relying heavily on the treatment of the Incarnation in St John Damascene's *De Fide Orthodoxa*, Thomas argues in the *Summa Theologiae* that the Son of God assumed human nature, not the person of man, nor 'a man', that is, human nature was assumed in an existing individual person (the Person of the Word), not as abstracted from all individuals, i.e., as a pure concept, nor, finally, collectively as a species or 'concrete universal' including all its instances.

He cites Damascene to the effect that 'The Son of God assumed human nature *in atomo*, i.e., in an individual, which is no other than the uncreated suppositum, the Person of the Son of God.'[19] For Thomas, the Incarnation took place only in the undivided person of Jesus Christ, not in the human nature as it would have existed prior to union with the divine nature. In the *Summa Theologiae* (III Q. 2, Art. 2), he concludes that:

> whatever adheres to a person is united to it in person, whether it belongs to its nature or not. Hence if the human nature is not united to God the Word in person, it is nowise united to Him; and thus belief in the Incarnation is altogether done away with, and Christian faith wholly overturned. Therefore, inasmuch as the Word has a human nature united to Him, which does not belong to His Divine Nature, it follows that the union took place in the Person of the Word, and not in the nature.

Thomas assumes here as elsewhere that 'nature' can be taken in two ways, 'first, as if it had being of itself, apart from matter, as the Platonists held', and, 'secondly, as existing in an intellect either human or divine'.[20]

With regard to the first possibility, Thomas turns to Aristotle, asserting that human nature 'cannot subsist of itself, as the Philosopher proves (*Metaphysics* 7: 26, 27, 29, 51) because sensible matter belongs to the specific nature of sensible things, and is placed in its definition, as flesh and bones in the definition of man. Hence human nature cannot be without sensible matter'.[21] Next, Thomas argues that human nature could not have been assumed by the Son of God as it exists in the Divine intellect, 'since it would be none other than the Divine Nature, and, according to this, human nature would be in the Son of God from eternity.'[22] As we shall see, this is in fact the thesis that Eckhart would adopt, proceeding from a Neo-platonic rather than an Aristotelian position. Finally, Thomas maintains, it cannot be said 'that the Son of God assumed human nature as it is in a human intellect, for this would mean nothing else but that he is [merely] understood to assume a human nature; and if he did not assume it in reality, this would be a false understanding, nor would this assumption of the human nature be anything but a fictitious incarnation, as Damascene says.'[23]

The soteriological consequence of Thomas's position is clear: 'The incarnate Son of God is the common savior of all, not by a generic or specific community, such as is attributed to the nature separated from the individuals, but by a community of cause, whereby the incarnate Son of God is the universal cause of human salvation.'[24] Such a cause, moreover, cannot be intrinsic, whether material or formal, but must be extrinsic, either efficient or final. And as exemplary 'leader' of the human race, Christ's causal influence on humanity can only be efficient.[25]

In Article 5 of the same question, Thomas directly addressed the major alternative to his position, namely that the Word of God assumed human nature in all individuals, a thesis at least similar to that later espoused by Eckhart. Again, he cites John Damascene, for whom the Son of God 'did not assume human nature as a species, nor did he assume all its hypostases' (*De Fide Orthod.* 3:11). Thomas then argues that

It was unfitting for human nature to be assumed by the Word in all its supposita. First, because the multitude of supposita of human nature, which are natural to it, would have been taken away. For since we must not see any other suppositum in the assumed nature, except the Person assuming, as was said above (A. 3), if there was no human nature except what was assumed, it would follow that there was but one suppositum of human nature, which is the Person assuming.[26]

Even more pointedly with regard to Eckhart's doctrine, Thomas's second argument insists that the assumption of human nature in all its existing individuals 'would have been derogatory to the dignity of the Incarnate Son of God, as He is the first-born of many brethren, according to the human nature, even as he is the First-born of all creatures according to the divine, for then *all men would be of equal dignity*' (emphasis added).[27] This, of course, is precisely what Eckhart concludes, making this tenet the foundation stone of his theological ethics.

Thomas's final word in this regard might well be taken from his reply to an objection based on the all-encompassing love of God: 'God so loved the world as to give his only-begotten Son' (John 3:16). 'But love makes us give ourselves to our friends as much as we can,' his hypothetical objector continues, much as would Eckhart a generation later, 'and it was possible for the Son of God to assume several human natures, as was said above (Q. 3, A. 7), and with equal reason all. Hence it was fitting for the Son of God to assume human nature in all its supposita.'[28]

Thomas replies simply and tellingly,

> The love of God to men is shown not merely in the assumption of human nature, but especially in what he suffered in human nature for other men, according to Rom. 5:8: 'But God commends His charity towards us, because when we were yet sinners . . . Christ died for us', which would not have taken place had He assumed human nature in all its supposita.

Here perhaps lies the fundamental difference in the soteriologies of the two Dominicans, that of Thomas centred on the redeeming death of Christ, that of Eckhart on the Incarnation. It also accounts for the relatively minor role played by sin, suffering and death in Eckhart's teaching compared with that of Thomas. This crucial difference may count for more in the long run than the philosophical disparity in their approaches.

Eckhart's Return to Platonic Orthodoxy

It is evident from both the German sermons and the Latin works that Eckhart generally follows Thomas's teaching on the Incarnation.[29] For the Meister also, 'God did not only become man – he took on human nature.'[30] That is to say, with Aquinas, albeit for other reasons, that the Word did not assume a human person, a 'man': '. . . God took on human nature and united it with his own Person. Then human nature became God, for he put on bare human nature and not any man.'[31]

Here, however, the similarity between Thomas and Eckhart begins to falter. First, he understood the identity of himself and all human beings with the Son of God to be one of identity without distinction. In

Sermon 12, for instance, Eckhart says, recalling the ancient Christian teaching that grounds his Christology, 'All that the eternal Father teaches is His being and His nature and His entire Godhead, which He divulges to us altogether in His Son and teaches us that we are that same Son.'[32] Similarly, in Sermon 29, Eckhart directly appropriates the Athanasian motif of the Alexandrian Christology: 'Why did God become man? That I be born God the same.'[33] His mystical exegesis finds the theme throughout scripture: 'Now our Lord says, "None knows the Father but the Son, nor the Son but the Father" (Matt. 11:27).' Therefore, he concludes, 'In truth, to know the Father we must be the Son.'[34]

In Sermon 22, commenting on the opening words of the Gospel of John, Eckhart says,

> Here we are given to understand that we are an only Son whom the Father has been eternally begetting out of the hidden darkness of eternal concealment, indwelling in the first beginning of the primal purity which is the plenitude of all purity. There I have been eternally at rest and asleep in the hidden understanding of the eternal Father, immanent and unspoken.[35]

Here, Eckhart appears to have adopted a position that Aquinas had clearly rejected, one that places the Platonic Ideas in the mind of God but also identifies individual human natures with the human nature of the Word.

Second, Eckhart frequently weaves together the themes of the eternal birth of the Son in the soul and the identity of human natures in Christ and all human beings:

> The Father bears his Son in the inmost part of the soul, and bears you with his only-begotten Son, no less. If I am to be the Son, then I must be Son in the same essence as that in which he is Son, and not otherwise. If I am to be a man, I cannot be a man in the essence of an animal. But if I am to be this man, then I must be this man in this essence. Now St John says, 'You are the children of God' (1 John 3:1).[36]

In a very striking passage from Sermon 76, Eckhart amplifies this basic tenet of his theological anthropology:

> St John says: 'See how great is the love that the Father has shown us, that we are called and are the children of God' (1 John 3:1). He says not only

'we are called' but 'we *are*'. So I say that just as a man cannot be wise without wisdom, so he cannot be a son without the filial nature of God's Son, without having the same being as the Son of God has – just as being wise cannot be without wisdom. And so, if you *are* the Son of God, you can only be so by having the same being of God that the Son has. But this is 'now hidden from us'; and after that it is written: 'Beloved, we are the Sons of God.' And what do we know? – That is what he adds 'and we shall be like him' (1 John 3:2), that is, the same as he is: the same being, experiencing and understanding – everything that he is, when we see him as God. So I say God could not make me the son of God if I had not the nature of God's Son, any more than God could make me wise if I had no wisdom.[37]

For Eckhart, in short, it is the Incarnation that effects a substantial identity between God and human beings because of the human nature all share with Christ. Frank Tobin aptly summarizes this facet of Eckhart's teaching:

For Eckhart, man becomes the Son and *is* the Son. There is only one Son, and there is no distinction between the Son in man and the Word. The doctrine brings an immediacy of the divinity to man and, with an uncompromising radicality, reduces man's existence to the existence of God.[38]

The Human Image of God

The dialectical logic of deification requires a concept of image in order to accomplish the work set for it in classical Neoplatonic theology. Augustine, as we have seen, utilized the notion strategically. And Pope Leo I writes, '. . . the grace of the Father has adopted as heirs neither the contentious nor the dissident, but those who are one in thought and love. The hearts and minds of those who have been reformed according to one and the same image should be in harmony with one another.'[39] For Eckhart, similarly, the mediating role of Christ as *the* divine image enjoys a critical role:

The eternal Word did not take upon itself this man or that, but it took upon itself one free, indivisible human nature, bare and without image [*bilde*],[40] for the impartible form of humanity is imageless. And since in this assumption the eternal Word took on human nature imagelessly, therefore the Father's image [*bilde*], which is the eternal Son, became the image [*bilde*] of human nature. So it is just as true to say that man became God as that God became man. Thus human nature was transformed [*überbildet*] by becoming the divine image, which is the image of the Father. Therefore, in order to be one Son, you must discard and depart [*sô müezet ir abescheiden und abegân*] from whatever makes for distinction in you. For man is an 'accident'[41] of nature: so, do away with whatever is an accident in you and take yourselves in the freedom of your impartible human nature. But since this very nature wherein you take yourselves has become the Son of the eternal Father by the assumption of the eternal Word, thus you, with Christ, become the Son of the eternal Father by reason of taking yourselves by that same nature which has there become God.[42]

Clearly, then, much of Eckhart's understanding of the consubstantial identity of all human persons in Christ hangs on his concept of *image*, which he carefully integrates into both sermons and treatises. In Sermon 58 of Quint's modern German edition, Eckhart said, for example, '. . . the soul is the natural image of God'.[43] In Eckhart's view, such a natural image implies likeness, and likeness implies equality: '. . . the noble and humble man is not satisfied to be born as the only-begotten Son whom the Father has eternally borne, but he wants to be also the Father and to enter into the same equality of eternal paternity and to bear him, from whom I am eternally born'.[44]

For Thomas Aquinas, conversely, insofar as human beings are created in the image of God, it is decidedly not by way of a likeness of equality:

. . . an *image* is so called because it is produced as an imitation of something else . . . But equality does not belong to the essence of an image; for as Augustine says [*Octoginta Trium Quaest*, Q. 74] 'Where there is an image there is not necessarily equality', as we see in a person's image reflected in a glass. Yet this is of the essence of a perfect image; for in a perfect image, nothing is wanting that is to be found in that of which it is a copy. Now it is manifest that in man there is some likeness to God, copied from God as from an exemplar; yet this likeness is not one of equality, for such an exemplar infinitely excels its copy. Therefore there is in man a likeness to God; not indeed a perfect likeness, but imperfect.[45]

The Grace of Adoption

It is critical for understanding Eckhart's Christology to recognize the central role in his thought played by grace. It is grace that establishes a significant difference in our common Sonship in Christ. In Sermon 66 Eckhart says, 'a man who makes himself wholly free from self for God's sake, who belongs to none but God and lives for none save God alone, is in truth by grace the same as God is by nature'.[46] Here, Eckhart alludes to the theme of adoption by grace, a linch-pin in his own theological anthropology as well as that of Thomas and, indeed, the classical tradition.

In the Latin works, similarly, Eckhart more carefully nuances some of his more startling claims.[47] Commenting on verses 12 and 13 of the first chapter of John's Gospel ('As many as received him he gave the power of becoming sons of God; those who believe in his name, who were born not from blood, nor of the will of the flesh, nor of the will of man, but of God'), Eckhart wrote, 'the first fruit of the Incarnation of Christ, God's Son, is that man may become by the grace of adoption what the Son is by nature, as it says in the text here, "He gave them the power of becoming sons of God" . . .'[48]

Not surprisingly, then, Eckhart's resolution of the tension between substantial identity with the Son of God based on common human nature and the infinite distance between the creature and its Creator, takes the classical form of distinguishing between natural generation (of the Word) and the redemption or regeneration of human beings by incorporation into Christ 'by the grace of adoption'.[49] For instance, in the defence statement prepared at Cologne, he insisted that, 'It is the same Son without any distinction whom the Father has naturally begotten in the Trinity and whom He generates in us *through grace,* just as many parchments are marked with one seal and many images born in many mirrors from a single face.'[50]

Similarly, in attempting to clarify another of the propositions to which the Cologne censors had taken exception ('A man ought so to live that he is identified with God's Son and so as to be the only begotten Son. Between the only begotten Son and the soul there is no distinction'[51]), he appeals implicitly to grace rather than creative emanation and also introduces the concept of analogy:

'Between the only begotten Son and the soul there is no distinction.' This is true. For how could anything white be distinct from or divided from whiteness? Again, matter and form are one in being; living and working. Yet matter is not, on this account, form, or conversely. So in the proposition. A holy soul is one with God, according to John 17:11, 'That they may all be one in us, even as we are one.' Still, the creature is not the creator, nor is the just man God. Nor should it be thought that just men, in each case, are sons of God, by one son of God after another, but just as all good men are good by analogy from one and the same goodness. And just as God is one in all things by essence, so the Son is one God in all sons-by-adoption, and they through him, and in him, are sons-by-analogy, as has been shown often above.

It is perhaps questionable whether Eckhart's seemingly desperate effort to couch his radical Christology in terms his prosecutors might more easily comprehend did more good than harm. In his own mind, it was simply a way of restating his case. He concluded,

... Therefore it should not be thought that there is one Son, by whom Christ is God's Son and another by whom we are called and are sons of God but it is the same thing and the same person, who is Christ the Son naturally born, *while we are sons of God by analogy*, by cohering to him with whom we are joint-heirs. Nor should it be thought that God, the Son of God, is something outside or distant from us, to which we are likened, as the image cast into the mirrors, but that he, God, undivided and One by essence, is inmost and closest to each one of us. 'In him we live and move and have our being' (Acts 17:28).[52]

At Avignon, Eckhart did not appeal to analogy, having admitted that the statements under attack 'are erroneous as they sound, but [he] supports them by saying that it is the same Son of God who is the Only-Begotten in the Trinity and by whom all the faithful are sons of God *through adoption*'.[53] That this was not merely a saving qualification introduced to provide an orthodox interpretation of previous doctrine can be seen from other instances:

God put on our clothing so that truly, in a proper sense and substantially, he becomes man in Christ. The nature assumed, however, is common to all men without more or less. Therefore it is given to every man to become the Son of God in himself certainly, but in himself by means of grace by way of adoption.[54]

Clearly, 'the grace of adoption' occupies the central position in Eckhart's thinking, a notion hallowed by centuries of use and no little confusion. The ancient doctrine of 'adoptive sonship' (*huiothesia, huiopoien*), which developed in correlation to that of deification (*theosis/theopoein*), is based on Rom. 8:11–23, 29–30, 9: 4; Gal. 4:5; and Eph. 1:5. Although founded on the notion of *legal* adoption current in the classical world, St Paul never used the term in this fashion, but applied it in Jewish fashion *religiously* to God's original election of Israel and the redemptive salvation of those who believe in Christ. A better translation would have been 'filiation' or 'affiliation'.

It should also be remarked that later, especially medieval, usage tended to employ the term to affirm the distinction between the divine Sonship of Christ and that of believers, and to support the difference between nature and grace, which seems to be the opposite of its original function. The fact that the Greek term is sometimes translated 'sonship' rather than 'adoption' witnesses to the theological imprecision latent in discussions of what has come to be known as the 'redemptive incarnation'. The inherent ambiguity became eclipsed in subsequent Christological controversies, however, as the distance between Jesus as Son of God and Son of Man was increased by the metaphysical stresses distinguishing 'person' from 'nature'.[55]

Be that as it may, Eckhart found himself snarled in a semantic misunderstanding that reflected the tectonic paradigm shifts of the later Middle Ages as Aristotelian and Middle-Platonic philosophies clashed in the background of theological debates. Already, the rising tide of Nominalism threatened to wash away the entire classical tradition. In the semantic confusion, it is perhaps not too surprising that Eckhart's reformulation of the ancient Christology of Alexandrian orthodoxy went unrecognized.

Eckhart's Incarnational Dialectic

In the preceding analysis, I have attempted to show that Eckhart incorporated and elaborated upon the teaching of the early Church on Incarnation and divinization without departing from the orthodox tradition. He also utilized the language and conclusions of Thomas' incarnational theology, modifying it as it suited him. His central disagreement with Thomas concerns the extension or universality of the assumption of human nature by the Word of God, that is, its redemptive or salvific implication. Clearly, Eckhart agrees with Thomas with regard to the central importance of the Incarnation in effecting the redemption of fallen humankind. Unlike Thomas, however, Eckhart so emphasizes the Incarnation that it practically eclipses the passion, death and resurrection of Christ.

As with other volatile theological topics, Eckhart can be cited from a variety of sermons and treatises in support of apparently opposed positions concerning the Incarnation and its effects on us. It is also possible to find passages where he reconciles these antithetical statements by means of qualifications or distinctions, or even a surprising twist in the development of his argument. It is therefore tempting to portray Eckhart as a dialectician, and convincing arguments have been made to support that conclusion. But on the basis of the texts cited, it is only possible to show that Eckhart expressed himself in a variety of ways, some of them plainly at odds with each other, others seemingly resolving the contradictions. Whether or not Eckhart himself was a dialectician, nothing prevents us from approaching these statements dialectically. Viewed from such a perspective, the tension within Eckhart's incarnational theology, and therefore between it and that of Aquinas, can in large measure be resolved in a manner consonant with orthodox Christian tradition.

The exception may prove to lie in the divergence between Thomas and Eckhart with regard to the assumption of human nature by the Word in all its supposits. For Eckhart, the analogous unity all human beings share with the Son is not a unity of proper proportionality, but nevertheless proportional, or rather, infinitely *dis*proportionate.[56] Christ is the natural, Only-Begotten Son, and we are sons by adoption through grace. But for Eckhart there is only one Son, and we are the same Son as the Son of God, Jesus Christ.

Notes

1. Adapted from 'I am the Son of God: Eckhart and Aquinas on the Incarnation', *Eckhart Review* (June 1992): 27–46.
2. See for instance, Emil Cioron's *Des Larmes et des Saints* and other works.
3. See D. T. Suzuki, 'Meister Eckhart and Buddhism', in *Mysticism Christian and Buddhist* (New York: Harper and Row, 1971), pp. 3–38 and passim. See also his comments in 'The Basis of Buddhism', in Woods, *Understanding Mysticism* (1981), pp. 128–30, 135–43.
4. Bernard McGinn remarks, for instance, 'If "God became man so that man might become God", the ancient Christian adage at the center of Eckhart's view of redemption, then his teaching on the *grunt* must be seen as Christological at its core.' Bernard McGinn, *The Mystical Thought of Meister Eckhart* (New York:

Crossroad, 2001), op. cit., p. 51. For a recent and immensely valuable overview of Eckhart's Christological doctrine, see especially pp. 115–27.

5. 'The Defense (Rechtfertigungsschrift)', in Raymond Blakney, *Meister Eckhart* (1941), p. 268. Cf. Gabriel Théry, O.P., 'Édition critique des piéces relatives au procés d'Eckhart continues dans le manuscrit 33b de la Bibliotheque de Soest', *Archives d'histoire littéraire et doctrinal du moyen âge*, 1 (1926): 199. The reference in Blakney to ST [I-]II, 108, A. 1, is clearly wrong, however. The most relevant passages in the Summa are III, Q. 4, AA. 1–5; Q. 2, A. 8, and Q. 23, A. 2.

6. Among the 28 articles cited in the Avignon indictment, numbers 11, 12, 20, 21 and 22 directly concern the union of the Son of God and human persons (see *Meister Eckhart, The Essential Sermons, Commentaries, Treatises and Defense*, ed. and trans. by Bernard McGinn and Edmund Colledge (New York: Paulist Press, 1981), pp. 78–9):

    The eleventh article. Whatever God the Father gave to his Only-Begotten Son in human nature, he gave all this to me. I except nothing, neither union, nor sanctity; but he gave the whole to me, just as he did to him. [See Sermon 5a, DW I, in Walshe (1987), p. 109.]

    The twelfth article. Whatever holy scripture says of Christ, all that is also true of every good and divine man [Sermon 24, DW I, pp. 421–2].

    The twentieth article. That the good man is that Only-Begotten Son of God. [See 'The Book of Divine Consolation' in *The Essential Sermons*, ed. cit., p. 229.]

    The twenty-first article. The noble man is that Only-Begotten Son of God whom the Father generates from all eternity [Sermon 14, DW I, p. 239. See Comm. Gen. No. 22 (citing John 1:12) in *The Essential Sermons*, ed. cit., p. 90].

    The twenty-second article. The Father gives birth to me his Son and the same Son. Everything that God performs is one; therefore he gives me, his Son, birth without any distinction [Sermon 6 (*The Essential Sermons*, ed. cit., p. 187–8)].

7. *De Incarnatione*, 54. *Patrologia Graeca* 25, 192b.

8. Oratio 7, *in laudem Caesarii fratris*, 23–4. *Patrologia Graeca* 35, 786–7.

9. *Comm. on Gospel of John*, Lib. 11, 11. *Patrologia Graeca* 74, 559–62.

10. *On the Epiphany*, 2.6–8.10. *Patrologia Graeca* 10: 858–9.

11. Sermon 194, 3–4. PL 38: 1016–17.

12. *Treatise on John*, tract 65, 1–3; CCL 36, 490–2.

13. Sermon 6 *in Nativitate Domini*, 2–3, 5. *Patrologia Latina* 54, 213–16.

14. Sermon 42, PL 194, 1831–2. See also Sermon 51 (*Patrologia Latina* 194, 1862): 'The whole Christ and the unique Christ – the body and the head – are one: one because born of the same God in heaven, and of the same mother on earth. They are many sons, yet one son.'

15. McGinn observes (1981), p. 27, '. . . the Meister's own position on the relation of faith and reason is closer to the theological positions of Christian Platonists than to the new precisions of Thomas Aquinas'. On Eckhart as a Neoplatonist, see Woods, *Eckhart's Way* (2009), pp. 77–86 and Chapter Three above.

16. Thomas' teaching on the Incarnation is mainly found in the *Summa Theologiae*, III, Questions 2–4 and 23; see also the *Summa Contra Gentes*, IV, 1–49.

17. The *Index Thomisticus* (Frommann-Holzboog, 1976) lists only 50 instances of *deificatio* or its grammatical variations in all of Thomas's writings. The largest number seem to be found in his commentary on *The Divine Names*. Most are

scattered throughout his commentaries on Aristotle, scripture, the Sentences of Peter Lombard, the *Compendium Theologiae*, etc. Moreover, none of the six instances in the *Summa Theologiae* refer to the goal of human spiritual development, but to Christ (See III, Q. 2, A. 1, ad 3; Q. 16, A. 3, and A. 5 ad 2). Thomas is reserved, to say the least, about the extension of the predicate in the second half of Athanasius's famous dictum. For a recent discussion of the Neoplatonic influences in Thomas's theology, see W. J. Hankey, *God in Himself: Aquinas' Doctrine of God as Expounded in the Summa Theologiae* (Oxford and New York: Oxford University Press, 1987).

18. I, Q. 85, A. 2, ad 2.
19. III, Q. 4, A. 2, Reply 1.
20. III, Q. 4, A. 4. Thomas continues, hypothetically, 'Nevertheless, [even] if human nature were subsistent in this way, it would [still] not be fitting that it should be assumed by the Word of God. First, because this assumption is terminated in a Person, and it is contrary to the nature of a common form to be thus individualized in a person. Secondly, because to a common nature can only be attributed common and universal operations, according to which man neither merits nor demerits, whereas, on the contrary, the assumption took place in order that the Son of God, having assumed our nature, might merit for us. Thirdly because a nature so existing would not be sensible, but [only] intelligible. But the Son of God assumed human nature in order to show himself in men's sight, according to Baruch 3:37: "Afterwards He was seen upon earth, and conversed with men."'
21. Ibid.
22. Ibid. Here Thomas is appealing to the same principle Eckhart would later employ with such great effect, 'What is in God, is God.' See Sermon 75 in the Stuttgart edition (No. 88 in Walshe's English translation [1987], p. 279).
23. Ibid. See also III, Q. 4, A. 4: '. . . Damascene says (*De Fide Orthod.* 3:11): "God the Word incarnate did not assume a nature which exists in pure thought; for this would have been no incarnation, but a false and fictitious incarnation." But human nature as it is separated or abstracted from individuals "is taken to be a pure conception (*in nuda contemplatione cogitatur*), since it does not exist in itself", as Damascene says (ibid.). Therefore, the Son of God did not assume human nature as it is separated from individuals.'
24. Ibid., Reply 1.
25. In Reply 2, Thomas anticipates what might have been Eckhart's objection: 'Self-existing (per se) man is not to be found in nature in such a way as to be outside the singular, as the Platonists held, although some say Plato believed that the separate man was only in the divine intellect. And hence it was not necessary for it to be assumed by the Word, since it had been with him from eternity.' Similarly, 'Although human nature was not assumed in the concrete, as if the *suppositum* were presupposed to the assumption, nevertheless it is assumed in an individual, since it is assumed so as to be in an individual' (Reply 3).
26. Compare III, Q. 2, A. 5, ad 2: '. . . Neither can it be said that the Son of God assumed human nature as it is in all the individuals of the same species, otherwise he would have assumed all men. Therefore it remains, as Damascene says further on (*De Fide Orthod.* 3:11) that He assumed human nature *in atomo*, i.e., in an individual; not indeed in another individual which is a *suppositum* or a person of that nature, but in the Person of the Son of God.'

27. III, Q. 4, A. 5. Thomas apparently regards this egalitarian consequence to be obviously untrue. His third argument is the weakest, proceeding from the principle of proportional symmetry: 'it is fitting that as one Divine suppositum is incarnate, so He should assume one human nature, so that on both sides unity might be found'.

28. Ibid., obj. 2.

29. The most extensive treatment of Eckhart's incarnational theology is that of Shizuteru Ueda, see esp. pp. 39–50. For an extensive account of Eckhart's patristic sources, see Hugo Rahner, S.J., 'Die Gottesgeburt. Die Lehre der Kirchenväter von der Geburt Christi im Herzen der Glaübigen', *Zeitschrift für katholische Theologie* 59, 3 (1935): 333–418. Shorter discussions can be found in McGinn and Colledge, Davies, Tobin and Woods. But see especially McGinn (2001), pp. 115–27.

30. Sermon 5b (Walshe No. 13b, Vol. I, p. 115).

31. Sermon 24 (Walshe No. 92, Vol. II, p. 313).

32. Sermon 12 (Walshe No. 57, Vol. II, p. 83, DP 13). Cf. Sermon 11 (Walshe No. 68, Vol. II, p. 157, DP 12).

33. DW II, 84, 1–2. Cf. Sermon 28: 'We are that very Son, and His birth is His indwelling and His indwelling is His birth. It remains ever the One, that continually wells up in itself' (Walshe No. 17, Vol. I, p. 145) and Sermon 38 (DW II, 227, 6–228, 3): 'Why did God become man? . . . To this purpose: that God be born in the soul and that the soul be born in God.' See also Sermon 6 (Walshe No. 65, Vol. II, p. 135), and Woods (2009), p. 115.

34. Sermon 26 (Walshe No. 11, Vol. I, p. 100, DP 49).

35. Sermon 22 (Walshe No. 53, Vol. II, p. 63, DP 23).

36. Sermon 30 (Walshe No. 18, Vol. I, p. 148). See also Sermon 102 (Walshe No. 2, p. 15, DP 58): '. . . this eternal birth occurs in the soul precisely as it does in eternity, no more and no less, for it is one birth, and this birth occurs in the essence and ground of the soul'.

37. Sermon 76 (Walshe No. 7, pp. 63–4. See also p. 65. DP 35) See also Sermon 46: 'you are of the same essence and same nature as Father and Son . . .' (DW II, 379, 6–382, 3), and Sermon 76: 'we become without any differentiation the same being and substance and nature that he is himself' (DW III, 320, 5–6).

38. Tobin (1986), p. 115.

39. Sermon 6 *in Nativitate Domini*, 2–3, 5. PL 54, 213–16.

40. Lit. 'form', or even 'picture'. In a note, Walshe observes that in this passage, 'bilde' means 'individual characteristics', not a Platonic Idea. Frank Tobin translates the term as 'definite characteristics'. Tobin (1986), p. 103.

41. Eckhart is here following St Thomas and, of course, Pseudo-Bede [*Sent. Phil. ex Arist*], 'who says, "the being of an accident is to inhere". Hence no accident is called being as if it had being, but because by it something is. Hence it is said to belong to a being rather than to be a being (*Metaph.* 7, text 2).' *Summa Theologiae*, I-II, Q. 110, A. 2, ad 3.

42. DW II, 383, 6–7. Walshe translation, No. 47, Vol. II, pp. 27–8. For an alternative translation, see Tobin (1986), p. 103, who comments on this passage (p. 104), 'Because God created man in his image and himself assumed human nature, the process of becoming the Son can be described as an uncovering of the divine image already existing by nature in individual human beings.' He then cites a

supporting text from Sermon 40: 'When a man lays bare and uncovers the divine image that God created in him naturally, God's image becomes evident in him.' (DW II, 275, 4–276, 1.)

43. Sermon 102, DP 58 (Walshe No. 2, Vol. I, p. 15).

44. Sermon 14 (Walshe No. 50, Vol. II, p. 46). Walshe comments, 'This seems to be the source of article 22 of the bull of 1329.' Ibid., p. 48, n. 18.

45. *Summa Theologiae*, I, Q. 93, A. 1.

46. Sermon 66; DW III, 109, 7–10 (Walshe No. 58, Vol. II, p. 89).

47. In his Latin works, Eckhart's teachings on deification do not differ essentially from that in the German works with regard to sameness without distinction. In Sermon LV, for example, the soul 'is transformed into that divine being [esse] by which God himself exists and lives' [Sermon LV, 4, n. 556, LW IV, n. 465 (Tobin translation). See also Sermon LIV, n. 527, LW IV, 444.] In both sets of texts, however, there are examples of more careful qualification, as in German Sermon 4: 'When the Father bears his Son in me, I am the same Son and not another: true we are different in humanity, but *there* I am the same Son and none other.' Sermon 4 (Walshe No. 40, Vol. II, p. 285, DP 4).

48. In Ioh., n. 106; LW III, 90 (Tobin translation). Cf. n. 123; LW III, 107: 'He is the Only-Begotten, coming from the Father alone; we are begotten, but not from one Father. He is a Son through the generation that leads to existence, species, and nature, and therefore he is the natural Son; we are sons through the rebirth [*regenerationem*] that leads to conformity with this nature' (McGinn translation).

49. Cf. Tobin (1986), p. 108: '. . . frequently the clear distinction is made between the sonship of Christ and that achieved by man by references to our becoming through the grace of adoption [*per gratiam adoptionis*] what Christ is by nature [*per naturam*]'.

50. McGinn, ed. cit. (1981), p. 52, n. 208, citing Franz Pelster, S.J., ed., 'Articuli contra Fratrem Aychardum Alamannum', Vat. lat. 3899, f. 123r–130v, in 'Ein Gutachten aus dem Eckehart-Prozess in Avignon', *Aus der Geistewelt des Mittelalters, Festgabe Martin Grabmann*, Beiträge Supplement 3, Munster, 1935, p. 1117 (emphasis added). See also Théry, art. cit., pp. 177, 242 and p. 199, 243–4).

51. Proposition 59 from Eckhart's *Rechtfertigungsschrift* (Daniels ed., 1923), Blakney translation, (1941), pp. 303.

52. Ibid., pp. 303–4. Emphasis added.

53. Pelster, p. 1117, McGinn translation (1981), p. 53, n. 214, emphasis added. See also Pelster, p. 1120, n. 13; and Théry, art. cit., pp. 198–9, 201, 214–15, 220, 229–35, 243–4, 265–6. Similarly, 'from the first intention, the Word assumed human nature, that is, this nature in Christ, for the sake of the whole human race. By assuming that nature, in him and through him he bestowed the grace of sonship and adoption on all men.' *Defense*, Théry, art. cit., pp. 230–1. See McGinn (1981), p. 46.

54. Sermon LII, n. 523, commenting on Rom. 13:14 – 'Put on the Lord Jesus Christ', Tobin (1986), p. 81, who recasts this sentence to provide clarity: 'Therefore it is given to every man to become the Son of God in [Christ] himself certainly, but in [man] himself [*in se*] [it happens] by means of grace by way of adoption.' See also LW IV, 437. Similarly, in his Commentary on John, 'where the idea that we become co-heirs (*coheredes*) is added to that of adoption', Eckhart 'stresses that

we are one with Christ *per gratiam adoptionis* as members of the church whose head is Christ.' In Ioh., n. 117; LW III, 102–3. Ibid. See also n. 184, LW II, 154. Ibid, p. 111, n. 78.

55. For Thomas Aquinas, the term 'adoption' refers generally to the distinction between the sonship of Christ, which is that of the 'natural' son of the Father, the eternal, only-begotten son of God, and the sonship of other human beings by grace, i.e., a free act of God elevating human beings in time to the status of brothers and sisters of Christ and co-heirs of the promises. Such adoption is effected by participation in the sonship of Christ, but not by identification in a common nature, i.e., essence. Christ remains the only-begotten son. We participate in the sonship of Christ primarily by incorporation into the Christian community through baptism. Moreover, such adoption is proper to the entire Trinity of Persons, not to one Person only.

56. Here see Caputo (1978), p. 221: 'In Eckhart's metaphysics there is no allowance for the proper and proportionate being of creatures. There is only the mystic's insistence on the dependence and shadowy reality of created things. In Eckhart, there is no analogy of proportionality, but only of what the scholastics call "attribution". Creatures have being because they are related to God who is being.' And thus, 'Just as Eckhart modified Aquinas' teaching that God is His own being to his own liking, so does he modify Aquinas's teaching on grace. He stresses not that the soul has a separate and proportionate share of God's divine life, proportioned to the capacity of the created nature to receive this supernatural elevation; rather he stresses the unity of the soul with the Son. There is only one Son (just as there is only one being, which is God) and we are made sons through and in that Son. We draw our being as sons from the Son.' Ibid., p. 220.

Chapter 6

Detachment for Commitment[1]

Relying upon a thorough knowledge of scripture, the ancient spiritual theology of Christian Alexandria, the teachings of the Cappadocian Fathers of the fourth century, and the anonymous Dionysian writings of a century later, Eckhart infused both Thomistic and Jewish elements into what became an encompassing mystical synthesis. His central teaching concerns the birth of the Word of God in the heart or soul of the just. In one sermon, Eckhart asked,

> Why do we pray, why do we fast, why do we do all our works, why are we baptised, why (most important of all) did God become man? I would answer, in order that God may be born in the soul and the soul be born in God. For that reason all the scriptures were written, for that reason God created the world and all angelic natures . . .[2]

For Eckhart, as for the ancient mystical theology of the Church, God is uniquely present in the depths of the soul, waiting to break forth into joyful consciousness: 'As surely as the Father in his simple nature bears the Son naturally, just as surely He hears him in the inmost recesses of the spirit, and *this* is the inner world. Here God's ground is my ground and my ground is God's ground.'[3]

Such total and blissful awareness is forestalled by the three 'obstacles' Eckhart frequently enumerates – scatteredness or 'multiplicity', materiality or 'corporeality', and temporality. Differently conceived, these ontological categories can be construed in the moral and spiritual order as inattentiveness, greed or acquisitiveness and impatience. Similarly, in a slightly different order,

> . . . there are three things that favor the union of God with the soul. The first is that the soul should be simple and undivided: for if she is to be united with God, she must be simple as God is simple. Secondly, that

she should dwell above herself and above all transient things and adhere to God. The third is that she should be detached from all material things and work according to her primal purity.[4]

Such is the *process* of detachment – *abgescheidenheit* in Eckhart's lexicon. (The word literally means 'cutoffness'.)

Despite the difficulty of achieving true detachment, Eckhart remained incurably optimistic in the face of God's boundless love and mercy:

> Often I feel afraid, when I come to speak of God, at how utterly detached the soul must be to attain to union with Him. But no one should think this impossible: nothing is impossible for the soul that possesses God's grace. Nothing was ever easier for a man than it is for the soul that has God's grace to leave all things . . .[5]

Detachment thus becomes the key that will unlock the door to Eckhart's way, so far as such a 'way' exists for him. 'When I preach,' Eckhart said,

> it is my wont to speak about detachment, and of how man should rid himself of self and all things. Secondly, that man should be informed back into the simple good which is God. Thirdly, that we should remember the great nobility God has put into the soul, so that man may come miraculously to God. Fourthly, of the purity of the divine nature, for the splendour of God's nature is unspeakable.[6]

Radically negative or apophatic in his mystical approach (as might be expected of someone so thoroughly schooled in Christian Neoplatonism), Eckhart asserted that nothing could describe either God or the soul. '. . . the hidden darkness of the eternal light of the eternal Godhead is unknown and shall never be known. And the light of the eternal Father has eternally shone in this darkness, and the darkness does not comprehend the light (John 1:5).'[7]

'But if God is neither goodness nor being nor truth nor one,' he asks rhetorically, 'what then is He? He is pure nothing: he is neither this nor that. If you think of anything He might be, He is not that.'[8] Yet, paradoxically (and for Eckhart, all language about God is paradoxical), 'God is in all things; but as God is divine and intelligible, so God is nowhere so truly as in the soul, and in the angels if you will, in the inmost soul, in the summit of the soul.'[9]

Such language could – and did – drive Eckhart's medieval critics to desperation. Yet his striking images only made more vivid age-old Christian teaching that attaining radical spiritual simplicity was the condition for the realization of a union which transcended all categories of understanding. Thus, becoming one with God by ridding the mind of all images and the heart of all attachments was the true and only work to which the human spirit was called.

> For whoever would enter God's ground, His inmost part, must first enter his own ground, his inmost part, for none can know God who does not first know himself. He must enter into his lowest and into God's inmost part, and must enter into his first and his highest, for there everything comes together that God can perform.[10]

Such a spiritual 'way' called for no special practices, heroic penances, pilgrimages, or other merely human works. Eckhart's spirituality remained a 'wayless way' as he described it colourfully:

> Indeed, if a man thinks he will get more of God by meditation, by devotion, by ecstasies or by special infusion of grace than by the fireside or in the stable that is nothing but taking God, wrapping a cloak around His head and shoving Him under a bench. For whoever seeks God in a special way gets the way and misses God, who lies hidden in it. But whoever seeks God without any special way gets Him as He is in Himself, and that man lives with the Son, and he is life itself.[11]

In the end, sanctification is God's work, union with God the work of grace, transformation into God the work of divine mercy. Eckhart remained a God-centred mystic, finding all things in God, and God in all things: '. . . God is unseparated from all things, for God is in all things and is more inwardly in them than they are in themselves'.[12] Thus, Eckhart insists,

> A man may go out into the fields and say his prayers and know God, or he may go to church and know God: but if he is more aware of God because he is in a quiet place, as is usual, that comes from his imperfection and not from God: for God is equally in all things and all places, and is equally ready to give Himself as far as in Him lies: and he knows God rightly who knows God equally (in all things).[13]

Ultimately, our destiny lies in God alone, and to God alone we should direct all our attention, our energy, our striving:

> Since it is God's nature not to be *like* anyone, we have to come to the state of being *nothing* in order to enter in to the same nature that He is. So, when I am able to establish myself in Nothing and Nothing in myself, uprooting and casting out what is in me, *then* I can pass into the naked being of God, which is the naked being of the spirit. All that smacks of *likeness* must be ousted that I may be transplanted into God and become one with Him: one substance, one being, one nature and the Son of God.[14]

Hence the question of detachment, which for many spiritual seekers today still seems to savour of the worst aspects of late medieval spirituality and the refined 'renunciations' and 'mortifications' of late eighteenth- and nineteenth-century devotionalism. But what Eckhart proposes is far removed from all that.

Detachment

In an unusual passage for a spiritual guide not much given to system, Eckhart identified four stages or 'steps' that the soul takes into God:

> The first is that fear, hope and desire grow in her. Again she steps on, and then fear and hope and desire are quite cut off. At the third stage she comes to a forgetfulness of all temporal things. At the fourth stage she enters into God where she will eternally dwell, reigning with God in eternity, and *then* she will never again think of temporal things or of herself, being fused with God and God with her. And what she then does, she does in God.[15]

Unlike later writers, Eckhart was not particularly concerned about how many steps or stages one took on the path towards union with God, but generally indicated that it was in some sense a progressive ascent, or, as he sometimes described it, a journey into 'the desert of the Godhead'. In sermon 74, Eckhart again identified four degrees or dimensions of true detachment as the steps on this path:

This virtue [detachment, spiritual poverty] has four degrees. The first breaks through and makes a way for a man from all transient things. The second takes them away from a man altogether. The third not only takes them away, but causes them to be altogether forgotten as if they had never been and this is part of the process. The fourth degree is right in God and is God Himself.[16]

It can be reasonably argued that these steps, which Eckhart insists are realities of present life, represent the classical stages of spiritual progress: conversion or awakening; the purgative period of active detachment, *Abgescheidenheit*; the passive purification and illumination of the soul – *Gelassenheit*, which is especially the 'letting-go' of preconceived ideas about God; and, ultimately, union with God or 'breaking through' into the silent wilderness of the Godhead. Eckhart's indebtedness to another strand of ancient Christian teaching is revealed in a similar passage with its echoes of St Gregory the Great, and the Augustinian spiritual masters Hugh and Richard of St Victor:

Whoever would achieve perfection in this triple love [of Father, Son and Holy Spirit] must needs have four things. The first is true detachment from all creatures. The second, the true life of Leah, that is to say the active life which is set in motion in the ground of the soul by the touch of the Holy Ghost. The third is the true life of Rachel, the contemplative life. The fourth is an aspiring spirit.[17]

This division of the spiritual life, which finds expression in almost all medieval writers, can be traced back to the Alexandrian school and in particular to Evagrius of Pontus. 'Entering into God', the ultimate stage of the soul's return, itself includes three distinct but related aspects or moments for Eckhart: the birth of the Word in the soul, the first, mystical 'breaking through' [*durchbrechen*] into God as Trinity, and the second, eschatological 'breaking through' into the hidden Godhead. The question raised by Eckhart's emphasis on detachment must therefore revolve around the interplay of grace and human volition – what role do human practices play in our detachment from the world? Can they in fact give us the ultimate freedom we seek?

Apatheia and Aphairesis

Detachment and moderation were prominent in ancient Christian catechesis. In the second century, Clement of Alexandria described the Christian life as 'a ceaseless conflict with the downward pull of the passions, and the disciple must learn to rise through the "moderation" of Aristotelian ethics to achieve the passionlessness (*apatheia*) of the Stoics, a calm tranquility of silent worship which is a life of continual joy in prayer like that of the angels'.[18] As would be the case with his remote spiritual descendant, Eckhart, Clement did not mean that we should squelch the emotional life, but rather that we need to order it appropriately in order to acquire tranquility of mind and spirit.

As we have already seen, Eckhart also preached the necessity and excellence of service. Love in action is itself a form of self-renunciation. In Sermon 6, Eckhart said,

> Whatever the Father has to give He bestows on the soul, that is, if she is no more like to herself than to another, and she should not be closer to herself than to another. Her own honour, her advantage or anything that is hers, she should no more desire or heed than what is a stranger's. Whatever is anyone's property should not be distant or alien to her, be it bad or good. All the love of this world is based on love of self. If you had let go of *this*, you would have let go of the world.[19]

Eckhart was uncompromising in his insistence that loving activity must take precedence over detached religiosity:

> The inwardly born and interior word . . . must shine forth, too, in your deeds. As Christ said, 'Let your light shine forth before others' (Matt. 5:16). He had in mind those who care only for the contemplative life and neglect the practice of charity, which, they say, they have no further need for, having passed that stage. It was not these Christ meant when he said: 'The seed fell on good soil and yielded fruit a hundredfold' (Matt. 13:8). He meant *them* when he said: 'The tree that bears no fruit shall be cut down' (Matt. 3:10, 7:19).[20]

And thus in Sermon 9, Eckhart tells us, contrary to most medieval piety, that in truth and justice only one thing is needful:

Martha feared that her sister would stay dallying with joy and sweetness, and she wished her to be like herself. Therefore Christ spoke as if to say: 'Never fear, Martha, she has chosen the best part: this will pass. The best thing that can befall a creature shall be hers: she shall be blessed like you.'[21]

He then explains, 'Martha was so well grounded in her essence that her activity was no hindrance to her: work and activity she turned to her eternal profit . . . Mary was a "Martha" before she was a Mary.'

Eckhart was consistent in his ethical commitment to the primacy of mercy, even when it involved stretching the boundaries of the intellectual tradition of his own order. Thus, with regard to the relative importance of love and knowledge, an issue which sharply divided the Dominican and Franciscan orders at the time, Eckhart said in Sermon 72,

The best masters declare that intellect strips everything off and grasps God bare, as He is in Himself, pure being. Knowledge breaks through truth and goodness and, striking on pure being, takes God bare, as He is, without name. I say that neither knowledge nor love unites. Love takes God Himself, insofar as He is good, and if God were to lose the name of goodness, love could go no further. Love takes God under a veil, a garment. Understanding does not do this: understanding takes God as He is known to it; [but] it can never grasp Him in the ocean of His unfathomableness. I say that above these two, understanding and love, there is mercy: there God works mercy in the highest and purest acts that God is capable of.[22]

It is in our acts of mercy that we come to reveal our closest likeness to God. For, as Eckhart says in Sermon 39, paraphrasing the First Epistle of John, '. . . the just man is like God because God *is* justice. Therefore: whoever is in justice is in God and is God.'[23] True justice realizes itself in perfect friendship, an equality of persons that finds expression in works of mercy where any kind of disparity or want threatens to disrupt the peace of spirit and mind that is due to all. Thus, even as a young prior speaking to the newest members of his community, Eckhart said in his *Talks of Instruction*, 'As I have often said, even if someone were in a rapture like St Paul, and knew a sick person who needed some soup, I should think it far better you left the rapture for love and would serve the needy man in greater love.'[24]

And as we have seen earlier, for Eckhart we owe our first debt of justice to God, and it is to God we now return. In Sermon 65, Eckhart said,

> God's due is His glory. Who are they that glorify God? Those who, having gone out of themselves, seek not their own in anything whatever it may be, whether great or small, who look for nothing under them nor over them nor beside them nor inside them, not clinging to possessions, honors, comfort, pleasure, advantage, nor inwardness nor holiness nor reward nor heaven, having gone out of all this, all that is theirs: from these people God has glory, and they truly glorify God and render him what is His due.[25]

Eckhart's Way

Ultimately, Eckhart's way was what he himself called 'ordinary':

> . . . if a man seeks God's will alone, whatever flows from that or is revealed by that he may take as a gift from God without ever looking or considering whether it is by nature or grace or whence it comes or in what wise: he need not care about that. It is well with him and he need only lead an ordinary Christian life without considering doing anything special. He should take just one thing from God, and whatever comes, accept it as the best for him, having no fear that by this limitation he will be hindered in any way, inwardly or outwardly. Whatever he may do, if only he is aware of having the love of God within him, that suffices.[26]

In practical terms, then, but not in terms of 'practices', Eckhart's spirituality can be described as a progressive 'stripping' of the self – physically, mentally and spiritually, that is, the purifying of knowledge and emotion, desire and imagination. Through such radical de-tachment (*Abgescheidenheit*), God eventually comes to be born in us, but not until we have also become detached not only from whatever is not God, but even from God as well. Eckhart thus advises us to negate our ideas of God as well as creatures and the self. Thus he even prays that 'God will rid me of God.' As with his indirectly affirmative 'nihilism', Eckhart's 'a-theism' must not be mistaken for the simple denial of God that constitutes the ultimate blindness in life. Again, Eckhart takes us to the opposite extreme from what to him would have seemed nonsense.

By stripping ourselves bare spiritually and psychologically in order to reveal our own inner transparency, we discover the abiding presence of God within us. It is thus that our radical no-thingness, the pure and receptive unself-consciousness of our deepest self as 'the mirror of the soul' is the truest and most creative image of God. And that is why Eckhart tells us that when the powers of the soul have been stripped naked, when no-thing can further prevent the shining through of the eternal splendour, then God's presence, he goes so far to say, *must* be revealed in loving, conscious immediacy, for it is God's eternal will and nature to be so 'born' in the human heart.

The Way of Spiritual Detachment: Some Impediments

An inquiry into the practical implications of Eckhart's teaching today, especially with regard to the poor and oppressed, must begin with the frank admission that there *are* problems with his approach, and some of them are serious ones for people today. As a Christian mystic and theologian who consciously worked within the philosophical tradition of Neoplatonism, there is an inescapable bias in Eckhart's teaching against the world of matter, history, and what he called multiplicity – what we might call diversity and pluralism. It is especially difficult to reconcile much of what Eckhart has to say about letting go of things and detachment with our growing concern for the body, earth and matter.

Another area of difficulty concerns human and divine suffering, what many Christians down the centuries have generally referred to as the Cross of Christ. The issue of suffering, even vicarious suffering, is well treated in Eckhart.[27] But what seems to be absent is the ancient notion of reconciliation achieved through the blood of the cross.

It might be helpful here to bear in mind that Eckhart's Christology is a Christmas faith – thoroughly incarnational and ending in glory, like the Mass at dawn on Christmas Day. It is more difficult to relate Eckhart to Lent and Easter. He was fully aware of the sufferings of Jesus, and the resurrection of Christ was the foundation of his faith. But Eckhart seems to have been so dazzled by the implications of the Incarnation, particularly the assumption of human nature into, not merely *by*, the divine person of the Word of God, that the humble, earthy, sometimes dirty and ultimately weak and aching humanity of Jesus gets overshadowed. In that respect, Eckhart's attitude towards Christ is more like that of the disciples on the Mount of Transfiguration than the faithful women on Calvary.

Despite all this, there is so much that is healthy and robust in Eckhart's spirituality, especially compared to the exaggerated emphasis of his times (and especially the period just after him) on the suffering humanity of Christ. Eckhart's theology and spirituality are never world-hating, or even world-denying. He simply sees through the world and all its beauty to the brilliant, even blinding glory of God.

With regard to today's issues – justice, peace, and the preferential option for the poor and oppressed – Eckhart has much to offer. Perhaps the most telling and promising message we hear from his sermons is the great principle of radical equality. For Eckhart, we are not only all one in Christ, we are all equal before and in God because of the common humanity we share with Jesus. Therefore, anything that diminishes the well-being of others, no matter how insignificant they may seem in the world's view of things, is an affront to the dignity of Christ, and an assault on the very glory of God.

Justice, then, means establishing the right order of things, assuring that everyone has equal access to the true gifts that God has given to everyone – and in today's world this must include health, education, and a life of purpose and value among people who are loving, peaceful and generous, as well as fundamental security and a world of clean air, pure water, and living space free from industrial pollution. Guaranteeing such rights and divine endowments for all, especially those who are dispossessed and in want, will require significant detachment on the part of the wealthy and powerful.

In the centuries after his death, Eckhart's more mystical followers embarked on the Gentle Way, the path of non-violence, friendliness. Many of his disciples formed into a loose-knit association called the Friends of God who strove to live in poverty, simplicity and peace. Eckhart's most immediate followers were the Dominican nuns of southern Germany and northern Switzerland, whose monasteries became the centre and sometimes the refuge for all sorts of people – from beggars and merchants to princes and bishops – who sought a place of spiritual light and refreshment in those turbulent times. Hundreds of years later, their ideals were still present in the teachings of the Mystical Anabaptists of Luther's time, the ancestors of the Mennonites, the Amish Brethren, the Hutterites, and the later Quakers.

With regard to the Catholic Church's emphasis after the Second Vatican Council on God's fundamental option for the poor, which we were urged to emulate, Eckhart teaches us again that the appropriate response to deprivation and misery is not spiritual romanticism, but a real and practical concern for the poor based on simplicity of life, frugality and generosity.

Thus some of Eckhart's weaknesses can also be seen as strengths – his lack of cultural and historical imbeddedness has made him a master for all seasons and even for all peoples. In our even more materialistic world, he continues to point beyond physical satisfaction, materialism and the tyranny of time to intangible values that constitute the most precious of all legacies for the human race – truth, justice, freedom and love. His doctrine contains universal implications for human rights, and his awareness of the inclusive scope of true social justice has particular importance for women's issues and the struggle of minority peoples everywhere.

Perhaps his greatest gift to us, however, is, in the last analysis, the vision that most troubled his prosecutors: his conviction of the radical equality of all human beings, the common and equal dignity of every man and woman. And this, he was convinced, was because of the Presence of God in the depths of all human experience, and the possibility of the Birth of the Word in our Hearts – our coming to consciousness of the great dignity and glory that is the birthright of every living person.

Notes

1. Portions of this chapter are adapted from a lecture for the Alister Hardy Research Centre at Maria Assunta Centre, London, 21 April 1993, and 'Meister Eckhart: Mystic under Fire', *Priests and People* 8, 11 (Nov. 1994): 433–8.
2. Sermon 38 (Walshe No. 29, Vol. I, p. 215).
3. Sermon 5b (Walshe No. 13b, Vol. I, p. 117, DP 6).
4. Sermon 85 (W 85, p. 264). Eckhart characterizes these obstacles and their remedies variously in different sermons, but they always focus on the same issues. Cf. Sermon 23 (Walshe No. 54, Vol. II, p. 72): 'Observe which are the three heavens. The first is detachment from all bodily things, the second is estrangement from all imagery, and the third is a bare understanding in God without intermediary.'
5. Sermon 73 (Walshe No. 73, Vol. II, p. 196, DP 33).
6. Sermon 53 (Walshe No. 22, Vol. I, p. 177).
7. Sermon 51 (Walshe No. 83, Vol. II, p. 254).
8. Sermon 23 (Walshe No. 54, Vol. II, p. 72). Cf. Sermon 73 (Walshe No. 73, Vol. II, p. 194).
9. Sermon 30 (Walshe No. 18, Vol. I, p. 147).
10. Sermon 54b (Walshe No. 46, Vol. II, p. 20).
11. Sermon 5b (Walshe No. 13b, Vol. I, pp. 117–18). See also Sermon 5a (Walshe No. 13a, Vol. I).
12. Sermon 77 (Walshe No. 49, pp. 38–9).
13. Sermon 68 (Walshe No. 69, Vol. II, p. 167, DP 36).
14. Sermon 76 (Walshe No. 7, Vol. I, p. 66, DP 35).
15. Sermon 84 (Walshe No. 84, pp. 259–60). Eckhart's description of transformation

into God was condemned in article 10, identification with the Son in articles 11, 12, 20, and 21, and identification (Union) with God in articles 13 and 14. Sermons in which these themes are prominent include: Redditus Return to God (Walshe nos. 4, 6, 9, 44, 45, 51, 56, 85, 88); Reformation into God 22, 43, 47, 95; Identity with the Son 7, 11, 14b, 43, 46, 47, 53, 57, 66, 71, 87, 89, 92; Becoming the Son 11, 43, 95; Breakthrough into God 11, 16, 48.

16. Sermon 74 (Walshe No. 74, Vol. II, p. 202). For a fuller treatment of the spiritual itinerary, see Chapter 7, 'Eckhart and the Wayless Way'.

17. Sermon 75 (Walshe No. 88, Vol. II, pp. 282–3).

18. Henry Chadwick, *Early Christian Thought and the Classical Tradition* (Oxford: Clarendon Press, 1984 edn), p. 63. Cf. pp. 61f.

19. Sermon 6 (Walshe No. 65, Vol. II, p. 134, DP 7).

20. Sermon 104 (Walshe No. 3, Vol. I, p. 29). Although Quint doubted the authenticity of this sermon, a parallel sermon exists in Latin (LW IV, 102) and a similar treatment is found in Sermon 4 (Walshe No. 40). It is now included in the critical edition (DW IV) as Predigt 104.

21. Sermon 86 (Walshe No. 9, Vol. I, pp. 86–7, DP 29).

22. Sermon 7 (Walshe No. 72, Vol. II, p. 189, DP 8).

23. Sermon 39 (Walshe No. 59, Vol. II, p. 98).

24. *Talks of Instruction* (Counsels of Discernment), Graef trans., in Ancelet-Hustache, op. cit., p. 79.

25. Sermon 6 (Walshe No. 65, Vol. II, p. 131, DP 7).

26. Sermon 62 (Walshe No. 55, Vol. II, p. 76, DP 48).

27. See Chapter 11 in this collection.

Chapter 7

Eckhart and the Wayless Way[1]

In 1984, when I was asked by Michael Glazier to undertake a book on Meister Eckhart in his series 'The Way of the Mystics', the most and perhaps only appropriate title that came to mind was 'Eckhart's Way'. As I began organizing my material, it fell more or less naturally into subdivisions – the Friar's Way, the Master's Way and the Preacher's Way. Without particular reflection, I presumed that Eckhart *had* a way, a presupposition that seems to run counter to some of Eckhart's plain statements, as when in German Sermon No. 86 he promotes what he calls 'a wayless way, free and yet bound, raised, rapt away well-nigh past self and all things, without will and without images . . .'[2]

On the basis of this passage and others, Robert Forman has argued that Eckhart not only proposed a spiritual path or method, at least implicitly, but somewhat like Matthew Fox, also claims that Eckhart's path was one of ecstatic awareness of union with God.[3] Forman further asserts that Eckhart attempted to articulate a structured series of stages of spiritual development. In this chapter I propose to address both of these claims. First, was Eckhart's 'way' one of ecstatic rapture or, rather, of contemplative mindfulness? Second, did Eckhart advance a staged set of methodologically driven approaches to union with God?

Ecstasy and Mindfulness: The Contemplative Way

Despite other differences among them, many commentators such as Oliver Davies, C. F. Kelley, Richard Kieckhefer, Bernard McGinn, Reiner Schürmann and Frank Tobin concur that insofar as Eckhart proposed a spiritual method, it was the classical route of the *via negativa* – the way of *agnosia*, or 'unknowing'. According to these writers, moreover, far from endorsing ecstasy, Eckhart attempted to dissuade his hearers from pursuing what was at the time a popular tendency among the beguines and many other would-be mystics. (Although from a later period, the figure of Margery Kempe inevitably comes to mind in the latter respect.)[4]

Richard Kieckhefer, for example, maintains that

> Eckhart did not view ecstatic or abstractive union with God as integral to the life of the soul, or even as a goal to be sought or particularly treasured. The state to which he invites his reader is that of habitual and nonabstractive union; he nowhere says that other forms are necessary or even helpful to the attainment of that goal.[5]

I think Kieckhefer is correct, although Forman proposes several interesting ideas about Eckhart's attitude towards ecstatic rapture that warrant consideration. He admits that 'Eckhart's "principle" emphasis is not on . . . ecstatic moments, but rather towards something more permanent'. He adds, rightly moreover, that 'It is not true that Eckhart disparages rapture.'[6]

It is something else, however, to maintain that Eckhart teaches a method that entails an endorsement of ecstatic rapture, and this is ultimately what Forman wants Eckhart to do. He even criticizes Eckhart for not making such an emphasis more explicit:

> From the vantage point of today, it is unfortunate that Eckhart saw fit to discourage his listeners or readers from taking up some effective technique. It is naive to think that people can transform themselves in the deep and fundamental way he/she seeks without effective tools. Throughout the centuries many such tools have been developed and are available to us now. Some are presumably more effective than others. Which are most effective is a judgment each individual must make for himself or herself. But there is no doubt that an advocacy of a more efficacious path would have made Eckhart a more productive spiritual adviser in his own time, and certainly more useful to us.[7]

Fundamentally, as I read Eckhart, the weight of evidence falls on the side of Kieckhefer, McGinn, Tobin, *et al.* Further, I suspect that had Eckhart endorsed what might have been considered 'more effective tools' in his own time, he would have been a much *less* productive adviser in ours. Nevertheless, in light of the interesting and sometimes persuasive arguments Forman offers, the question can still be raised whether or not Eckhart's way is so wayless after all.

In Pursuit of a Way

Questions of method and stages along the way are very old in Christian spirituality, as they are in other spiritual traditions. The common Hebrew word *derek* came to be a metaphor for human experience or the direction of one's life as a whole (Gen. 6:12), as well as the more ancient theme of the Way of the Lord (Ex. 32:8; Deut. 5:23). Later use reflects the Wisdom tradition's notion of the Two Ways, that of the wise and that of the fool (Pr. 4:11, 18; 14:12, 16:7; Wis. 5:6).

The Greek equivalent, *hodos*, is used in the same manner in Christian scripture, where Jesus talks of the narrow way that leads to life and the wide way that leads to destruction (Matt. 7:13). The earliest Christian writings are filled with references to the Way of Salvation, the Way of God, and so forth. In John 14:4–6 and Hebrews 9:8 and 10:19, Jesus himself is seen as the Way to salvation and ultimately to God. Christianity itself was first known as The Way (see Acts 9:2, 19:9, 23; and 24:14, 22).[8] In other religious traditions there are similar concepts, such as those in Chinese Taoism (*Tao* means 'road' or 'path') and Japanese Shinto (*Shen Dao*, 'the Way of the Ancients'), as well as 'the Way of the Masters' in Sufism, and even the Shining Path of Peruvian Maoism.

In Christian spirituality, the development of what Forman calls 'tools' or, rather more ominously, 'techniques', occurred early. The concept of method, a word etymologically related to 'way', was widely favoured among both pagan and Christian Greeks. The prefix *meta* with *hodos* produces the terms *methodeia* and *methodos*, which mean 'proceeding according to a rule'. In regard to what is later known as the spiritual life, such terms meant a rule for the whole of life. (Significantly, *methodeia* also meant 'craft' and 'wiliness'.) Thus, certain physical dispositions for prayer which came to preoccupy (some would add obsessively) the desert saints of the fourth and fifth centuries now strike us as odd, repugnant, or even pathological *methods*, such as those of the stylites, dendrites, adamites, enkratites and others. Even the discipline of moderate ascetics such as Anthony and Pachomius are worrisome today – including social isolation, extreme fasting and other severe bodily and mental practices.

One way or another, spiritual 'methodists' have included charismatics, prophets and seers of every type, from the Donatists, Montanists and Priscillianists of the ancient Church to the flagellants and Lollards of the Middle Ages, to the Quakers and Quietists, Anabaptists, Shakers and Spiritualists of later times. Some never bathed or cut their hair, others shaved their heads bald. There have been nuns, monks, hermits, mendicants, gyrovagues and vagabonds, hesychasts, virgins, libertines, vegetarians, Crusaders, nurses, holy fools and clowns. Jesuits and Franciscans, Puritans and Catholics, Jansenists, Abolitionists, Prohibitionists, Fundamentalists, Pentecostals, evangelicals, liberals, modernists, Unitarians, Mormons, Jews for Jesus, Old Catholics, Born-again Christians, Lefeverites . . . all have had their favourite forms of devotion, and many have not infrequently proposed that these are not only suitable for everyone but requisite for salvation.

The question whether Eckhart espoused or promoted such a 'way' in the sense of a method is thus not an idle one. From my perspective, the answer is complex. As usual when dealing with the mystics, it seems to be both 'Yes' and 'No'. That is, 'Yes he does, but it is not what one might think' – whether the 'it' is God, the self, the soul, or the way to union with God.

Eckhart's Wayless Way

The spirituality of the Order of Preachers is distinguished, like God in Eckhart's way of thinking, by being indistinct – it features no particular method like the Spiritual Exercises of St Ignatius, the Jesus Prayer, the practices of Teresa of Àvila, much less those of later spiritualities. What Eckhart would have received as his Dominican legacy is an emphasis on contemplation in the widest sense, which leads to apostolic activity, specifically preaching.

The 'way' Eckhart proposes, so far as he does so at all, follows the apophatic route of classical Christian contemplation favoured in the Order of Preachers during his formative years and as taught by his close contemporary St Gregory Palamas in the East and practitioners of the *via negativa* in the West such as Richard of St Victor. What Eckhart in fact teaches is that the silent repose of contemplation, the polar opposite of ecstatic rapture, is the 'place of rest' where one encounters the divine Presence in the ground of the soul.

The elements of spirituality Eckhart would have learned as a young friar are reflected in this passage from the *Summa Theologiae* of St Thomas Aquinas, which Eckhart would have known well: 'Contemplation is the soul's clear and free dwelling on the object of its gaze; meditation is the survey of the mind while occupied in searching for the truth; and cogitation is the mind's glance, which is prone to wander.'[9]

The legitimate heirs of such a 'path' are the author of the *Cloud of Unknowing*, St John of the Cross, and John Main, even the Anabaptists and early Baptists, rather than the first Quakers or latter-day Pentecostals and other ecstatics. For early Christian spirituality, the discipline of *aphairesis* refers to stripping away concepts, not surrender to the inner light.

On the Circle of Eternity

Turning to Eckhart's teaching then, it is helpful to begin with the dense and rather obscure passage Forman cites in favour of Eckhart's supposed acceptance of ecstatic approaches to the spiritual life. It appears in the famous sermon in which Eckhart inverts the usual medieval symbolism of Mary the contemplative and Martha the active.[10] It begins with typical insistence that God can truly be approached only in immediate and direct experience, without conceptual mediation:

> . . . he who works in the light rises straight up to God free of all means: his light is his activity and his activity is his light.
>
> Thus it was with dear Martha, and so it was that [Jesus] said to her '*One* thing is needful', not two. When *I* and *you* are once embraced by the eternal light, that is *one*. Two-in-one is a fiery spirit [*brinnender geist*], standing over all things, yet under God, on [or within] the circle [brink, border, precincts] of eternity [*dem umberinge der êwicheit*].[11] This is two, for it sees God but not im-mediately. Its knowing and being, or its knowing and the object of knowledge will never be one. God is not seen except where He is seen spiritually, free of all images . . .

At this point, Eckhart introduces what may be called his threefold path towards union with God:

> Mark now what the circle of eternity means [*waz umberinc sî der êwicheit*]. The soul has three ways into God. *One* is to seek God in all creatures with manifold activity and ardent longing. This was the way King Solomon meant when he said 'In all things have I sought rest' (Eccles. 24:7). The *second* way is a wayless way [*wec âne wec*], free and yet bound, raised, rapt [*gezucket*] away well-nigh past self and all things, without will and without images, even though not yet in essential being. Christ meant that when he said, 'You are blessed, Peter, flesh and blood have not illumined you, but being caught up into the higher mind.

When you call me God, my heavenly Father has revealed it to you'
(Matt. 16:17). St Peter did not see God unveiled, though indeed he was
caught up by the heavenly Father's power past all created understanding
[*in*]to the circle of eternity [*den umberinc der êwicheit*] . . . You should
understand therefore that St Peter stood on [within] the circle of eternity [*dem umberinge der êwicheit*], but was not in unity beholding God
in His own being.

The *third* way is called a way, but is really being at home, that is:
seeing God without means [*âne mittel*] in His own being. Now Christ
says, 'I am the way, the truth and the life' (John 14:6): one Christ as
Person, one Christ the Father, one Christ the Spirit, three-in-one: three
as way, truth and life, one as the beloved Christ, in which he is all.
Outside of this way [*wege*] all creatures circle [around], and are *means*
[*umberingent und vermittelnt*]. But led into God on this way by the
light of His Word and embraced by them both in the Holy Spirit – that
passes all words.

Modeless Mode: Without Means or Images

For Eckhart, the Wayless Way is characterized, first, by immediacy. As God
is without mode or measure, the way to God must also be without mode
or measure, that is, without means, immediately. (For Eckhart, 'means' in
this regard are not merely creatures but especially conceptual tools –
ideas, images, even sensory representations.) This is because, first of all,
God has neither medium nor modes. 'We must take God as mode without
mode, and essence without essence, for He has no modes.'[12] Elsewhere
Eckhart preached similarly that

The joy of the Lord is the Lord Himself and no other, and the Lord is
living, essential, actual intellect which understands itself and is living
itself in itself and is *the same*. (In saying this) I have attributed no mode
to Him: I have taken from Him all mode, for He is Himself modeless
mode, living and rejoicing in that which he is.[13]

Further, therefore, 'God works without means and without images, and
the freer you are from images, the more receptive you are for His inward
working, and the more introverted and self-forgetful, the nearer you are
to this.'[14] Consequently, 'If we are to know God it must be without means,
and then nothing alien can enter in. If we do see God in this light, it must

be quite private and indrawn, without the intrusion of anything created. *Then* we have an immediate knowledge of eternal life.'[15]

Therefore, with regard to attaining the Birth of the Word in the soul, the climax of the spiritual journey, detachment (*Abgescheidenheit*) is required, the mental discipline of 'stripping', what the ancient tradition knew as *aphairesis* – the active purification of the senses and the imagination as well as the mind: 'A man cannot attain to this birth except by withdrawing his senses from all things. And that requires a mighty effort to drive back the powers of the soul and inhibit their functioning. This must be done with force, without force it cannot be done.'[16]

This is a theme found abundantly elsewhere: '. . . a master says, "To achieve an interior act, a man must collect all his powers as if into a corner of his soul where, hiding away from all images and forms, he can get to work." Here he must come to a forgetting and an unknowing [*unwizzen*]. There must be a stillness and a silence . . .'[17] Similarly, 'For you to know God in God's way, your knowing must become a pure unknowing, and a forgetting of yourself and all creatures.'[18]

This, of course, is also the central theme of the *Cloud of Unknowing*, that anonymous work of English spirituality written about 50 years later – and the only one from this period that reflects the influence of Eckhart and the Rhineland tradition. Such 'unknowing', moreover, is not merely a stripping away of concepts (*aphairesis*), but a complete stilling of the mind. For Eckhart, therefore, the truest kind of prayer is thus no prayer, 'in which the soul knows nothing of knowing, wills nothing of loving, and from light it becomes dark'.[19]

Practical Implications and Applications: The Ordinary Way

Concepts and sense images are not the only kind of means to which Eckhart objects. There are also practical means, and these too must be abandoned on the Wayless Way. Here, too, Eckhart says, a distinction must be made:

There are two kinds of means [*mittel*]. One means, without which I cannot get to God, is work or activity in time, which does not interfere with eternal salvation. 'Works' are performed from without, but 'activity' is when one practises with care and understanding from within. The other means is to be free of all that.[20]

Means also include ends, insofar as our purposes are less than ultimate and therefore less than one. Here again we turn to one of Eckhart's sermons cited by Forman:

> I say truly, as long as you do works for the sake of heaven or God or eternal bliss, from without, you are at fault. It may pass muster, but it is not the best. Indeed, if a man thinks he will get more of God by meditation [*innerkeit*], by devotion, by ecstasies [*in süezicheit* = 'sweetness'] or by special infusion of grace than by the fireside or in the stable, that is nothing but taking God, wrapping a cloak around His head and shoving Him under a bench. For whoever seeks God in a [special] way [*wîse, weise*: manner, way, method, fashion, habit] gets the way and misses God, who lies hidden in it. But whoever seeks God without any [special] way [*wîse*] gets Him as He is in Himself, and that man lives with the Son, and he is life itself.[21]

The way Eckhart proposes is, in fact, not extraordinary, much less ecstatic. It can be called, simply, the Ordinary Way, which requires both freedom and discretion, rather than a set of predetermined practices. In a passage that also presages the doctrine of the *Cloud* author, Eckhart observes that,

> Christ fasted for forty days. Imitate him by considering what you are sure that you are most inclined and ready to do; apply yourself to this and observe yourself closely. It is often more profitable for you to refrain from these things than to go without any food. Similarly, it is sometimes harder for you to suppress one word than to keep completely silent. So it is harder at times for a man to endure one little word of contempt, which really is insignificant, when it would be easy for him to suffer a heavy blow to which he had steeled himself, and it is much harder for him to be alone in a crowd than in the desert, and it is often harder for him to abandon some little thing than a big one, harder for him to carry out a trifling enterprise than one that people would think much more important. Thus a man in his weakness can very well imitate our Lord, and he need never consider himself far off from him.[22]

Eckhart rarely refers to penitential practices and nowhere else as comprehensively as in his *Talks of Instruction* to the Dominican novices at his priory in Erfurt, when he describes 'the ordinary way' of Christian living. True penitence, he says, is a complete lifting up of the mind away from all things into God, and whatever the works may be in which you have found and still find that you can most perfectly achieve this, do them with no constraint; and if you are impeded in this by any exterior works, whether it be fasting, keeping vigil, reading or whatever else, give it up and do not be afraid that in this you may be foregoing any of your penitence, because God has no regard for what your works are, but for what your love and devotion and intention in the works are.[23]

Action, Being and Holiness

For Eckhart, the 'way' he advocates can best be described as an intensified development of the normal life of a Christian rather than a distinct and separate form of living. He tells his hearers at one point,

> if someone seeks God's will alone, whatever flows from that or is revealed by that he may take as a gift from God without ever looking or considering whether it is by nature or grace or whence it comes or in what wise: he need not care about that. It is well with him and he need only lead an ordinary Christian life without considering doing anything special.[24]

Eckhart actually seems at times to be attempting to set people's minds at ease about 'spiritual perfection' rather than daring them to scale unimaginable heights of sanctity:

> People ought never to think too much about what they could do, but they ought to think about what they could be. If people and their way of life were only good, what they did might be a shining example. If you are just, then your works too are just. We ought not to think of building holiness upon action; we ought to build it upon a way of being, for it is not what we do that makes us holy, but we ought to make holy what we do. However holy the works may be, they do not, as works, make us at all holy; but, as we are holy and have being, to that extent we make all our works holy, be it eating, sleeping, keeping vigil or whatever it may be.[25]

In a sermon attributed to Eckhart, we learn finally that such holiness of life is so ordinary that it frequently goes without notice or may even be mistaken for laxity:

When the man of the soul is in true possession of his eternal bliss, when the powers [of the soul] are cut off, then that man meets with no opposition from anything. But note, you must pay heed, for such people are very hard to recognize. When others fast, they eat, when others watch, they sleep, when others pray, they are silent – in short, all their words and acts are unknown to other people; because whatever good people practise while on their way to eternal bliss, all that is quite foreign to such perfected ones. They need absolutely nothing, for they are in possession of the city of their true birthright.[26]

Spirituality without Technique

In regard to the second issue raised at the beginning of this chapter, I would like to consider more briefly Eckhart's 'Way' in terms of Stages of Development. Did Eckhart in fact advance a staged set of methodologically driven approaches to union with God as were soon to become common as 'spiritual exercises'?

Robert Forman correctly observes that Eckhart frequently described the progress of his pilgrim in terms of steps. These, however, do not represent stages of spiritual development in the modern sense, but reflect, first, Eckhart's awareness that spiritual growth inevitably occurs as we come closer to God, but also that such growth is not so much temporal as intentional. The number of such changes or states, second, often reflect the source Eckhart was currently considering and tend to be arbitrary, whether three, four, six, seven or, especially in his Latin works, far more. For instance, Eckhart proposes a simple sequence of three helps or steps that we may take in our approach to God: 'Observe which are the three heavens. The first is detachment from all bodily things, the second is estrangement from all imagery, and the third is a bare understanding in God without intermediary.'[27]

Elsewhere he argues that just as there are three obstacles to our union with God in this life, multiplicity, temporality and materiality,

So too there are three things that favour the union of God with the soul. The first is that the soul should be simple and undivided: for if she is to be united with God, she must be simple as God is simple. Secondly, that she should dwell above herself and above all transient things and adhere to God. The third is that she should be detached from all material things and work according to her primal purity.[28]

Eckhart does not restrict himself to trinitarian patterns. Here he describes four 'steps' into God:

> The soul takes four steps into God. The first is that fear, hope and desire grow [*wahsent*] in her. Again she steps on, and then fear and hope and desire are quite cut off. At the third stage she comes to a forgetfulness of all temporal things. At the fourth stage she enters into God where she will eternally dwell, reigning with God in eternity, and *then* she will never again think of temporal things or of herself, being fused with God and God with her. And what she then does, she does in God.[29]

Consider a similar passage that conveys much of the same understanding of a progressive approach to divine union:

> This virtue [detachment = *Abgescheidenheit*] has four degrees. The first breaks through and makes a way for a man from all transient things. The second takes them away from a man altogether. The third not only takes them away, but causes them to be altogether forgotten as if they had never been – and this is part of the process. The fourth degree is right in God and is God Himself.[30]

In a somewhat different vein, Eckhart elsewhere itemizes four 'things' needed for perfection in love of God:

> Whoever would achieve perfection in this triple love [of Father, Son and Holy Spirit] must needs have four things. The first is true detachment from all creatures. The second, the true life of Leah, that is to say the active life which is set in motion in the ground of the soul by the touch of the Holy Ghost. The third is the true life of Rachel, the contemplative life. The fourth is an aspiring spirit.[31]

Each of the preceding passages focuses in one way or another on detachment. The number of steps described are relative to the number of points Eckhart was making and have little, if any, other significance. It would appear rash to suggest that they represent discrete structures of the spiritual life. Along the same lines, consider these five properties he indicates that characterize those who abide in God:

The first is that between him and God there is no difference, they are one [*unum*] . . . between man and God there is not only no difference, there is no multiplicity, only one. The second is that he gains his blessedness in the same utter purity where God gets it and maintains Himself. The third is that he has one knowing with God's knowing, and one action with God's action, and one awareness with God's awareness. The fourth is, that God is all the time being born in that man . . . The fifth thing is that this man is all the time being born in God.[32]

And yet in another sermon he identifies six prerequisites for seeing God:

. . . the natural mind can never be so noble as to be able to touch or seize God without means, unless the soul has these six things of which I have spoken: First, to be dead to all that is unlike; second, to be well purified in light and in grace; third, to be without means; fourth, to be obedient to God's word in the inmost part; fifth, to be subject to the divine light; the sixth is what a pagan master says: blessedness is when one lives according to the highest power of the soul, which should always be striving upwards and receiving her blessedness from God.[33]

The teaching remains fundamentally the same; the number of steps or stages varies considerably and seemingly arbitrarily. There actually is something almost playful about Eckhart's enumeration of stages, states, qualities and requisites of various kinds. But despite possible correlations between various lists, deciding upon any kind of consistent, much less definitive, system or structure appears to be a futile quest.

Conclusion: Eckhart's Way

To the question 'Does Eckhart propose a way or spiritual path?', the answer is, I think, twofold, as I mentioned earlier. In the sense of a 'way' as a more or less distinctive and formal system of procedures or rules whereby a disciple undertakes to follow in the steps of a master, the answer is 'No'. The only 'way' Eckhart would have recognized here would have been what to him was the classical or traditional spiritual life as described and practised from at least the fourth century with its various component elements and functions – contemplation and action, purification, illumination, unification, etc. But taken in the sense of a more or less progressive if indeterminate series of steps or stages whereby the soul, or heart, or essential spiritual character of a person is transformed into the true image of God by ever closer realization of the presence of God in the very core of human experience and existence, the answer is a qualified 'Yes'.

This is not to say that Eckhart ever proposed a structured schema of the stages of spiritual perfection even as loose as the drawing by Henry Suso, one of Eckhart's students, which Forman appends to his text.[33] As I read Eckhart, both the nature and number of these stages vary and are relatively unimportant in themselves – he talks about three, four, five or six stages, depending on what he is discussing at the time. It should be noted, also, that in none of them is ecstasy or rapture endorsed, or even, with one possible exception, mentioned. But what *is* clearly present in his overall scheme is the centrality of what he calls the Birth of the Word in the Soul of the Just Person, and our breaking through into God. This progressive realization of unity with God is preceded by a serious effort to live one's life in accordance with the ordinary obligations and opportunities of a seriously committed Christian.

Insofar as a path or way to God exists, for Eckhart it is the *via negativa*, the simplification and unification of consciousness. It has two lanes, so to speak – one is *aphairesis*, stripping away all ideas, images and concepts of God so as to rest in Truth, the simple apprehension of God's grounding presence. The other is *apatheia* – the achievement of emotional calmness by detachment from all possessiveness, dividedness and self-centredness, so as to abide in the selfless love of God and neighbour.

The rest may not be silence, but it is the work of mercy and grace, beyond all human worth or effort, God's work. The Birth of the Word of God within the soul or the depths of human experience, the Ground or apex of the soul, is not in itself nor does it lead to ecstatic rapture, although such experiences may occur. The Birth of the Word leads, rather, to two 'breakthrough' experiences – our birth into God in this life, and our eternal birth into God beyond the limits of life and death, our disappearance into the trackless desert, the void of the Godhead into which no distinction of Father, Son, or Holy Spirit ever peeped, and where seer and seen, knower and known, lover and beloved experience undifferentiated and perpetual unity.

Notes

1. Portions of this chapter are based on a lecture presented to the Ibn' Arabi Society at Chisholme House, Hawick, Scotland, 23 May 1992.

2. Sermon No. 86 (Walshe No. 9, Vol. I, p. 83).

3. Robert Forman, *Meister Eckhart: Mystic as Theologian* (Rockport, MA/Shaftesbury, Dorset: Element Books, 1991). See also Matthew Fox, O.P., ed., *Breakthrough: Meister Eckhart's Creation Spirituality in New Translation* (Garden City, NY: Doubleday, 1980).

4. See Louise Collis, *The Apprentice Saint* (London: Michael Joseph, 1964).

5. Richard Kieckhefer, 'Meister Eckhart's Conception of Union with God', *Harvard Theological Review* 71 (1978): 224.

6. Forman, p. 20. See also Frank Tobin: 'Eckhart nowhere condemns visions and ecstasies; rather, he pays them scant attention while, at the same time, emphasizing the astonishing union with God possible to souls based simply on their nature as his creatures.' 'Mechthild and Meister Eckhart: Points of Comparison', in *Meister Eckhart and the Beguine Mystics,* Bernard McGinn, ed. (New York: Continuum, 1994), p. 45. Forman reluctantly concedes Richard Kieckhefer's contention that Eckhart deliberately de-emphasizes ecstasy (p. 64). Later, however, he attempts to qualify Kieckhefer's point, along with the judgements of McGinn, Schürmann and Kelley (p. 114).

7. Forman, op. cit., p. 94.

8. Cf. Acts 16:17 (the way of salvation), 18:25 (the Way of the Lord) and 18:26 (the Way of God). Also see Luke 24:35 ('on the way').

9. *Summa Theologiae,* II-II, Q. 180, a. 1., following Richard of St Victor.

10. Sermon 86 (Walshe No. 9, Vol. I, pp. 83–5).

11. *Um* = 'about', 'around', 'for', etc. In Middle Low German *brinc* meant ' edge', 'border', etc. Compare Modern German *im bering(e) der Stadt*: 'within the borders of the town', *im bering(e) eines Schlosse*: 'within the confines of the castle'.

12. Sermon 71 (Walshe No. 19, Vol. I, p. 160). 'In medieval philosophy and theology, "mode" (Latin: *modus*, "measure" or "manner") generally referred to the proportion or measure determining the relationship of the constitutive principles of some compound thing. Since God is not composed of principles of whatever kind, God can have no mode. Cf. Thomas Aquinas, *Summa Theologiae*, 1, Q. 5, a. 5.' Richard Woods, *Eckhart's Way* (2009), p. 117, n. 21.

13. Sermon 66 (Walshe No. 58, Vol. II, p. 95).

14. Sermon 57 (Walshe No. 1, Vol. I, p. 8, DP 57). Not found in the original critical edition, this sermon was included in Josef Quint's Modern German edition, *Meister Eckehart: Deutsche Predigten und Traktate* (Munich: Carl Hanser, 1955) and is now considered to be authentic (hereafter DP). In the critical edition edited by Georg Steer, DW IV, it is numbered as Predigt 101. Cf. also *Talks of Instruction (Counsels of Discernment)*, in *The Essential Sermons, Commentaries, Treatises and Defense*, ed. and trans. by Bernard McGinn and Edmund Colledge (New York: Paulist Press, 1981), p. 212.

15. Sermon 71 (Walshe No. 19, Vol. I, pp. 158–9).

16. Sermon 104 (Walshe No. 3, Vol. I, p. 25).

17. Sermon 102 (Walshe No. 2, Vol. I, p. 20, DP 58).

18. Sermon 103 (Walshe No. 4, Vol. I, p. 40f., DP 59).

19. *On Detachment*, Walshe ed., Vol. III, p. 292.

20. Sermon 86 (Walshe No. 9, Vol. I, p. 82).

21. Sermon 5b (Walshe No. 13b, Vol. I, pp. 11718).

22. *Talks of Instruction* (Colledge trans.), c.17, ed., cit., p. 268.

23. Ibid., c. 16, p. 265. Compare *The Letter on Discretion in Stirrings of the Soul*, in *The Cell of Self Knowledge*, ed. by Martin Gardner (Baltimore, MD: Christian Classics, 1983). See also *The Pursuit of Wisdom and Other Works by the Author of the Cloud of Unknowing*, translated and annotated by James Walsh, S.J. (New York: Paulist Press, 1988), pp. 134–43.

24. Sermon 62, DP 48 (Walshe No. 55, Vol. II, p. 76). He adds, 'He should just take one thing from God, and whatever comes, accept it as the best for him, having no fear that by this limitation he will be hindered in any way, inwardly or outwardly. Whatever he may do, if only he is aware of having the love of God within him, that suffices.'

25. *Talks of Instruction*, ed. cit., c.4, p. 250.

26. Pfeiffer Sermon 37 (Walshe No. 37, Vol. I, pp. 270–1, considered doubtful by Quint).

27. Sermon 23 (Walshe No. 54, Vol. II, p. 72).

28. Sermon 85 (Walshe No. 85, Vol. II, p. 264).

29. Sermon 84 (Walshe No. 84, Vol. II, pp. 259–60).

30. Sermon 74 (Walshe No. 74, Vol. II, p. 202).

31. Sermon 75 (Walshe No. 88, Vol. II, pp. 282–3).

32. Sermon 40 (Walshe No. 63, Vol. II, pp. 118).

33. Sermon 45 (Walshe No. 30, Vol. I, p. 226).

34. A reproduction can also be found in Henry Suso, *The Exemplar, with Two German Sermons*, Frank Tobin, trans. and ed., preface by Bernard McGinn (New York: Paulist Press, 1989), p. xiv.

Chapter 8

Eckhart on Contemplation[1]

Eckhart of Hochheim should be viewed as a practical mystic, if not *rather* than, then certainly *more* than a theoretical one. To categorize Eckhart as a speculative mystic diminishes or even dismisses him as a spiritual guide, except in the sense that the word 'theory' reflects the Greek *theoria*, which is usually taken to mean *contemplation*. Yet it is as a spiritual guide that Eckhart has found his greatest following today, and, it seems evident, in his own day as well.[2]

Eckhart was, of course, a profound thinker and, indeed, in the tradition of Albert the Great and Thomas Aquinas, a philosopher as well as a saint. So it should not be surprising that there are at least three levels of meaning in Eckhart's teaching – first, the practical or pastoral instruction, which is all too easily overlooked in our eagerness to delve into the deeper layers, the theological, second; and third, the philosophical, which encompasses at least epistemological and ontological dimensions. Among these levels also run rich strata of psychology and linguistics. Here, I want to excavate from the top down because I think it is important to understand Eckhart first of all as a spiritual master rather than mainly a theologian or philosopher. He was, after all, a preacher, a Dominican who, like his master Dominic, willingly if not wholly subordinated his speculative and even contemplative interests to the demands of ministry. And here he also follows Thomas Aquinas.

Insofar as Eckhart proposed a way of life that can be described as contemplative, what did he mean by that? Or, more to the point, how did he exhort his listeners to be contemplative? Seeing God is, of course, what the ancient Greek term *theoria*, which we translate *contemplation*, means. The word is based on the verb 'to see' in the sense of looking at something or someone. Ultimately, our question must be couched in terms of what it meant for Eckhart to look for and ultimately to 'see' God. It should not surprise anyone that he did not mean what we might think he means at first glance.

Eckhart's Teaching on Contemplation

First of all, it is not an idle question to ask whether Eckhart did in fact say anything about contemplation, or whether he advocated a way of living that we describe in our terms, but not his, as contemplative? Was his teaching in this regard orthodox and traditional? Or was he radical and eccentric as some critics claim?

Since in his German works Eckhart himself did not use the Latinate word 'contemplation', we might well begin carefully here. Where he appears to refer to contemplation in his sermons, usually without elaboration, the term is supplied by his translators.[3] In Modern German, the ordinary term is *Betrachtung*. The terms Eckhart used are, usually, *betrachtung, andaucht,* 'devotion' or 'meditation' and sometimes both (e.g., Sermon 5a, Sermon 41); *beschauung* (e.g., Sermon 75); and *eschauung* (e.g., Sermon 49), the latter three conveying in both Middle High and Modern German the sense of 'looking at something intently'. Modern translators render these and similar terms accurately enough by 'contemplation', meaning 'concentrated attention upon God'.[4]

In the Middle Ages, at least prior to the fourteenth century, contemplation did not imply a lack of thinking but conveyed, rather, a sense of sustained awareness of whatever kind. But under the influence of Eckhart and the author of the *Cloud of Unknowing*, among others, the sense of non-discursive awareness of the presence of God begins to replace the notion of sustained reasoning *about* God. Eckhart's notion perhaps most closely resembles the Buddhist concept of *mindfulness,* which might be a good translation of *innerkeit* – although with a Christian addendum: 'a man must learn to acquire an inward desert, wherever and with whomever he is. He must learn to break through things and seize his God in them, and to make His image grow in himself in essential wise.'[5]

The more or less received tradition regarding contemplation in the High Middle Ages was formulated largely in terms derived from Richard of St Victor. Drawing on much earlier sources, Richard distinguished contemplation from meditation and reasoning, not, however, exactly as we do today. St Thomas follows Richard closely in this, understanding by contemplation a kind of sustained intellectual concentration on truth; specifically, on God as truth.

According to Richard, in his *Benjamin Major*,

Thinking, slow footed, wanders hither and thither along by-paths, caring not where they will lead. Meditation, with great mental industry, plods along the steep and laborious road keeping the end in view. Contemplation, on a free wing, circles around with great nimbleness wherever the impulse takes it. Thinking crawls along, meditation marches and sometimes runs, contemplation flies around and when it wills, it hovers upon the height. Thinking is without labor and bears no fruit. Meditation labors and has its fruit. Contemplation abides untoiling and fruitful. Thinking roams about; meditation investigates; contemplation wonders.[6]

Thomas Aquinas, following Richard closely, writes in reverse order, 'Contemplation is the soul's clear and free dwelling on the object of its gaze; meditation is the survey of the mind while occupied in searching for the truth; and cogitation is the mind's glance, which is prone to wander.'[7]

So far as I can tell, Eckhart nowhere cites either Richard of St Victor or St Thomas directly, although he obviously knew this tradition and is probably referring to it in this passage from his *Talks of Instruction*:

a man should be pervaded with God's presence, transformed with the form of his beloved God, and made essential by Him, so that God's presence shines for him *without any effort*; rather he will find emptiness in all things and be totally free of things. But first there must be thought and attentive study, just as with a pupil in any art.[8]

Eckhart's emphasis here focuses on what later writers would refer to as passive, receptive or even 'infused' contemplation.[9] His initial stress on this aspect serves to remind us that although he speaks of progress in the art of contemplation, he never loses sight of what is an effortless and essentially gratuitous awareness of God's presence. Eckhart's most extensive treatment of what can be called the contemplative life is found in his *Talks of Instruction*, discourses most likely given to novices and younger members of the community when he was prior at Erfurt. Many of the themes in Eckhart's later sermons find parallels in these colloquies, sometimes developing them in surprising directions.

In his instructions to these beginners in the spiritual life, Eckhart is generally concerned with two items – first, our preparation and the mental activity involved in learning how to 'see' God, and, second, God. He is very little interested in what later writers would describe, often at great length, as mystical experiences, the interface between human consciousness and the divine presence. If anything, Eckhart strives to deflect attention away from experiences *of* God, as we shall see, in order to foster simple awareness of God's total presence, here and now. Or, rather, just simple awareness, since to be aware of God *as* God, that is, as other, bespeaks the difference between 'the eye by which I see God and the eye by which God sees me' and retreats from the union of vision which is truly beatific.[10] God, Eckhart says, is in *all* things, everywhere, and all things are in God at all times and all places. That is where we will 'find' God, but not by looking for God in the ordinary sense of that phrase.

This is what Meister Eckhart said to his novices:

> . . . in all his acts and in all things a person should consciously use his reason, having in all things a perceptive awareness of himself and his inward being, and in all things seize God in the highest possible way. For a man should be as our Lord said, 'Like people on the watch, always expecting their Lord' (Luke 12:36). For indeed, people who are expectant like that are watchful, they look around them to see where he whom they expect is coming from, and they look out for him in whatever comes along, however strange it may be, just in case he should be in it. In this way we should consciously discover our Lord in all things. This requires much diligence, demanding a total effort of our senses and powers of mind; then those who manage this are in a right state: taking God equally in all things, they find God in equal measure in all.[11]

By 'reason' here, Eckhart means much more than calculating correctly. He is referring to the use of all our wits, paying attention, being watchful, recognizing what is really the case with things. And for Eckhart, this can only awaken us to the presence of God in and around us and all things, including our work and play. From the outset, Eckhart never counsels turning our backs on the world in order to find God:

> For anyone who would be in a right state, one of two things must happen: either he must seize God in activities, and learn to have Him, or she must abandon all works. But since in this life no one can refrain

from activities, which are human and manifold, so one should learn to have his God in all things and remain unhindered in *all* acts and places. And so, when a beginner has to deal with people, he should first arm himself strongly with God and fix Him firmly in his heart, uniting all his intentions, thoughts, will and strength with Him, so that nothing else can arise in his mind.[12]

This, for Eckhart, is the beginning and basis of contemplation. He also taught his novices, that after some practice, when feelings of peace and happiness accompany moments of quiet attentiveness,

> ... one must sometimes leave such a state of joy for a better one of love, and sometimes to perform a work of love where it is needed, whether it be spiritual or bodily. As I have said before, if a man were in an ecstasy as St Paul was (2 Cor. 12:2–4), and if he knew of a sick person who needed a bowl of soup from him, I would consider it far better if you were to leave that rapture out of love and help the needy person out of greater love.[13]

When Eckhart does acknowledge what might be called stages of development in the discipline of contemplation, he does not devote much attention to them nor, especially, does he espouse any form of method or spiritual exercises such as found in later periods. In fact, Eckhart scorns particular methods of mental prayer, forms of which must have been known both to his Dominican students and the sisters he later instructed. In this, he reflects the original tradition of the Order. Simon Tugwell observes that

> ... the early Dominicans were not particularly concerned, either for themselves or for others, with what has come to be called the 'interior life'. Some of them, certainly, were great men of prayer, but their prayer was simple, devotional, and largely petitionary. But there is no hint of any methodical 'mental prayer', such as we find in later centuries, nor is there any sign of any theory of mystical progress attached to these simple prayers. When thirteenth-century Dominicans do comment on the ascent of the soul to God, it is in intellectualist terms that belong more within the domain of speculative theology than in the kind of mystical theology we have since become used to.[14]

With Eckhart, at the end of the thirteenth century, this has begun to change. Yet it would be wide of the mark to claim that Eckhart, or even his immediate followers such as Suso and Tauler, proposed a particular method of prayer or spiritual exercises. However, insofar as Eckhart clearly had particular, practical advice with regard to contemplation, he represents a bridge between earlier and later Dominican tradition, and between the spirituality of the earlier beguines and the later Dominican nuns. In Sermon 5a, for instance, Eckhart says,

> We find people who like the taste of God in one way but not in another, and they want to have God only in one way of contemplation [*Andaucht*], not in another. I raise no objection, but they are quite wrong. If you want to take God properly, you should take Him equally in all things, in hardship as in comfort, in weeping as in joy, it should be all the same to you.[15]

He makes the point even more emphatically in Sermon 5b:

> . . . if a man thinks he will get more of God by meditation [*innerkeit*], by devotion, by ecstasies [*süezicheit* – sweetness] or by special infusion of grace than by the fireside or in the stable – that is nothing but taking God, wrapping a cloak around His head and shoving Him under a bench. For whoever seeks God in a special way [*wîse*] gets the way and misses God, who lies hidden in it. But whoever seeks God without any special way gets Him as He is in Himself, and that man lives with the Son, and he is life itself.[16]

On the other hand, he was concerned with what might be called discipline or training in contemplation in order to arrive at a point at which an awareness of the presence of God was a more or less constant feature of one's ordinary life. First of all, to arrive at a contemplative attitude, assuming that one is living according to the Christian faith, one needed to develop what Eckhart called a 'bare mind'. Such a frame of mind allowed one to be aware of God in all things and to see all things in God.

> Now if a man truly has God with him, God is with him everywhere, in the street or among people just as much as in church or in the desert or in a cell. If he possesses God truly and solely, such a man cannot be disturbed by anybody. Why?

He has only God, thinks only of God, and all things are for him nothing but God. Such a man bears God in all his works and everywhere, and all that man's works are wrought purely by God – for he who causes the work is more genuinely and truly the owner of the work than he who performs it.[17]

For Eckhart, training in contemplation essentially means learning how to 'see' rightly – both mentally and spiritually. Thus, the first stage in his spiritual discipline involved stripping oneself of all attachments, not merely to material comforts, or even especially so, but, rather, mental constructs, ideas of God which actually hinder our actual perception of God's presence. In his *Talks of Instruction,* Eckhart said,

. . . true possession of God depends on the mind, an inner mental turning and striving towards God – but not in a continuous and equal thinking of Him, for that would be impossible for nature to strive for, very difficult and not even the best thing. A man should not have, or be satisfied with, an imagined God, for then, when the idea vanishes, God vanishes! Rather, one should have an essential God, who far transcends the thought of man and all creatures. Such a God never vanishes unless a man wilfully turns away from Him.[18]

Eckhart's way is the way of unknowing, the *via negativa* or 'apophatic' discipline that developed in the early Christian community in Egypt and spread through the Greek-speaking Mediterranean church. (Among other things, *apophasis* meant 'denial' or 'negation'.) In this, Eckhart perhaps most resembles St Gregory of Nyssa and the Pseudo-Dionysios both in his emphasis on simplicity and rigor. He also sounds very much like St Basil the Great writing to his brother, St Gregory Nazianzus:

One should aspire at keeping the mind in quietude [*hesychia*]. The eye that wanders continually around, now sideways, now up and down, is unable to see distinctly what lies under it; it ought rather to apply itself firmly to the visible object if it aims at a clear vision. Likewise, the spirit of man, if it is dragged about by the world's thousand cares, has no way to attain a clear vision of the truth . . . There is only one escape: withdraw from the world altogether. Now this withdrawal [*anaxoresis*] does not mean that we should leave the world bodily, but rather break loose from the ties of 'sympathy' of the soul with the body. This means to be without a city, without a house, without anything of our own, without property, without possessions, without resources, without affairs, without contracts, without being taught by men, but making ready to receive in our heart the imprint of divine teaching.[19]

Any number of excerpts from Eckhart could parallel St Gregory's teaching. For instance, Eckhart observes in his *Talks of Instruction*,

For him who would be in a right state, one of two things must happen: either he must seize God in activities, and learn to have Him, or he must abandon all works. But since man cannot in this life refrain from activities, which are human and manifold, so a man should learn to have his God in all things and remain unhindered in all acts and places. And so, when a beginner has to deal with people, he should first arm himself strongly with God and fix Him firmly in his heart, uniting all his intentions, thoughts, will and strength with Him, so that nothing else can arise in that man's mind.[20]

And in Sermon 75, Eckhart says, as we have seen elsewhere,

Three things prevent the soul from uniting with God. The first is that she is too scattered, that she is not unitary for when the soul is inclined towards creatures, she is not unitary. The second is when she is involved with temporal things. The third is when she is turned towards the body, for then she cannot unite with God.

So too there are three things that favour the union of God with the soul. The first is that the soul should be simple and undivided: for if she is to be united with God, she must be simple as God is simple. Secondly, that she should dwell above herself and above all transient things and adhere to God. The third is that she should be detached from all material things and work according to her primal purity.[21]

Eckhart is no less insistent on the matter of pictorial concepts or images, the kind of actively imaginative exercises promoted in later centuries by St Ignatius Loyola and others. For, Eckhart explains, 'God works without means and without images, and the freer you are from images, the more receptive you are for His inward working, and the more introverted and self-forgetful, the nearer you are to this.'[22]

In his *Talks of Instruction*, Eckhart amplifies this insight in a passage that deserves to be cited at length:

You should learn to be unattached in your works. But for an unpractised man it is an uncommon thing to reach the point where no crowd and no task hinders him – it calls for diligent application – so that God is ever present to him and shines before him completely unveiled, at all times and in all company. Skilful diligence is required for this, and in particular two things. One is that a man has shut himself off well inwardly, so that his mind is on its guard against the images without, that they remain without and do not unfittingly keep company and walk with him, and that they find no resting-place in him. The second is that he should not let himself be caught up by his *internal* imagery, whether it be in the form of pictures or lofty thoughts, or outward impressions or whatever is present to his mind, nor be distracted nor dissipate himself in their multiplicity. A man should train and bend all his powers to this and keep his inner self present to him.[23]

Anticipating an objection, he says,

Now you might say a man must turn outwards if he is to do external works, for no task can be done but according to its own form. That is true. But the externality of form is nothing external for the practiced man, for to the inward-turned man all things have an inward divinity. This above all is necessary: that a man should train and practice his mind well and bring it to God, and then he will always have divinity within. Nothing is so proper to the intellect, nor so present and near as God. It never turns in any other direction.[24]

In the end, for Eckhart,

He who has God thus essentially, takes Him divinely, and for him God shines forth in all things, for all things taste divinely to him, and God's image appears to him from out of all things. God flashes forth in him always, in him there is detachment and turning away, and he bears the imprint of his beloved, present God.[25]

Action and Contemplation

As a Dominican, and a man himself greatly involved in administration as well as preaching and teaching, Eckhart was keenly aware of the practical as well as the theoretical tension between action and contemplation. In a sermon attributed to Eckhart, but not included in either of Quint's collections, yet which has parallels in other German and Latin sermons of his, we read,

> St Thomas says the active life is better than the contemplative, in so far as in action one pours out for love that which one has gained in contemplation. It is actually the same thing, for we take only from the same ground of contemplation and make it fruitful in works, and thus the object of contemplation is achieved. Though there is motion, yet it is all one; it comes from one end, which is God, and returns to the same, as if I were to go from one end of this house to the other; that would indeed be motion, but only of one in the same. Thus too, in this activity, we remain in a state of contemplation in God. The one rests in the other, and perfects the other. For God's purpose in the union of contemplation is fruitfulness in works: for in contemplation you serve yourself alone, but in works of charity you serve the many.[26]

Here, Eckhart is somewhat seditiously paraphrasing rather than directly quoting St Thomas, whose comment merits citing in full:

> The work of the active life is twofold. One proceeds from the fullness of contemplation such as teaching and preaching. [. . .] And this work is more excellent than simple contemplation. For even as it is better to enlighten than merely to shine, so it is better to give to others the fruits of one's contemplation than merely to contemplate. [. . .] Accordingly, the highest place in religious orders is held by those which are directed to preaching and teaching, which moreover are nearest to the episcopal perfection . . . The second place belongs to those which are directed to contemplation, and the third to those which are occupied with external actions.[27]

Elsewhere, Thomas is specific about the superiority of contemplation:

It is more acceptable to God that one apply one's own soul and the souls of others to contemplation than to action . . . the work of the active life conduces to the contemplative by quelling the interior passions which give rise to the phantasms by which contemplation is hindered.[28]

Thomas also affirms, citing Augustine as his authority, that works of charity take precedence over solitary contemplation. For Thomas, however, this is more by way of concession than for Eckhart. According to Thomas, 'Sometimes a person is called away from the contemplative life to the works of the active life on account of some necessity of the present life, yet not so as to be compelled to forsake contemplation altogether.' And here he cites Augustine: 'if it be imposed on us, we must bear it because charity demands it of us . . .' (*de Civ. Dei*, xix, 19). Hence it is clear that when a person is called from the contemplative to the active life, this is done not by way of subtraction, but of addition.[29]

Ultimately, the basis of Eckhart's teaching on the possibility of seeing God in all things, and all things in God, is, like much of his teaching, the intimate relationship between God as Creator-Mind and the creature as the embodiment of a divine idea. And here, we find ourselves on the threshold of the ontological dimension of his doctrine: 'When God contemplates a creature He gives it its being: when a creature contemplates God, it derives its being from Him. The soul has a rational, noetic being: therefore wherever God is, the soul is, and wherever the soul is, God is.'[30]

Meditation and Contemplation Today

The impetus towards a recovery of the contemplative dimension of a full human life has not been limited to religious sources, as has also been the case with the practice of meditation, which is taught and widely practised for its medical and psychological benefits, as in the Relaxation Response – Dr Herbert Benson's adaptation of the manta yoga, otherwise known in the West as Transcendental Meditation.

One of the often-cited remedies to our hectic lifestyle today is 'to stop and smell the roses'. I'm not sure where that started, but it has the scent of contemplation about it. Meister Eckhart was one of the first mystical writers to use the rose as a symbol of the simple presence of nature as a contemplative medium pointing to God. In German Sermon 8, he says,

There is no life so feeble but, taken as it is being, it is nobler than anything that ever lived. I am certain that if the soul had knowledge of the least thing that has being, she would never depart for an instant from that thing. The meanest thing, known in God – if one were but to know a flower as it has being in God – that would be nobler than the whole world. To know the meanest thing in God as it is one being is better than to know an angel.[31]

One of Eckhart's seventeenth-century followers, the young poet Johannes Schaeffler, who called himself Angelus Silesius, put Eckhart's notion into verse:

> The rose blooms because she blooms,
> She does not consider why
> Nor does she preen herself
> Just to catch my eye.[32]

For Eckhart, and for the Zen Buddhists who find him so fascinating, the flower just *is*. But in its simple is-ness, the rose beckons us to enter our own reality. For Eckhart, that is the way to the discovery of God in all things – and all things in God.

Knowing and Unknowing God

We began our questioning by asking whether Eckhart said anything about contemplation, or whether later translators read later notions about the spiritual life back into Eckhart's doctrine. I also asked whether his teaching in this area was orthodox and traditional or, rather, radical and eccentric.

In regard to the first question, it seems evident that Eckhart not only referred to contemplation in his sermons and discourses in terms consistent with the teaching of Richard of St Victor and St Thomas Aquinas, but in many respects was even more traditional insofar as he returned more wholeheartedly than they to the ancient teaching of the spiritual masters of Alexandria, Antioch and Cappadocia. However, Eckhart's strongly apophatic emphasis on knowing and seeing God eventually put him at odds with partisans of a more positive, not to say Aristotelian, approach.

Following Augustine, Eckhart teaches us that God is closer to us than we are to ourselves, that is, always present, here and now. It is we who are absent, who pay no attention:

Therefore I say that there is no blessedness without a man's being aware and well knowing that he knows God . . . Therefore it was very well said by our Lord that 'a nobleman went away to a distant country to gain a kingdom for himself, and returned'. For man must be one in himself and must seek it in himself and in one – that is, to see God alone; and 'returning' is being aware and knowing that one knows God and is aware of it.[33]

However, it is not reflexive awareness itself that constitutes our ultimate happiness:

I say that when a man, the soul, the spirit, sees God, he realises and knows himself as knowing. That is, he knows that he sees and knows God. Now some people have thought, and it seems credible, that the flower and kernel of bliss lies in that knowledge, when the spirit knows that it knows God;[34] for if I had all joy and did not know it, what good would that be to me, and what joy would that be? But I definitely deny that that is so.[35]

Rather, '. . . our Lord says in very truth that eternal life is knowing God alone as true God, and not in knowing that one knows God (John 17:3)'.[36]

The tension in Eckhart's teaching here is not that between contradictory positions. In his sermons, Eckhart frequently stressed that beatitude lies in *knowing* God, not only in possessing God or being one with God, but 'knowing' in a very particular sense:

A master declares – and the best of our masters with him – that blessedness depends on our understanding and knowing, and we have a compulsive urge to know the truth. I have a power in my soul which is ever receptive to God. I am as certain as that I am a man, that nothing is so close to me as God. God is closer to me than I am to myself: my being depends on God's being near me and present to me. So He is also in a stone or a log of wood, only they do not know it. If the wood knew God and realised how close He is to it as the highest angel does, it would be as blessed as the highest angel. And so man is more blessed than a stone or a piece of wood because he is aware of God and knows how close God is to him. And I am the more blessed, the more I realise this, and I am the less blessed, the less I know this. I am not blessed because God is in me and is near me and because I possess Him, but because I am aware of how close He is to me, *and that I know God*.[37]

In *The Nobleman*, however, Eckhart further explains his point:

> Though it is true that the soul cannot be happy *without* that [knowledge], yet felicity does not depend on it; for the *first* condition of felicity is that the soul sees God naked. From that she derives all her being and her life, and draws all that she is, from the ground of God, knowing nothing of knowledge, nor of love, nor of anything at all. She is utterly calm in God's being, knowing nothing but being there and God. But when she is aware and *knows* that she sees, knows and loves God, that is a turning away and a reversion to the former stage according to the natural order . . .[38]

By whatever name we call it, for Eckhart, happiness, bliss or beatitude consists less in becoming conscious of the fundamental unity we share with God, not only in the depths of our own experience, but more in the simple fact of our being, than in forgetting it: losing ourselves in God and, it might be added, God in ourselves. In the words of a modern master whose debt to Eckhart was deep and sincere:

> The contemplative way is, in fact, not a way. Christ alone is the way, and he is invisible. The 'desert' of contemplation is simply a metaphor to explain the state of emptiness which we experience when we have left all ways, forgotten ourselves and taken the invisible Christ as our way.[39]

Notes

1. Portions of this section are based on 'Unknowing God: Meister Eckhart on Contemplation', an address to the Eckhart Society Conference, Plater College, Oxford, 1 September 1995 and subsequently published in the *Eckhart Review* 5 (Spring 1996) and selected talks to various groups of Dominican sisters and associates.
2. Even C. F. Kelley, who would deny Eckhart the title of mystic, nevertheless acknowledges him as a spiritual guide, one of the greatest in European history. See C. F. Kelley, *Meister Eckhart on Divine Knowledge* (New Haven, CT: Yale University Press, 1977. Reprinted with a foreword by William Stranger, New York: DharmaCafé Books, 2009), p. 1.
3. Instructive examples include Sermon 104 (Walshe No. 3, Vol. I, p. 28, Pfeiffer 3), considered dubious by Quint despite parallels and now accepted as genuine;

Sermon 5a (Walshe No. 13a, Vol. I, p. 112); Sermon 23, (Walshe No. 54, Vol. II, p. 73); Sermon 41, (Walshe No. 43, Vol. I, p. 4, DP 46,); Sermon 49 (Walshe No. 89, Vol. II, pp. 290–1).

4. For instance, Wiligis Jäger, who wrote '... "contemplation" always refers to a form of Christian prayer that is not focused on an object. In other words, it never means meditation on a content. It signifies rather an experiential state that is not accessible to the faculties which dominate in our everyday consciousness.' Wiligis Jäger, *The Way to Contemplation: Encountering God Today* (New York: Paulist Press, 1987), p. 3.

5. *Talks of Instruction*, No. 6, Walshe ed., Vol. III, p. 20.

6. Richard of St Victor, *Benjamin Major*, in *Richard of Saint-Victor, Selected Writings on Contemplation*, trans. and intro. by Clare Kirchberger (London: Faber and Faber, 1957), p. 136. Cf. *Patrologia Latina* 196:66C.

7. *Summa Theologiae*, II–II, Q. 180, a. 1.

8. Walshe ed., Vol. III, p. 19. Emphasis added.

9. Cf. this passage from the twentieth-century philosopher and theologian, William Ernest Hocking: 'Contemplation, as used by the medieval mystics implies that the effort of "meditation", in which one holds the object before the mind by force of will, gives way to a state in which the object attracts and holds attention without further conscious effort.' William Ernest Hocking, *The Meaning of God in Human Experience* (New Haven: Yale University Press, 1963), p. 371.

10. The reference here is to Sermon 12 (Walshe No. 57, Vol. II, p. 87): 'The eye with which I see God is the same eye with which God sees me: my eye and God's eye are one eye, one seeing, one knowing and one love.' For the same doctrine, see Sermon 62 (Walshe No. 55, Vol. II, p. 78): 'Whoever sees anything in God does not see God. A righteous man has no need of God. What I have, I am not in need of. He serves for nothing, he cares for nothing: he has God, and so he serves for nothing.' See also Sermon 10 (Walshe No. 66, Vol. II, p. 139).

11. *Talks of Instruction*, No. 7 (Walshe, Vol. III, p. 20).

12. Ibid., p. 21.

13. Ibid., No. 10 (Walshe, Vol. III, pp. 24–5).

14. *Early Dominicans: Selected Writings*, ed. by Simon Tugwell, O.P. (New York: Paulist Press, 1982), 'Introduction', pp. 3–4.

15. Sermon 5a (Walshe No. 13a, Vol. I, p. 112).

16. Sermon 5b (Walshe No. 13b, Vol. I, pp. 117–18).

17. *Talks of Instruction*, No. 6 (Walshe ed., Vol. III, p. 16).

18. Ibid., pp. 17–18.

19. St Basil to Gregory of Nazianzus, *Letter* 2 (*The Fathers Speak*, George Barrois, ed. [Crestwood, New York: St Vladimir's Seminary Press, 1986], pp. 47–8).

20. See above, n. 12.

21. Sermon 75 (Walshe No. 85, Vol. II, p. 264).

22. Sermon 101 (Walshe No. 1, Vol. I, p. 8, DP 57).

23. *Talks of Instruction*, No. 21 (Walshe ed., Vol. III, pp. 45–6).

24. Ibid.

25. Ibid., No. 6, p. 18.

26. Pfeiffer 3 (Walshe No. 3, Vol. I, p. 28). Although Quint doubted the authenticity of this sermon, it is now included in the critical edition (DW IV) as Predigt 104.

27. *Summa Theologiae*, II–II, Q. 188, A. 6.

28. Ibid., II–II, Q. 182, A. 2 ad 3.

29. Ibid., Q. 182, A. 1 ad 5. The likely reference here is to being ordained bishop, however, as Thomas is speaking of a change in the state of life rather than simple acts of charity which obligate all Christians.

30. Sermon 10 (Walshe No. 66, Vol. II, p. 145): Dâ got die crêatûre anesihet, dâ gibet er ir wesen; dâ diu crêatûre got anesihet, dâ nimet si er wesen. Diu sêle hât ein vernünftic bekennelich wesen; dâ von, swâ got ist, dâ ist diu sêle, und swâ diu sêle ist, dâ ist got. DW I, p. 173. The verb *anesihet* which Quint recognizes as a homœteleuton, comes from *ansehen*, 'to look at' or 'for'.

31. Sermon No. 8 (Walshe No. 82, Vol. II, p. 245).

32. Die Ros ist ohn warum: sie bluhet, well sie bluhet. Translation by Frederick Frank, *The Book of Angelus Silesius with Observations by the Ancient Zen Masters* (New York: Alfred A. Knopf, 1976), p. 66.

33. *The Nobleman*, Walshe ed., Vol. III, p. 114. Cf. Quint's Modern German version in the *Deutschen Predigten*: 'So also sage ich, daß es zwar Seligkeit nicht gibt, ohne daß der Mensch sich bewußt werde und wohl wisse, *daß* er Gott schaut und erkennt . . . Denn der Mensch muß in sich selber Eins sein und muß dies suchen in sich und in Einen und empfangen in Einen, das heißt: Gott lediglich schauen; und <zurückkommen>, das heißt: wissen und erkennen, daß Man Gott erkennt und weiß. (*Von Edeln Menschen*, DP, p. 148.)

34. Walshe here cites Thomas Aquinas, *Summa Theologiae*, I-II, Q 3, and also *LW* III, 93, 6ff.

35. *The Nobleman*, Walshe, Vol. III, p. 112.

36. Ibid., p. 113.

37. Sermon 68 (Walshe No. 69, Vol. II, pp. 165–6), emphasis added. See also the following in regard to experiential knowledge or knowledge *of*, rather than *about*, God: 'If a man dwelt in a house that was beautifully adorned, another man who had never been inside it might well speak of it: but he who had been inside would *know*.' Sermon 68 (Walshe No. 69, Vol. II, p. 169.) '. . . as for the man who has no acquaintance with inward things, he does not know what God is, just as a man who has wine in his cellar: if he has not drunk it or tried it, he does not know that it is good. So it is with people who live in ignorance: they do not know what God is, and yet they think and imagine that they are living. That knowing is not from God . . .' Sermon 10 (Walshe No. 66, Vol. II, p. 141).

38. *The Nobleman*, Walshe ed., Vol. III, p. 112. Also see above, n. 10.

39. Thomas Merton, *Contemplative Prayer* (New York: Doubleday Image Books, 1996), p. 92.

Chapter 9

Eckhart on Prayer: A Brief Excursion

Prior to ending one of his most interesting sermons with a distinctively brief prayer, Eckhart commented,

> People often say to me 'Pray for me.' And I think, 'Why do you go out? Why do you not stay within yourself and draw on your own treasure? For you have the whole truth in its essence within you.' That we may thus truly stay within, that we may possess all truth immediately, without distinction, in true blessedness, may God help us. Amen.[1]

Much as Eckhart both advocates and dispenses with contemplation, so also he prays and encourages prayer, not least at the end of every sermon. But he likewise dispenses with prayer. Or seems to. Meister Eckhart said to his novices,

> The most powerful prayer, one well-nigh omnipotent to gain all things, and the noblest work of all is that which proceeds from a bare mind. The more bare it is, the more powerful, worthy, useful, praiseworthy and perfect the prayer and the work. A bare mind can do all things.

Eckhart then asks (and answers) a question that may well have risen in the minds of his hearers at that point: 'What is a bare mind?'

> A bare mind is one which is worried by nothing and is tied to nothing, which has not bound its best part to any mode, does not seek its own in anything, that is fully immersed in God's dearest will and gone out of its own. A man can do no work however paltry that does not derive power and strength from this source. We should pray so intently, as if we would have all members and all powers turned to it – eyes, ears, mouth, heart and all the senses; and we should never stop until we find ourselves

129

about to be united with Him whom we have in mind and are praying to: that is – God.[2]

For many people, praying, like contemplation, is a quest for something. No matter how noble our intention, such prayer tends to invert Christ's petition in the Lord's Prayer, and we end up by saying, 'My will be done.'

Eckhart resisted the implication that in meditation or contemplation God appears as a thing among other things, visible, palpable, audible and, above all, useful, a view which set him apart from those inclined to pursue religious experience through visions and ecstatic states. Eckhart said:

> some people want to see God with their own eyes as they see a cow, and they want to love God as they love a cow. You love a cow for her milk and her cheese and your own profit. That is what all those men do who love God for outward wealth or inward consolation – and they do not truly love God, they love their own profit. I truly assert that anything you put in the forefront of your mind, if it is not God in Himself, is – however good it may be – a hindrance to your gaining the highest truth.[3]

And so, with regard to prayer, Eckhart says,

> Alas, how many are there who worship a shoe or a cow and encumber themselves with them – they are foolish folk! As soon as you pray to God for creatures, you pray for your own harm, for creature is no sooner creature than it bears within itself bitterness and trouble, evil and distress. So they get their deserts, these people who reap distress and bitterness. Why? They prayed for it.[4]

For Eckhart, prayer, like contemplation, is simply attentiveness to God. Moreover, all true prayer is contemplative prayer, whether in church, at home or in the marketplace. Thus, the perfection of prayer is attending to God completely, in all things, and attending to all things in God. In the ancient words of the Church fathers, to pray is to raise the mind and heart to God. When we pray, we should attend first to God, not to our needs and wants, or even those of other people.

> A man should never pray for any transitory thing: but if he would pray for anything, he should pray for God's will alone and nothing else, and then he gets everything. If he prays for anything else, he will get nothing.[5]

The reason, of course, is that in themselves, apart from God, all creatures are in fact nothing. Here, Eckhart is only saying what Jesus said, 'Do not be anxious, saying, "What shall we eat?" or "What shall we drink?" or "What shall we wear?" For the Gentiles seek all these things; and your heavenly Father knows that you need them all. But seek first his kingdom and his righteousness, and all these things shall be yours as well' (Matt. 6:31–33). And thus Meister Eckhart says, 'I never pray so well as when I pray for nothing and nobody, not for Heinrich or Konrad. Those who pray truly, pray to God in truth and in spirit, that is to say, in the Holy Ghost.'[6]

Anticipating a reasonable objection to what appears to be a denigration of the life of prayer, in another sermon Eckhart assumes the role of interlocutor:

> Now you might say, 'But sir, what must a man do to be void as a desert in respect of himself and all things? Should a man wait all the time for God to work and do nothing himself, or should he do something in the meantime, like praying or reading or some other good occupation such as listening to sermons or studying scripture? Since such a man is not supposed to take anything in from without, but only from within, from his God, does he not miss something by not doing these things?[7]

Step by step, Eckhart develops his theology of prayer in a dense passage that at least skirts the borders of what many worried churchmen would later characterize as 'quietism':

> Now listen. All outward works were established and ordained to direct the outer man to God and to train him to spiritual living and good deeds, that he might not stray into ineptitudes: to act as a curb on his inclination to escape from self to things outside; so that when God would work in him He might find him ready and not have to draw him back from things alien and gross. For the greater the delight in outward things the harder it is to leave them, the stronger the love the sharper the pain when it comes to parting.

He then returns to his point about 'practices', pre-eminently among them, prayer:

> See then: All works and pious practices – praying, reading, singing, vigils, fasting, penance, or whatever discipline it may be – these were invented

to catch a man and restrain him from things alien and ungodly. Thus, when a man realizes that God's spirit is not working in him and that the inner man is forsaken by God, it is very important for the outer man to practice these virtues, and especially such as are most feasible, useful and necessary for him; not however from selfish attachment, but so that, respect for truth preserving him from being attracted and led astray by what is gross, he may stay close to God, so that God may find him near at hand when He chooses to return and act in his soul, without having to seek far afield. But if a man knows himself to be well trained in true inwardness, then let him boldly drop all outward disciplines, even those he is bound to and from which neither pope nor bishop can release him.[8]

This final reference is, in medieval terms, undoubtedly an allusion to the vows of religious life. Although this still sounds at least somewhat shocking, and was meant to, Eckhart is invoking a principle that had even legal force in the Middle Ages: the greater always includes the lesser. Thus, he argues, true contemplative prayer already encompasses all that the human spirit can aspire to in this life. He explains,

> From the vows a man has made to God none can release him, but they can be turned into something else: for every vow is a contract with God. But if a man has taken solemn vows of such things as prayer, fasting or pilgrimage, if he then enters some [religious] order, he is released from them, for in the [religious] order he is vowed to goodness as a whole, and to God Himself.[9]

Eckhart's teaching here is consistent with his instructions to the novices at Erfurt, which also greatly resemble the doctrine found in the spiritual counsels of the author of *The Cloud of Unknowing*:[10]

> Turn all your study to letting God grow great for you, so that all your sincerity and striving is directed towards Him in all that you do or leave undone. In truth, the more you have of this, the better all your works, of whatever kind, will be. Hold fast to God, and He will fasten all goodness to you. If you seek God, you will find God and all goodness.[11]

Ultimately, therefore, Eckhart is not devaluing prayer, but exalting it, not least by insisting that when and where we pray is not important, only *that* we pray, and pray always:

A man may go out into the fields and say his prayers and know God, or he may go to church and know God: but if he is more aware of God because he is in a quiet place, as is usual, that comes from his imperfection and not from God: for God is equally in all things and all places, and is equally ready to give Himself as far as in Him lies: and he knows God rightly who knows God equally (in all things).[12]

In Sermon 86, Eckhart preached, similarly,

Three things especially are needful in our works: to be orderly, understanding, and mindful. 'Orderly' I call that which corresponds in all points to the highest. 'Understanding' I call knowing nothing temporal that is better. 'Mindful' I call feeling living truth joyously present in good works. When these three points are one, they bring us just as near and are just as helpful as all Mary Magdalene's joy in the wilderness.[13]

Did Eckhart himself pray – even for Heinrich or Konrad? Very likely, but the prayers of Eckhart that have come down to us are those with which he typically ended his sermons.

Some Brief Prayers of Meister Eckhart

The Augustinian tradition of brief prayer enshrined in *The Cloud of Unknowing* and other spiritual classics was practised by Eckhart as he preached – literally. Almost every sermon ends with a brief prayer, often in tune with the liturgical season. Taking a number of them together as a representative sample, we get a glimpse of how Eckhart prayed.

May the God who has been born again as human assist us to this birth, eternally helping us, weak men and women, to be born in him again as God. Amen.[14]

That we may be thus caught [on the hook of love] and freed, may He help us who is love itself. Amen.[15]

May we all attain this love of which I have spoken. So help us our beloved Lord Jesus Christ. Amen.[16]

And that Jesus may come into us and clear out and cast away all hindrances of body and soul and make us one, as he is one with the Father and the Holy Ghost, one God, that we may become and remain eternally one with Him, so help us God. Amen.[17]

That we may attain to this perfection [of detachment], may God help us. Amen.[18]

That we may outstrip and cast behind us all things unpleasing to the newborn King, may He help us who became a human child in order that we might become the children of God. Amen.[19]

That we may ever be a 'by-word' to the Word of God, may the Father and this same Word and the Holy Ghost help us. Amen.[20]

May God help us to love justice for its own sake and God without 'Why'. Amen.[21]

May we find ourselves in the day and the time of understanding, in the day of justice, and the day of blessedness: so help us the Father and the Son and the Holy Ghost. Amen.[22]

Notes

1. Sermon 5b (Walshe No. 13b, Vol. I, p. 119, DP 6). Possibly a variant of Sermon 5a, it expounds on the same passage of scripture and contains parallel passages. It also concludes in Eckhart's typical fashion, a feature lacking in Sermon 5a.
2. *The Talks of Instruction*, No. 2, 'Of the Most Powerful Prayer and the Highest Activity', Walshe, Vol. III, pp. 12–13.
3. Sermon 16b (Walshe No. 14b, Vol. I, p. 127).
4. Sermon 26 (Walshe No. 11, Vol. I, pp. 97–8).
5. Sermon 62 (Walshe No. 55, Vol. II, p. 76).
6. Sermon 67 (Walshe No. 70, Vol. II, p. 174).
7. Sermon No. 3 in the Pfeiffer ed., *In his quae Patris mei sunt* (Walshe No. 3, Vol. I, pp. 32–4, passim.). Although considered dubious by Quint, Sermon 3 is now recognized as authentic and is listed in the critical edition (DW IV) as Predigt 104.
8. Ibid., p. 34.
9. Ibid., pp. 34–5.
10. See 'The Letter on Discretion in Stirrings of the Soul' in *The Pursuit of Wisdom and Other Works by the Author of the Cloud of Unknowing*, translated and annotated by James Walsh, S.J. (New York: Paulist Press, 1988), pp. 134–43. Also see above, Chapter 7, p. 105, n. 22.

11. *Talks of Instruction*, ibid., Ch. 5, p. 15.
12. Sermon 68 (Walshe No. 69, Vol. II, p. 167).
13. Sermon 86 (Walshe No. 9, Vol. I, p. 85).
14. Sermon 101 (Walshe No. 1, Vol. I, p. 120, DP 57).
15. Sermon 103 (Walshe No. 4, Vol. I, p. 47, DP 59).
16. Sermon 65 (Walshe No. 5, Vol. I, p. 52).
17. Sermon 1 (Walshe No. 6, Vol I, p. 61).
18. Sermon 30 (Walshe No. 18, Vol. I, p. 152).
19. Sermon 102 (Walshe No. 2, Vol. I, p. 23, DP 58).
20. Sermon 9 (Walshe No. 67, Vol. II, p. 155, DP 10). 'Beiwort' is Middle High German for 'adverb' as well as modern German for 'adjective', a word dependent on a principle word.
21. Sermon 6 (Walshe No. 65, Vol. II, p. 137, DP 7).
22. Sermon 10 (Walshe No. 66, Vol. II, p. 146).

Chapter 10

Eckhart's Imageless Image: Art, Spirituality and the Apophatic Way[1]

Eckhart asked,

> How can a man be always being born in God? Take note: As this image is revealed in a man, so that man grows in likeness to God, for in that image the man is like the image of God as He is according to His naked essence. And the more a man lays himself bare, the more like he becomes to God, and the more like he becomes to God, the more he is made one with Him. Thus a man's being ever born in God is to be understood to mean that that man is refulgent with his image in God's image, which is God in his bare essence, with which that man is one. Thus this oneness of man and God is to be understood as a likeness of image, for man is Godlike in his image. So, when we talk of man being one with God, and being God according to that unity, we refer to that part of the image in which he is Godlike, and not to his created nature.[2]

'Image' is clearly an important term in Eckhart's mystical vocabulary, around which he constructs some of his most characteristic and difficult themes. Despite its depth, difficulty and medieval tenor, there is nothing quaint or musty about Eckhart's concern with the notion of image, and in particular the human person as *Imago Dei* – the image of God. This ancient Christian doctrine is still very much at the front of theological disputation, as indicated in the Santa Clara lecture by Mary Catherine Hilkert, '*Imago Dei: Does the Symbol Have a Future?*'[3] In it, Hilkert summarized much of the theological debate surrounding the theme and offered constructive suggestions for rehabilitating it in an era in which feminist, liberation and ecological pressures require a reassessment of both the concept, the language in which it has been formulated, and its historical and current implications for spirituality and ethics.[4]

Hilkert does not cite Eckhart, nor does Eckhart address issues that are of special importance to Hilkert and many people today, such as human arrogance in regard to other species and the planet as a whole, gender disparity, and the oppressive inequity between rich nations and poor nations. Still, Eckhart's approach to the image, and the *Imago Dei* in particular, offers insights that are surprisingly similar to many of Hilkert's observations and, I think, contain a wealth of spiritual wisdom.

Eckhart did not approach this subject in a vacuum, of course. He drew on resources of both the biblical and philosophical traditions of the past, as well as theological speculation. Since I do not have much to add by way of textual exegesis to what has been thoroughly discussed by Bernard McGinn, Bruce Milem, Loris Sturlese, Wolfgang Wackernagel, Emilie Zum Brunn and others,[5] in this chapter I propose, first, to provide some context for understanding Eckhart's doctrine of the image, specifically its origins in Hebrew and Christian Scripture and the ancient Greek philosophical tradition. Second, I will address Eckhart's treatment of these themes briefly in respect to art and artistic pursuits, and, finally, explore some of the implications of Eckhart's doctrine for ordinary spirituality.

The Doctrine of the Image in Context

Eckhart's treatments of the image reflect some if not most of the previous thousand years of religious and scholarly development and controversy, not least the Iconoclast movement that disrupted the Eastern Church for over 200 years and was instrumental in bringing the works of the pseudonymous Christian writer Dionysius the Areopagite to the West. Scholars are not wholly in agreement about the extent to which Eckhart's doctrine was shaped by these varied elements of the tradition. Still, it is abundantly evident that he was deeply influenced by the apophatic tradition of Alexandrian Christianity which, drawing on the Wisdom tradition of later Judaism and the doctrine of Philo, was developed by Gregory of Nyssa, Dionysius the Areopagite, Maximus the Confessor, and many other great theological and spiritual writers.

It would be well to bear in mind that we are necessarily dealing with translations from ancient Hebrew, New Testament Greek, medieval Latin and Eckhart's Middle German. Standard translations of biblical and philosophical texts are sufficiently reliable, and Eckhart's Latin works tend to be consistent and clear enough to identify his remarkable philosophical and theological training as well as his occasional flashes of originality.

But even contemporary German scholars must cope with Eckhart's German, which comes down to us in textual variants thanks to the various dialects of his audiences, mainly Dominican nuns and beguines, who came from all parts of the area then known as 'the Germanies' and the southern Rhineland we know today as northern Switzerland, and transcribed their memories and notes of Eckhart's sermons in those dialects.

To begin with, and very briefly, the Middle High German word *bild* has many of the same nuances as the modern German term, which primarily means 'image' or 'picture' as well as 'form' or 'shape'. The earlier word also meant 'form', a meaning largely missing in Modern German, but retained in the verb *bilden*, which means 'to form, shape or fashion' rather than 'to image', which is rendered in Modern German by *einbilden*. The English word 'imagination' is *Einbildung* in German. (*Glîchnis*, by which Eckhart and Modern German usually mean 'similitude' or 'simile', could also mean 'equality' for Eckhart, although he ordinarily used for that the noun *Glîchheit* [Modern German *Gleichheit*].) The terms Eckhart uses, if not coins, for this process are *widenbilden* and *überbilden*, which may be translated as *reformation* (or *re-imaging*) and *transformation* (or *transfiguration* or even *trans-imaging*). Sometimes, Eckhart also uses the rare Latinism *transformieren*. Eckhart also uses the term *entbilden*, which would have meant 'unform', 'disfigure' or even 'de-form', but in the sense that an image is erased, as in this passage from Sermon 40: '. . . when a man surrenders himself nakedly to God, he is then unformed [*entbildet*], informed [*inbildet*] and transformed [*überbildet*] into the divine uniformity [*einformigkeit*] in which he is one with God'.[6]

The richness or possible ambiguity of these terms gave Eckhart plenty of scope for word-play. But it is also easy to misread him for that reason. Context usually supplies the key to understanding, as when, for instance, Eckhart emphasizes the equality of the Word as the image of the Father, or the human person as the image of Christ. In German Sermon 42, for instance, Eckhart preaches that

> The eternal Word did not take upon itself this man or that, but it took upon itself one free, indivisible human nature, bare and without image, for the impartible form of humanity is imageless. And since, in this assumption, the eternal Word took on human nature imagelessly, therefore the Father's image, which is the eternal Son, became the image of human nature. So it is just as true to say that man became God as that God became man.[7]

And in Sermon 6 he says, cryptically enough, 'They who are like nothing are Godlike. God's being is like nothing: in it is neither image nor form.'[8] On the other hand, he also dismisses images and likeness as completely inadequate to represent the unknown and unknowable *Gotheit*, by which he means that all mental and graphic images – concepts and pictures: 'God works without means and without images,' he insists, 'and the freer you are from images, the more receptive you are for His inward working, and the more introverted and self-forgetful, the nearer you are to this.'[9]

Ferreting out the different and sometimes conflicting meanings of the term 'image' in Eckhart's German works thus requires care. Scholars generally seem to agree that there are at least three fundamental levels or layers of meaning in Eckhart's sermons – different, but related. But Eckhart's teaching varies from work to work. What he stresses in one place, he may ignore, if not deny, elsewhere. In short, how Eckhart developed his teaching in one sermon does not mean that it is therefore a key to understanding his teaching in others.

Sources: Scriptural Origins

Eckhart never developed a comprehensive theory of the image, but it is highly significant, as Sturlese pointed out several years ago, that his most systematic teaching on the subject is found in three of his Latin scriptural commentaries – those on Genesis, Wisdom and John – and Latin Sermon 49.[10] But as we shall consider shortly, Eckhart's understanding was shaped also by the philosophical tradition of Aristotle, the reconstructed Platonism of Proclus and Thomistic thought, for all of whom the notion of image was also critically important.[11]

Eckhart's frequent emphasis on the linked terms 'image' and 'likeness' has obvious connections with Genesis 1:26 and 27, passages on which he also commented in his two books on Genesis:

> Then God said, 'Let us make humanity in our image, after our likeness; and let them have dominion over the fish of the sea, and over the birds of the air, and over the cattle, and over all the earth, and over every creeping thing that creeps upon the earth.' So God created humanity in his own image, in the image of God he created him; male and female he created them.

Countless commentaries have been written over the centuries on the famous passages in Genesis which describe the creation of Adam and Eve and thereby all human beings in the 'image' and 'after the likeness' of God. The Hebrew terms are *tselem* for 'image', and *demuth* for 'likeness'. The theological significance of the passages loomed enormous in the Christian era, but in their original form the terms were less remarkable. They are used later, as in Genesis 5:3, for the ordinary process by which a child is said to resemble or be 'like' his or her parents: 'When Adam had lived a hundred and thirty years, he became the father of a son in his own likeness [*demuth*], after his image [*tselem*], and named him Seth.' But the deeper significance was not forgotten, as in this passage from the account of God's Covenant with Noah after the Flood: 'Whoever sheds the blood of man, by man shall his blood be shed; for God made man in his own image [*tselem*] (Gen. 9:6).'

Although Hebrew scripture affirms unequivocally that the human person is made in the image and likeness of God, the scriptures do not, on the other hand, tell us *what* that similarity consists of. Scriptural emphasis is moral, rather than metaphysical, as witnessed in the passage concerning the Noachic covenant mentioned above. In Exodus, Leviticus, Deuteronomy and other books of the Hebrew Scriptures, this moral and eventual cultic understanding is reflected primarily in the prohibition against graven images, on one hand, for nothing created can be like God.[12] Nothing, that is, except the human person. Thus, on the other hand, the dignity and value of human life is sanctioned as the moral and spiritual consequence of the inexpressible greatness of the Creator God.

In Christian scripture, following the Septuagint tradition, *tselem* was normally translated by the Greek term *eikon* (see Col. 1:15, etc.). 'Likeness' was rendered by *homoiosis* or *homoioma* and their cognates, a linguistic fact that would bear difficult fruit in the great Christological controversies that split the early Church between Orthodoxy and Arianism.[13] *Eikon*, of course, is the same as 'icon' in English, and still refers to a sacred image. It is worth noting that the centuries-long dispute in the Eastern Church, as well as later in Puritan England and New England regarding the propriety of sacred images, has its roots in the apophatic rejection of any representations of the unseen, invisible, incomprehensible God.

The ancient Hebrew rejection of images as *eidola*, idols, thus had its positive dimension as well as the negative, although the positive was often implicit – no graven or 'made' image of God was permissible, not simply because God is unrepresentable, but also because the human person is the sole valid image of God. The biblical insight which grounds the moral dignity and value of the human person thus also establishes the basis for a spirituality of deification, as the great mystical theologians of the fourth and fifth centuries quickly realized. And it was that mystical tradition that found its way to Eckhart.

Philosophical and Theological Sources

But Eckhart was not only a mystic and spiritual master; he was a scholar, theologian and philosopher who was keenly aware of the rich and often nuanced heritage of ancient Greek and contemporary Latin thought with respect to the doctrine of images. Even adequately exploring this aspect of Eckhart's intellectual resources could result in a very long digression. Suffice it to say here that, beginning with Plato and Aristotle, the philosophical journey of the image is complex and difficult. However, this hardly deterred Eckhart from attempting a grand synthesis of the philosophical and scriptural meanings and, in large measure, he succeeded in creating a surprisingly coherent doctrine.

What Eckhart took from the Greek philosophical ancestors was, first of all, a psychological or epistemological notion of the image, based on the physical image of objects involved in the act of vision as understood in the Middle Ages. Almost all the Greek and Latin words that signify image or likeness, such as *eidos*, *eidolon*, *idea* and *species*, refer to seeing – specifically how a thing 'looks' or appears to an observer. Significantly, Eckhart's teacher, predecessor and friend, Dietrich of Freiburg, whose teaching on the image was more systematic and comprehensive than Eckhart's, was the greatest medieval authority on optics as well as a leading Neoplatonic scholar. While etymologizing, it's worth noting that both the English word 'image' and the Latin *imago* mean 'copy', and are related to the word *imitare*, 'imitate'.

The fundamental meaning of the Greek *eikon,* which literally means 'copy', or 'resemblance', was that of the physical shape, figure, or appearance of something, a character expressed in later Latin translation by several terms – *figura, forma* and *species* among them, as well as the direct borrowing which has come down to us also in English. For the philosophers, in all of these cases the physical image or appearance of an object conveyed by light to the eye and eventually to the mind by way of the imagination, common sense and memory, was also the analogue of the mental image or concept, the *idea* formed by abstraction from all sensible particulars. So important was the mental image in Aristotle's philosophy and psychology that he believed that 'it is impossible even to think without a mental picture'.[14] Today, we refer to such 'mental pictures' as 'eidetic imagery', to distinguish them from formal or abstract concepts.

Eckhart frequently utilizes these notions throughout his works without greatly bothering to draw out their logical, psychological or philosophical implications. But they also ground the discussion that did concern him keenly, the theological dimension and, by extension, its spiritual application. Not surprisingly, it is the theological aspect of Eckhart's doctrine of the image that has understandably attracted most scholarly attention.

As Loris Sturlese, Bruce Milem and other scholars have demonstrated, in Sermon 16b and elsewhere, Eckhart employed two paradigms of the soul as the image of God – the Trinitarian or epistemological, based on the three higher powers of the soul traceable to St Augustine – intellect, will and memory; and the ontological or onto-theological, founded on the absolute dependency of the soul upon God, a notion not of Eckhart's own creation, but frequently original in his formulation of it – so original that it was cited by the censors in Cologne as heretical. Following Sturlese and other commentators, I think it is clear that Eckhart regarded the onto-theological image as both fundamental and superior.

But Eckhart also distinguished between the uncreated image and the created image. In Sermon 16a and elsewhere, Eckhart clearly and consistently identified Christ as the exclusive *Imago Dei*, the uncreated image, and the human person as created *ad imaginem Dei*, as in the biblical account. But in the same sermon and elsewhere, Eckhart also identified not only himself, but all human persons with that same Son, first by reason of the Incarnation, in which the Word of God assumed not a particular person, but human nature, and, secondly, by a process of transfiguration or transformation [*überbildung*], whereby the divine image of God, deformed or disfigured [*entbildet*] whether by 'falling' into temporal, spatial, material existence, or by sin, is changed into the image of Christ and thereby into God. In a striking passage in Sermon 16b, Eckhart says,

. . . some complain that they have no inwardness nor devotion nor rapture nor any special consolation from God. Such people are still not on the right way: one can bear with them but it is second-best. I declare truly that, as long as *anything* is reflected in your mind which is not the eternal Word, or which looks away from the eternal Word, then, good as it may be, it is not the right thing. For he alone is a good man who, having set at naught all created things, stands facing straight, with no side glances towards the eternal Word, and is imaged and reflected there in righteousness. That man draws from the same source as the Son, and is himself the Son. Scripture says, 'No man knows the Father but the Son' (Matt. 11:27). Therefore, if you would know God, you must not merely be *like* the Son, you must *be* the Son yourself.[15]

Thus, we are created both *Imago Dei* and *ad imaginem Dei*, the second as creatures distinct from but wholly dependent upon God for our existence, and the first as identical with the Word of God and thus indistinct from God in the depths of the divine nature itself. Eckhart sometimes emphasizes one of these aspects, and at other times its complement, depending on his present agenda.

In summary, then, various levels of image can be distinguished in Eckhart's thinking: first, the *physical* image, whether a natural product, such as a reflection in a pond or a mirror, or the product of human art – a painting or other representation. Second, Eckhart shares with his contemporaries a *psychological* notion of the image as shape, form or figure conveyed by light-rays to the eye or other senses and recognized as what we would call a percept by a concurrence of imagination, memory and the unifying or common sense. Third, an *epistemological* concept or mental image is produced by a process of abstraction through which the sensible particulars of the physical image are stripped away, revealing the universal form or idea.

In addition, fourth, Eckhart recognizes two fundamentally different kinds of *theological* image: first, the Trinitarian image of intellect, will and memory, by which the human person formally resembles God as a spiritual being; and, second, the onto-theological image by which God expresses the divine nature by a process of formal emanation, giving birth to the Son and all things out of the infinite matrix of divine ideas in the mind of God. Eckhart's distinction of the created image familiar to us as a work either of nature or of human artifice from the uncreated image, which is an expression or outflowing of the formal nature of God, cuts across the other distinctions. The uncreated image is primarily and essentially the Eternal Word, the Second Person of the Trinity, and secondarily, created beings, especially spiritual entities – angels and human souls as these exist primordially (or in Kelley's term 'principially') in God.[16]

Why any of this is important is because Eckhart frequently refers to images without indicating which level of image he is referring to. Thus, at times he seems to disparage images completely, as when he rejects all images of God as misleading, referring here to pictorial, psychological, and even theological paradigms or models of God which, by stipulation, fall infinitely short of conveying anything to us of the utter simplicity, purity, nobility and unity of God. (Even these latter terms signify negatively rather than positively, by denying their opposites.) So, Eckhart tells us, we must strip away *all* such concepts and images of God, 'seizing God bare and naked in his dressing room', in his famous homely metaphor.[17] And here Eckhart has recovered the ancient Christian notion of *aphairesis*, which is related to the notion of 'unknowing', *agnosia,* both pivotal elements in his spiritual theology.

But when Eckhart turns his attention to the uncreated *Imago Dei*, whether the primary, essential Image that is the exclusive character of the Son, or the shared image in which all intellectual creatures share, his tone is very different. Here, Eckhart extols the identity of the Word with the Father and our identity *through* the Word with the Father – first as the creative expression of God's eternal idea, and then as reformed or transfigured into the image of Christ by the spiritual process of 'breaking through' (*durchbrechen*).

I will return to this aspect of Eckhart's teaching in the concluding section, as it seems to be less noticeable in some of the more recent discussions of Eckhart's doctrine of images. But it is the most relevant to the spiritual life, and more fully expresses Eckhart's dynamic vision of the return of all things to God. At this point it seems appropriate to ask, what has Eckhart's nuanced understanding of image to do with art itself?

Eckhart and the Artless Image

Eckhart lived more than a century before the great flowering of Dominican art and artists in the Florentine Renaissance inaugurated by Blessed John Dominici (1357–1419). Thus, while there are many references to art and artists in his extant writings, it is not surprising that Eckhart left no treatises on aesthetics. It is possible to construct a more or less systematic philosophical account from his general remarks and the medieval principles that underlie much of his teaching, as that of the great Indian philosopher and critic Ananda Coomaraswamy in 1934, more than a decade before reliable translations of many crucial passages were available, and many works ascribed to Eckhart were shown to be attributed to him falsely.[18] But Coomaraswamy's effort, while brilliant and worthy of fuller attention by Eckhart scholars, remains – as must all such attempts – largely conjectural. On a much more modest basis, however, we can consider how Eckhart's remarks and examples taken from the world of art illustrate his doctrine of the image and vice versa, for that is how he usually approached the subject.

As a mystic and theologian who favoured the negative or apophatic approach of the ancient Christian tradition, one might expect Eckhart to take a dim view of art. In fact, while he disparages mental images of God as inadequate and misleading, consistently advising his followers to strip away all sensible particulars so as to encounter God in the no-thingness of inner presence and the darkness of unknowing, nowhere does Eckhart reject art or speak disparagingly of artists. Rather, he often uses art and artistic processes as examples of theological and spiritual detachment and discovery. This is especially the case with his doctrine of the image.

In German Sermon 19, for instance, Eckhart craftily combines the two motifs:

> Our teachers ask, '*What* praises God?' Likeness does. Thus everything in the soul that is like God, praises God. Whatever is unlike God does not praise God; just as a picture praises the artist who has lavished on it all the art that he has in his heart, making it entirely like himself. The likeness of the picture praises the artist without words. That which one can praise with words is a paltry thing, and so is prayer with the lips.[19]

In his treatise *The Nobleman*, Eckhart anticipates Michelangelo in his comment on how the artist liberates the inner form by a process of stripping away, a direct analogy to the spiritual detachment necessary to reveal the true image of God within:

> if an artist wants to make an image from wood or stone, he does not put the image into the wood, but he cuts away the chips that had hidden and concealed the image: he gives nothing to the wood but takes from it, cutting away the overlay and removing the dross, and then that which was hidden under it shines forth. That is the treasure hidden in a field of which our Lord tells in the gospel (Matt. 13:44).[20]

In another sermon, Eckhart expounds on what might be called apophatic art appreciation, alluding to the process of 'stripping away' or *aphairesis*:

Now since something desirable appears in every creature, therefore people love now *this* and now *that*. Now put aside 'this' and 'that', and what remains is nothing but God. If a man paints a picture on the wall, the wall is the support of the picture; so, if anybody loves the picture on the wall, he loves the wall as well. If you took the wall away, the picture would be removed as well. But if you can remove the wall in such a way that the picture remains, then the picture is its own support. If anyone should then love the picture, he would love pure picture. So, you should love all that is lovable and not that *on which* it appears lovable, and then you will love nothing but God: that is an undoubted truth.[21]

Similarly, in Sermon 20a, Eckhart makes the artistic parallel explicit:

When the soul pronounces God, this utterance does not comprise the real truth about His essence: no one can truly say of God what He is. Sometimes we say one thing is like another. Now since all creatures contain next to nothing of God, they cannot declare Him. We can judge the skill of a painter who has made a perfect picture. And yet we cannot fully judge it from that. All creatures cannot fully express God, for they are not receptive to what He really is.[22]

The most perfect copy, likeness or image of a human subject, or any other for that matter, reveals but cannot exhaust the potential of the artist. But even a great artist must always deal with a limited aspect of a subject, so no creature, nor even the totality of creatures, can ever express what the infinite and incomprehensible God is truly *like*.

The duality of Eckhart's notion of Likeness is here the key to understanding the paradox. For in one respect, *nothing* is like God, and in another, *all* things are like God – they bespeak their Creator, but never fully, adequately or completely. In Sermon 50, Eckhart expounds the point from God's point of view, so to speak, drawing attention to the *Imago Dei*, the divine imprint in the soul which *is* the presence of God, a formal emanation in the language of the schools, rather than an effect:

There was a debate in the schools, and some masters maintained that God had imprinted His image in the soul as a picture is painted on a wall, which fades. This was refuted. Other masters said, with more truth, that God impressed His image as something permanent in the soul, like a lasting thought, such as: 'I have an intention today, and have the same thought tomorrow, and I shall keep this image alive by ever-present attention'. Therefore, they said, God's works are perfect. For if the carpenter were perfect at his work, he would not need any materials: for as soon as he thought it, the house would be ready. Thus it is with the works of God as soon as He has thought them, the works are perfected in the ever-present Now.[23]

In a difficult passage from Sermon 44, Eckhart extends his analogy further, explaining how the naked image, one not 'adorned' with accidentals of sensible colouration, expresses the nature of the one who made it.

Our best masters say, if an image in stone, or painted on a wall, had nothing added to it, then, taken as an image, that image would be one with him of whom it was an image. That is a fitting doctrine for when the soul enters the image, where there is nothing alien but just the image, with which it is one image.[24]

His point is theological, however, and he quickly passes on to consider how discovering and affirming the true image of the self simultaneously reveals God's presence:

If a man is placed in that image where he is like God, then he receives God, then he finds God. Where there is a splitting up, God cannot be found. When the soul enters her image and finds herself in the image alone, in that image she finds God; and the finding of herself and God is one and the same act, and is timeless – there she finds God. So far as she is therein, so far is she one with God. He means, as far as one is included there where the soul is God's image. As far as he is in there, so far is he divine – so far therein, so far in God, not included, not united, but *one*.[25]

Finally, at least so far as this brief excursion is concerned, in Sermon 77 Eckhart passes beyond the ordinary sense of 'likeness', meaning similarity, and argues that the human person is 'like God' in the opposite sense conveyed by the German *glîch* – the sameness of radical identity:

Let us now speak further of the angels, of whom I just said that they were an image of God, and that they are a mirror containing in itself the reflection of the goodness and purity of the stillness and mystery of

God, as far as that is possible. We should be like the angels, and so we would be an image of God, for God made us in His own image.

At this point, Eckhart shifts the analogy from the angels to art:

An artist who wants to make an image of a man does not copy Conrad or Henry. For if he made an image like Conrad or Henry, he would not be portraying man, he would be portraying Conrad or Henry. But if he made a picture of Conrad it would not be like Henry for, if he had the skill and ability, he would portray Conrad perfectly himself, exactly as he was. Now God has perfect skill and ability, and therefore He has made you just like Him, an image of Himself. But 'like Him' denotes something foreign and aloof. But between man and God there is nothing foreign and aloof, and therefore man is not 'like him' but he is altogether identical with Him and the very same as He is.[26]

In sum, there are at least four meanings or levels of meaning in Eckhart's teaching about the image:

- the physical – the appearance or 'look' of something, including artistic representations;
- the psychological – our perception of physical objects;
- the epistemological – our generation of concepts, the world of abstract ideas;
- and the onto-theological – the generation of the Word and the creation of the human soul as expressions of the divine nature.

To understand Eckhart at any point it is necessary to recognize which of these related but differing notions he is employing.

Spiritual Implications

In Eckhart's important Sermon 16b, toward the end the preacher appropriately turns from a theory-laden consideration of images to the spiritual consequences of understanding this doctrine for his audience. Here, too, I wish to consider very briefly the spiritual implications of Eckhart's teaching for us today. I must limit my remarks to only one aspect of his teaching, however, one that is often overlooked or at least underplayed by commentators – the dynamic or dialectical character of the process by which we are transformed into the imageless image of God.

As might be expected, there is nothing static about Eckhart's spirituality of the image or, rather, in this regard, transformation of the image. Although noted, but not especially stressed, by Bernard McGinn and other recent commentators, Eckhart draws frequently on the Pauline and early Christian notion of transformation into Christ, in which the human *Imago Dei* is reformed or transformed by grace into the image of Christ and thus becomes one with the imageless image of God. Since, Eckhart says, as we have already had occasion to note,

> . . . the eternal Word took on human nature imagelessly, therefore the Father's image, which is the eternal Son, became the image of human nature. So it is just as true to say that man became God as that God became man.' He adds, however, 'Thus human nature was transformed [*überbildet*] by becoming the divine image, which is the image of the Father.[27]

Incorporation into God through Christ is a major thematic in all of Eckhart's writings. In Sermon 6, he freely (and, as it turned out fatally) translates 2 Corinthians 3:18 – 'We are wholly transformed into God and changed.'[28] Here is an illustration. It is just the same as when in the sacrament bread is changed into Our Lord's body . . . I am converted into Him in such a way that He makes me *one* with His being, not *similar*. By the living God it is true that there is no distinction.'[29] To his judges, Eckhart's vision of transubstantiation smacked of heresy, if for him it was only an illustrative comparison. In that respect, we come back to Eckhart's notion of the imageless image.

Eckhart's Imageless Image

Eckhart delighted in paradoxical wordplay, coining oxymora to identify the themes particularly susceptible to his apophatic deconstruction, peppering his sermons with phrases such as unlearned learning, wayless way, beingless being, groundless ground, and in this respect, the 'imageless image' [*bildlös bild*], by which he referred in Sermon 50, for example, to the soul's original and final status in God. The following, somewhat dense, passage may serve as a summary of his whole spiritual dynamic:

I have often said that through this act in God, the birth wherein the Father bears His only-begotten Son, through this outflowing there proceeds the Holy Ghost, that the Spirit proceeds from both, and in this procession the soul is outpoured, and that the image of the Godhead is imprinted on the soul; and in the outflowing and return of the three Persons the soul is poured back, being reformed into her primal and imageless image.[30]

Imagelessness is not some peculiar property of the original image, however. It pertains to the nature of the image itself, as Eckhart explains more fully in Sermon 69, relying on physical analogies of vision as understood in the Middle Ages:

If I put my hand over my eye, I cannot see the hand. If I hold it out before me, I see it at once. This is due to the dense nature of the hand; accordingly it must be clarified and rendered subtle in the air and light, and conveyed to my eye as an image. You can observe this with a mirror: if you hold it before you, your image appears in the mirror. The eye and the soul are such a mirror, in that whatever is held before them appears therein. Hence I do not see my hand, or a stone, but rather I see an image of the stone. But I do not see that image in another image or in a medium. Rather, I see it without means and without image, for the image is the means and not another means. That is because an image is without image as motion is without motion, though the cause of motion, and magnitude is without size, though the cause of size. Thus too an image is imageless, in that it is not seen in another image.[31]

It is therefore because the Word is the perfect image of God that by being transformed (re-imaged) in the likeness of Christ we are ultimately transformed into the very Godhead. Eckhart continues,

The eternal Word is the medium and the image itself (which is without means or image), so that the soul may grasp God in the eternal Word, and know Him immediately and without any image.[32]

In Sermons 16a and 16b, as Loris Sturlese and Bruce Milem have shown, but in other places as well, Eckhart locates the ground for the *Imago Dei* in the onto-theological relation of creature to Creator, that of absolute dependency. We are what we are because we have been creatively thought by God, the Eternal Artist.[33] The human person is the realization in time, matter and place of the divine idea existing in eternity, purity and unity in the mind of God. By acknowledging, even embracing, that total dependency, we discover ourselves as the creative expression of God's own nature, for what is in God, *is* God. And with that, we begin the return journey to our final home in God, beyond time, place and particularity.

Conclusion: The Transforming Vision

Mary Catherine Hilkert observes in her Santa Clara lecture that the heritage of the *Imago Dei* doctrine strikes many people today as so problematic that many believe it should be abandoned altogether.

> The history of the transmission of that doctrine with its claims that women are not in the image of God, less equally in the image of God, most fully in the image of God when in union with a man, or in the image of God in her spiritual soul but not her carnal body, is by now not only well-documented, but officially disavowed as official teaching.[34]

Eckhart, unfortunately, is not without flaw in this regard, often subordinating the figure of woman to that of man precisely in regard to the faculties of the soul which most truly image the spiritual nature of God.[35] But just as Hilkert demonstrates that the exploitation of nature and the subjugation of women are not intrinsic to the doctrine of *Imago Dei*, I believe that Eckhart's most valuable insights can be disengaged from the standard sexist analogies of the Middle Ages without harm to his intention. Such detachment will, rather, serve to liberate his deeper teaching from the restrictions of its cultural expression.

It is in his discussion of the onto-theological dimension of the *Imago Dei*, rather than the Augustinian Trinitarian model, that Eckhart has most to offer us today, and here especially in terms of his dynamic model of transformation into the image of Christ and thence into God. But Eckhart's stringent qualifications in regard to mental images or concepts of God, his apophatic spirituality, also frees us from much of the doctrinal baggage of the past that on a personal level prevents spiritual growth in very significant respects. 'I pray God to rid me of God', was Eckhart's outrageous prayer.[36]

One thing seems clear enough from a consideration not only of Eckhart's works but also of the scholarly investigations of his doctrine of the image: Eckhart's teaching is neither incoherent nor contradictory. But it is also complex and nuanced. I don't think it is yet possible, whether it ever will be or not, to say with confidence that anyone has definitively captured all the richness of his teaching. I doubt if Eckhart himself would have been able to give a perfectly clear exposition of the doctrine.

Toward the conclusion of her lecture, Mary Catherine Hilkert asks, 'Does the symbol *Imago Dei* have a future in a world of violence, exclusion and ecological devastation? In the end, it appears that the answer is up to us.'[37]

Surely this is true. Eckhart drew on the great apophatic spiritual and theological tradition of the Hebrew and Christian faith as well as the psychological and philosophical insights of Plato and Aristotle, and even his own experience of art and artists, to create – if all too implicitly in many respects – a rich and liberating notion of the human person as created in the image and according to the likeness of God. For Eckhart, this image, divine in its origin, distorted in its fall into a material form disfigured by sin, has nevertheless been assumed and transformed by God's grace – the birth of the Word of God in the depths of our being, and our rebirth into the hidden desert of the Godhead – the wayless, imageless, incomprehensible Ground of Being where all is divinely one and yet each thing remains what it is.[38]

And for us now, as Hilkert says, 'The image of God continues to take flesh where Wisdom's children delight in creation and learn to live within limits that respect the common good of the whole community of the living.'[39] To this proposition, I believe that Eckhart, for whom all creation was a book about God, and for all human beings are one Son of God, transfigured, transformed or 'trans-imaged' in Christ, the true and only Image of God, could only respond with a great 'Amen.'

Notes

1. An earlier form of this chapter was given as a paper at the Eckhart Society Conference, 23–26 August 2002, Plater College, Oxford, and subsequently published in the *Eckhart Review* 12 (2003): 5–20.
2. Walshe No. 63, Vol. II, pp. 118–19.
3. Mary Catherine Hilkert, O.P., '*Imago Dei: Does the Symbol Have a Future?*', The Santa Clara Lectures, Santa Clara University, 8:3 (14 April 2002).
4. For a succinct account of medieval doctrine of humanity as *Imago Dei*, see Bernard McGinn, 'The Human Person as Image of God', in *Christian Spirituality, I: Origins to the Fifth Century*, Jean Leclercq, Bernard McGinn, John Meyendorff, eds (New York: Crossroad, 1985), pp. 312–30.

5. Among resources accessible from the *Eckhart Review* are Loris Sturlese's important article 'Mysticism and Theology in Meister Eckhart's Theory of the Image', Mark Atherton, trans., *Eckhart Review* 2 (1993); Emilie Zum Brunn's 'The Experience of God as Expressed in Eckhart's German Works', *Eckhart Review* (Spring 1994): 56–71; and Bruce Milem's prize-winning essay of 1998, 'Meister Eckhart and the Image: Sermon 16b', *Eckhart Review* 8 (Spring 1999): 47–59. See also Bernard McGinn, *The Mystical Thought of Meister Eckhart*, op. cit., pp. 106–13 and Bruce Milem, *The Unspoken Word, Negative Theology in the German Sermons of Meister Eckhart* (Washington: Catholic University of America Press), 2002.

6. Sermon 40 (Walshe No. 63,Vol. I, p. 119). For the significance of *entbilden* in Eckhart's thought, see Wolfgang Wackernagel, *Ymagine denudari: Ethique de l'Image et Métaphysique de l'abstraction*, (Paris: Vrin, 1991).

7. Sermon 46 (Walshe No. 47, Vol. II, pp. 27–8).

8. Die niht glîch sint, die sint aleine gote glîch. Götlich wesen enist niht glîch, in im enist noch bilde noch forme. Sermon 6 (Walshe No. 65, Vol. II, p. 134, DP 7).

9. Sermon 101 (Walshe No. 1, p. 8, DP 57).

10. In Gen. n. 115ff., LW I/1, pp. 270ff.; In Sap. n.143, LW II, pp. 480ff.; In Ioh. n. 23–6, LW III, pp. 19–21; Serm. XLIX 1–3 n. 505–12, LW IV, pp. 421–8. The relevant passages are Gen. 1:26, Wisdom 7:26, Col. 1:15. and Matt. 22:30. See Loris Sturlese, art. cit., p. 26.

11. See Sturlese (1993), p. 18: 'The collected sermons of Eckhart may be regarded as an attempt to convey in German to a German audience a sophisticated philosophy which had as its goal a redefinition of the relationship between God and humanity. The cornerstones of this project were Scripture, with its concept of *imago*, and classical philosophy, with its concept of intellect.'

12. See Ex. 20:4 and Lev. 26:1. In Deut. 4:16 and many other passages, the term employed for 'image' is often *maccekah* ('a molten thing', an idol) rather than *tselem*. But see Daniel 3:7, Nahum 1:14, etc. Habukkuk 2:14 employs both terms.

13. See Matt. 22:20, Mark 12:16, Luke 20:24, Acts 14:11, Rom. 8:3, 2 Cor. 3:18, Heb. 7:15, James 3:9, etc.

14. *On Memory and Recollection*, 450a.

15. Sermon 16b (W 14b, p. 126–277).

16. See C. F. Kelley, *Meister Eckhart on Divine Knowledge* (New Haven, CT: Yale University Press, 1977). Reprinted with a foreword by William Stranger (New York: DharmaCafé Books, Random House, 2009).

17. Sermon 40 (Walshe No. 63, Vol. II, pp. 117–18). See also Sermon 11 (Walshe No. 68, Vol. II, p. 160, DP 12) and Sermon 37 (Walshe No. 31, Vol. I, p. 231).

18. Ananda K. Coomaraswamy, *The Transformation of Nature in Art* (Cambridge: Harvard University Press, 1934, New York: Dover Publications, 1969 reprint); and Brian Keeble, 'Meister Eckhart's View of Art, Eckhart Society *Newsletter*, 3 (Summer, 1989): 2–5. I must here express my gratitude to Ashley Young for bringing both Brian Keeble's article on Coomaraswamy and the chapter on Eckhart in Coomaraswamy's study to my attention.

19. Sermon 19 (Walshe No. 35, Vol. I, p. 259).

20. *Von Edeln Menschen*, Walshe trans., III, p. 109.

21. Sermon 63 (Walshe No. 77, Vol. II, pp. 220–1, also Jundt 7).

22. Sermon 20a (Walshe No. 32a, Vol. I, pp. 235–6).

23. Sermon 50 (Walshe No. 93, Vol. II, p. 319).

24. Sermon 44 (Walshe No. 20, Vol. I, p. 164).

25. Ibid.

26. Sermon 77 (Walshe No. 49, Vol. II, pp. 39–40).

27. Sermon 46 (Walshe No. 47, Vol. II, pp. 27–8).

28. 'Wir werden alzemâle transformieret in got und verwandelt.' The passage in fact reads, 'And we all, with unveiled faces, beholding the glory of the Lord, are being changed [*metamorphoumetha*] into His likeness from one degree of glory into another; for this comes from the Lord who is the Spirit.'

29. Sermon 6 (Walshe No. 65, Vol. II, pp. 135–6, DP 7). This phrase was condemned in Avignon as Prop. 12.

30. Sermon 50 (Walshe No. 93, p. 318). Cf. Sermon 11 (Walshe No. 68, pp. 158–9, DP 12), and Sermon 22 (Walshe No. 53, Vol. II, p. 63, DP 23), among others.

31. Sermon 69 (Walshe No. 42, Vol. I, p. 295, DP 53).

32. Ibid., pp. 295–6.

33. See in this respect Josef Pieper, *The Silence of St Thomas*, trans. by John Murray, S.J. and Daniel O'Connor (South Bend, IN: St Augustine's Press, 1999 ed.), p. 57.

34. Hilkert, loc. cit, p. 4.

35. See Grace M. Jantzen, 'Eckhart and Women', *Eckhart Review*, 3 (Spring 1994 and above, pp. 12 and 23).

36. Sermon 52 (Walshe No. 87, Vol. II, p. 274).

37. Hilkert, loc. cit., p. 18.

38. For a fuller elaboration of this theme, see Chapter 3 above.

39. Ibid., pp. 18–19.

Chapter 11

Eckhart, Suffering and Healing[1]

When I met Ursula Fleming, the founder of the Eckhart Society, she was conducting courses in pain management in England. I came to know her much better in regard to the Society, to which she attracted me early in its history. Her two great passions were, of course, related. As she wrote in her little book *Meister Eckhart: The Man from Whom God Hid Nothing*, 'Most of what I know and teach about pain control comes from the study of Eckhart.'[2]

Our understanding of and attitude towards pain and suffering differ greatly from those in the Middle Ages, and there is reason to believe that even our experience differs considerably. Nevertheless, the apparent time-lessness of Eckhart's sermons and treatises has contributed to the applica-tion of his teaching today, and probably will in the future as well, not only in the West, but also in Asia. Nevertheless, some acquaintance with the context of Eckhart's teaching will help in understanding him, first by alerting us to the issues and preoccupations of those to whom his message was addressed and, second, by limiting the extent to which we read back into Eckhart and his times our own issues and preoccupations, many if not most of which would have seemed very odd to the late thirteenth-century Dominican.

Modern and Medieval Approaches to Pain and Suffering

First of all, it is important to bear in mind that how we regard pain and suffering today in Europe, North America and the rest of the so-called 'First World' differs significantly not only from many other places on the planet, but from medieval perceptions, and even those of our grand-parents. As Ivan Illich wrote many years ago in his breakthrough book, *Medical Nemesis*, 'Pain has changed its position in relation to grief, guilt, sin, anguish, fear, hunger, impairment and discomfort. What we call pain in a surgical or cancer ward is something for which former generations had no special name.'[3]

In his book *Spontaneous Healing*, Dr Andrew Weil remarks that 'Pain has two aspects: the physical sensation arising from some disturbance of body structure or function and the psychic perception of it.'[4] In more traditional terms, this points to the difference between pain and suffering, pain being primarily some form of often acute physical discomfort, the capacity for which people share with animals and, according to several researchers, even some forms of plant life. Suffering, however, entails not only an awareness of pain, but its meaning or lack of meaning in the scheme of life as a whole. It may well be that higher forms of animal life suffer in addition to experiencing pain, but as generally understood, suffering is both distinctively human and also largely a psychological and spiritual event.

It would not be an exaggeration to say that on a worldwide basis today, the human race is facing a situation of drastic dimensions, one involving pain and suffering on an unprecedented level. In the Western world, pain management has focused largely on the development and use of agents of analgesia and anaesthesia, mainly drugs. As Illich and others have observed, alcohol and opium have been used in this fashion for over a thousand years. But alleviation is not enough, even or perhaps *especially* in the face of modern anaesthetics and analgesics. It is here, I believe, that Eckhart can still make a difference. So let us turn back the clock to the early fourteenth century, first of all to situate Eckhart's teaching in the world he lived in and addressed.

The Medieval Situation

To some degree, all religions confront the inevitability of suffering and offer ways by which suffering can be overcome. In the Middle Ages, Meister Eckhart often turned his formidable powers of discernment to suffering, at one point devoting an entire work to it, the *Book of Divine Comfort*. In that and in many of his sermons and other treatises, he continued the classical tradition represented by Boethius's *Consolation of Philosophy* and other writings of antiquity. Eckhart's approach was exceptional, as might be expected.

First of all, it is important to bear in mind that Eckhart lived and died in a world very different even from the later fourteenth century, when the most severe epidemic in Western history ravaged Europe in successive waves, killing at least one-third of the population by the end of that century alone. His teaching is understandably more optimistic than that found in later literature, but he was no stranger to a world of illness, war, injury, hunger and oppression.

Generally speaking, three areas regarding pain and suffering were of focal concern in the High Middle Ages, including Eckhart's period:[5]

- the alleviation of pain and suffering caused by disease, injury and poverty;
- the infliction of pain to guarantee truthful testimony, i.e., the use of torture; and
- the voluntary acceptance or even production of pain as religious activity.

Religiously sanctioned pain, especially self-inflicted or at least accepted pain, included four major types:

- penitential: private and public expiation of one's sins, e.g., flagellants;
- devotional: identification with the suffering Christ;
- sacrificial: vicarious atonement, e.g., freeing souls from purgatory; and
- tactical: as an aid to prayer, e.g. desert stylites, Celtic monks, ecstatics and mystics of various periods and traditions.

The role of tactical pain in religious culture is not only greatly misunderstood, but largely ignored despite its psychological and spiritual importance for understanding religious experience. My concern here, however, is especially the penitential, devotional and sacrificial interpretations of suffering, all of which were paramount in the spirituality of an important constituency of Eckhart's preaching, the beguines and Dominican nuns of the late thirteenth and early fourteenth centuries. Their experience of pain and their attitude towards suffering had much to do with the evolution of Eckhart's doctrine.[6]

Women's Bodies and the Spirituality of Suffering

That Eckhart's preaching, especially in the latter part of his career, was intended mainly for religious women, communities of beguines and Dominican nuns, is not in dispute. In 1314 the Master of the Dominican Order had in fact placed him in charge of the spiritual direction of these groups of well-read, ardent and, in many cases, strong-willed women. For the next ten years, he made the city of Strassburg his headquarters, exercising an enormous influence on the great circle of monasteries and beguine houses in the southern Rhineland. There were over a dozen monasteries in that area and over 70 beguine communities in the city of Strassburg alone. Many of the nuns had themselves been beguines, being drawn to the Order by the irresistible confluence of mysticism and scholarship that characterized the Dominicans at this time. And not least among their concerns was bodily, mental and spiritual suffering.

The shift towards voluntary suffering on the part of women religious in the Middle Ages was an element in a complex reconfiguration of power relationships that affected medieval culture as a whole. As Jo Ann McNamara has shown, increasing restrictions on religious women in the high Middle Ages with regard to begging and the distribution of alms led to a spiritualization of both perceived need and voluntary deprivation, resulting in the development of an ethos of redemptive suffering, particularly as expressed in bodily mortification.[7] This was especially characteristic of, but not restricted to, houses of beguines and, later, convents of Dominican nuns. It was in this context that Eckhart, Henry Suso and John Tauler developed their approach to the problem of pain and suffering.[8] And that approach, particularly in the case of Eckhart, ran counter to the enthusiasm for self-inflicted penitential suffering in particular.

In short, Eckhart's teaching occupies a precarious position between the self-imposed suffering of women religious by which they achieved a sense of spiritual empowerment increasingly denied them in the later Middle Ages, and a spirituality of radical spiritual poverty that seemingly divests the soul of its autonomy. His solution to the pastoral dilemma was hardly less daring than the theological development it required, one which eventually gained Eckhart the unwelcome attention of the Inquisition of the Archbishop of Cologne.

The Problem of Pain

For Eckhart, the principal source of suffering lies in turning away from God to find comfort from creatures. His remedy for suffering is, therefore, to turn back to God in complete detachment from creatures. If this were all there was to it, his teaching would differ little from that of many other medieval spiritual writers. However, Eckhart approaches the problem of pain in a characteristically different manner. In effect, he teaches that the way of turning to God to find solace or, in modern terms, healing, is to accept rather than fear or flee from suffering. But unlike many of his contemporaries, most particularly the beguines and Dominican nuns of the period, Eckhart never counsels his disciples to *seek* suffering. The difference hangs on his understanding of the relation between God and suffering.

His doctrine can be perhaps too neatly summarized in three propositions that constitute a paradoxical dialectic:

- First, in God there is no suffering, only eternal and absolute joy.
- Second, nevertheless God suffers by sharing in our suffering.
- Third, therefore, to suffer rightly is to experience God, or in Eckhart's pithy phrase, God *is* our suffering.

Theologically, the first proposition is unobjectionable. Within the pure actuality of the Godhead, as in the Persons of the Trinity, there is only joy and love, beyond any shadow of alteration: 'in God,' Eckhart writes in *The Book of Divine Comfort*, 'there is no sorrow or suffering or distress. If you would be free from all adversity and pain, turn and cleave entirely to God.'[9]

The second proposition requires considerable explanation. The third, even more so. For as a preacher and spiritual director, Eckhart's primary interest lay in drawing out the implications of the startling conclusion of his dialectic. As a result, the distinctions that differentiate and unite joy and suffering in God (and us) remain somewhat undeveloped in his preaching and, it would not be unkind to say, sometimes opaque.

In order to cast light on the problem of God's suffering, it is essential, of course, to consult Eckhart's most mature work on the problem of pain, *The Book of Divine Comfort*, written by his own hand rather than transcribed, in which he most directly addresses the question of loss, pain, and especially emotional and spiritual suffering. Although it is the more focused of his teachings on suffering, it will nevertheless be helpful first to consider some of Eckhart's earlier and middle teachings. In all of them, it is important to bear in mind that for Eckhart pain and suffering were first of all facts of common experience to be accepted and overcome, not by grim endurance, but by transformation.

Early Teaching: The Talks of Instruction

When Eckhart was still a relatively young man in the declining years of the thirteenth century, he was responsible for the spiritual formation of the newest members of his community, most of whom would still have been teenagers. Despite the early date of this work, his *Talks of Instruction* contains the seeds of Eckhart's mature teaching on pain and suffering. When he takes up the matter of suffering in connection with the effects of sin, he does so in a very unconventional way:

> However great the suffering may be, if it comes through God, then God suffers first from it. Indeed, by the truth that *is* God, there never was so tiny a pang of sorrow that befell a man, not the least little discomfort or inconvenience, but if he placed it in God, then it would pain God incomparably more than that man, and incommode God more than the man himself.[10]

Clearly, for Eckhart, God is neither remote nor impassable, viewing human suffering with detachment if not actively inflicting it by way of punishment or warning. He goes on to explain that because God suffers with us, our suffering thus provides access to God not as we would have God, but as God would have us. Moreover, by welcoming suffering as a form of God's presence, we transcend all pain and bitterness. Eckhart says,

> But if God endures this [suffering] for the sake of such benefit as He intends for you thereby, and if *you* will endure that which God endures and which comes to you *through* Him, then it inevitably becomes godlike, so that shame is like honour, bitterness like sweetness and the blackest darkness like the brightest light. It takes all its savour from God and becomes godlike: for whatever comes to such a man conforms to God, because he seeks nothing else and has no taste for anything else. Accordingly, he gets hold of God in all bitterness just as in the greatest sweetness.[11]

His teaching here is a consistent application of his great maxim, 'Those who seek God rightly find God in all things equally and all things equally in God.'[12] Not surprisingly, Eckhart did not advise his novices to seek out pain and suffering as a special means of growing closer to God.[13] His resistance to, perhaps even rejection of, exterior penance as unhelpful in leading towards union with God is outlined clearly in the *Talks of Instruction*. But seeking and especially finding God may nevertheless lead someone to penance:

Many people think they are performing great works by outward things such as fasting, going barefoot, or other such things which are called penance. But the true and best penance is that whereby one improves greatly and in the highest degree; and that is that a man should experience a complete and perfect turning away from whatever is not entirely God and divine in himself and in all creatures, and have a full, perfect and complete turning towards his beloved God in unshakeable love, so that his devotion and yearning for Him are great. In whatever you do, the more of this is present, the more righteous you are; and the more this is the case, in the same measure will there be more penance, and it will wash away more sin and all pain. [. . .] This is true penance, and it comes especially and most perfectly through true suffering in the perfect penance of our Lord Jesus Christ.[14]

Eckhart's intent in all his teaching was not merely to reverse the polarities of power with regard to the economy of suffering and merit, but to subvert them. For him, suffering was never to be linked with barter, and he was clearly uncomfortable with the notion of vicarious atonement. As a consequence, his understanding of the imitation of Christ is nuanced quite differently even from that of a disciple such as Henry Suso, and strikingly different from that of the beguines. He says,

People may well be daunted and afraid because the life of our Lord Jesus Christ and the saints was so severe and painful, and a man cannot endure much of this or does not feel compelled to it. And so, when people feel themselves unequal to this, they often think they are far from God, as One whom they are unable to follow. No one should think this. [. . .] Even suppose, though, that your great shortcomings have carried you so far away that you cannot conceive yourself near to God, you should still regard God as near to you.[15]

Eckhart, moreover, cautions his young disciples not to undertake penances of their own devising, but to be prepared to accept the difficulties that come in the course of life – a maxim that will reappear 200 years later in the writings of St John of the Cross:

Let nothing touch your mind with power and love but God alone – it should be exalted above all else. Why? Because that would be a feeble kind of inwardness that the outward dress could correct. Rather should the inward correct the outer, if it rests entirely with you. But if it just comes to you, you can from your ground accept it as good, just as you would put up with it if it were different, and would be glad and willing to endure it. The same applies to food, friends and relations and with whatever else God gives you or takes from you.[16]

Eckhart next turns to what would become perhaps the greatest of all his themes, that of radical detachment, here expressed as letting go of our own will towards perfection and allowing God to get on with the universe.

> . . . I consider better than anything that a man should fully abandon himself to God when He would cast anything upon him, be it disgrace, trouble or whatever kind of suffering it might be, accepting it with joy and gratitude, allowing oneself rather to be led by God than plunging into it oneself. So just learn all things gladly from God and follow Him, and all will go well with you.[17]

Although Eckhart never embraces the spirituality of Christocentric suffering that would characterize his disciple Henry Suso and many other medieval mystics, he advises his young friars to imitate Christ in their suffering, not by identifying with them but by giving their pain to the body (as Ursula learned so well), and keeping the mind clear and aware of the presence of God.

> [Christ's] higher powers had possession and enjoyment of eternal bliss. But His lower powers were at the same time involved in the greatest suffering and struggle in the world, yet none of these works hindered the others in their sphere. That is how it should be in you, that the highest powers should be lifted entirely into God, and entirely surrendered and added to Him. Moreover, we should assign all suffering to the body, to the lower powers and the senses, but the spirit should raise itself up with all its strength and plunge unfettered into God.[18]

What Eckhart means by 'giving the pain to the body' is not altogether evident, but his counsel resonates with Zen Buddhist teaching, and found application in Ursula Fleming's work with cancer patients. If I understand Eckhart rightly, he is advocating a form of mental distancing – a refusal to allow pain to dominate consciousness but to isolate it, accept it and thus reduce its impact and monopolization of attention. In a passage that will find later echoes in *The Book of Divine Comfort*, Eckhart promises that, by learning to endure suffering rather than seeking it, we will find God in the suffering.

> You may say, 'I fear I am not earnest enough and don't try as hard as I could.' You should regret this and endure it with patience; regard it as discipline and be at peace. God gladly endures shame and misfortune and willingly forgoes His praise and service that those who love Him and belong to Him may be at peace. [. . .] In fact, however wrong we may be, if we duly accept from God whatever He does or does not do to us, and suffer for righteousness' sake, we are blessed. Therefore do not lament for anything, but bewail only the fact that you still do lament and are not satisfied.[19]

All this is for beginners in the spiritual life. I sometimes wonder how effective Eckhart was in getting his teaching across to those youngsters. Given the fact that some of the young men he taught, at least later in his career, were Henry Suso and John Tauler, some of them apparently were paying attention.

Middle Works: The German Sermons

Eckhart's later teaching is less exhaustive and, you may think, exhausting. But it is no less profound. With the exception of his Latin scriptural commentaries, the largest body of Eckhart's works is constituted by his German sermons. And these contain many references to pain and suffering, most of them dovetailing with or reiterating his doctrine in the treatises and *The Book of Divine Comfort*. The main difficulty with the sermons, since we do not know the order in which they were preached, is that at one point or another, Eckhart may mention one facet of his paradoxical teaching on pain and suffering, seemingly contradicting himself. Elsewhere, however, we find the corrective. Placed in the context of his earlier teaching and his mature doctrine, his views manifest a remarkable coherence.

In his sermons, Eckhart especially stresses what I have called the first of his dialectical propositions. As in *The Talks of Instruction* and, later, *The Book of Divine Comfort*, Eckhart affirms that God suffers in our suffering, in the sermons he insists that in God there can be neither real suffering nor tribulation, so that even in his agony, Jesus was able as the Son of God to transcend the suffering that as a human being transfixed him bodily. In this, Jesus is our model and exemplar rather than our substitute. In German Sermon 49, Eckhart says, for instance,

> I shall call [Christ's] noble soul for this time a grain of wheat which perished in the earth of his noble humanity in suffering and action, in grief and in death, as he said himself before he was to suffer, in these words 'My soul is grieved unto death' (Matt. 26:38). He did not then mean his noble soul according as this is intellectually contemplating the highest good, with which he is united in person and which he is according to union and person: that, even in his greatest suffering, he was continually regarding in his highest power, just as closely and entirely the same as he does now: no sorrow or pain or death could penetrate *there*. So it is in truth, for when his body died in agony on the cross, his noble spirit lived in this presence.[20]

To the extent that we have broken through into God, which for Eckhart means by transformation in and through Christ the Word, we are no less beyond the reach of all suffering and pain, as he says in Sermon 76:

> If I am fully transported into the divine essence, then God, and all that He has, is mine. [. . .] That is when I have true joy, when neither pain nor sorrow can take it from me, for *then* I am installed in the divine essence, where sorrow has no place. For we see that in God there is no anger or sadness, but only love and joy. [. . .] And so, when you have reached the point where nothing is grievous or hard to you, and where pain is not pain to you, when everything is perfect joy to you, *there* your child has really been born.[21]

Here he is referring to the birth of the divine Child, the Word of God, within us, the sign of our breakthrough into the heart of God. The Christian life, the wayless spiritual way that Eckhart preached, consists in our progression towards that unimaginable union with God and, in that, the transformation and transcendence of all pain and suffering. The ground of our ascent to that desert of the Godhead is the seed of God within us, the spark of the soul that features so prominently in Eckhart's spirituality and that of his followers:

There is another power, immaterial too, flowing from the spirit, remaining in the spirit, altogether spiritual. In this power God is fiery, aglow with all His riches, with all His sweetness and all His bliss. Truly, in this power there is such great joy, such vast unmeasured bliss that none can tell of it or reveal it fully. Yet I declare that if ever there were a single man who in intellectual vision and in truth should glimpse for a moment the bliss and the joy therein, then all his sufferings and all God intended that he should suffer would be a trifle, a mere nothing to him – in fact I declare it would be pure joy and comfort to him.[22]

At this point, Eckhart returns to the theme of God's suffering in us and for us, setting out the criterion by which we measure our conformity to God:

If you would know for certain whether your suffering is your own or God's then you can know by this: If you suffer for yourself, in whatever way, that suffering hurts and is hard to bear. But if you suffer for God and God alone, your suffering does not hurt and is not hard to bear, for God bears the load. In very truth, if there were a man willing to suffer purely for God's sake and for God alone, then although he were suddenly called upon to bear all the suffering that all men have ever endured, the collective sufferings of all the world, it would not hurt him or bear him down, for God would bear the burden. [...] In brief, whatever a man suffers for God and God alone, He makes light and pleasant.[23]

Far from advocating some kind of Stoic indifference or impassability, Eckhart maintains that pain, like pleasure, always remains part of the human condition. It is to be neither pursued nor avoided for its own sake, but accepted where necessary as an inevitable condition of life. The *only* important thing is conformity to God's will. In Sermon 25 Eckhart says,

If our will is God's will, that is good, but if God's will is our will, that is far better. If your will is God's will, then if you are sick you will not desire, against God's will, to be better – though you *would* wish it were God's will that you were better. And when things went wrong with you, you would wish it were God's will that they should go aright. But when God's will *is your will,* then if you are sick: 'In God's name!', if your friend dies: 'In God's name!' It is a certain and necessary truth that though it should entail all the pains of hell, of purgatory, and the world, the will in union with God would bear all this eternally, for ever in hellish torment, and take it for its eternal bliss; and resigning in God's will our Lady's bliss and all her perfection and that of all the saints, it would remain forever in eternal pain and bitterness, not wavering for an instant and with no thought of wishing things were otherwise.[24]

In Sermon 4, he explains less hyperbolically that:

You have neither sickness nor anything else unless God wills it. And so, knowing it is God's will, you should so rejoice in it and be content that pain would be no pain to you: even in the extremity of pain, to feel any pain or affliction would be altogether wrong, for you should accept it from God as the best of all, for it is bound to be best for you. For God's being depends on His willing the best. Let me then will it too, and nothing should please me better.[25]

Thus,

A man who is established thus in God's will wants nothing but what is God's will and what is God. If he were sick he would not want to be well. To him all pain is pleasure, all multiplicity is bare simplicity, if he is truly established in the will of God. Even though it meant the pains of hell it would be joy and happiness to him. He is free and has left self behind, and must be free of whatever is to come in to him . . .[26]

If Eckhart's teaching on transcending pain and suffering, and especially the voluntary acceptance of sickness and sorrow, remains undeveloped in individual sermons, taken as a whole, inasmuch as that is possible, it shows a remarkable consistency. But it is in Eckhart's most mature works that he most successfully, if never completely, brings these themes together in final form.

'On Detachment'

Although it is now questioned as a work of Eckhart's own hand rather than a product by a disciple, one of the most positive statements about suffering comes from the long sermon 'On Detachment', *Von Abgeschei- denheit*.[27] It begins in what might be called Eckhart's usual manner. He says,

. . . I extol detachment above love because love compels me to suffer all things for God's sake, whereas detachment makes me receptive of nothing but God. Now it is far nobler to be receptive of nothing but God than to suffer all things *for* God, for in suffering a man has some regard to the creatures from which he gets the suffering, but detachment is quite free of all creatures.[28]

But as he nears his conclusion, he subtly reverses his priorities, and extols the value of suffering as the product of detachment:

Now take note, all who have good sense! The swiftest steed to bear you to His perfection is suffering, for none will enjoy greater eternal bliss than those who stand with Christ in the greatest bitterness. Nothing is more gall-bitter than suffering, nothing more honey-sweet than having suffered. Nothing disfigures the body before men like suffering, and nothing beautifies the soul before God like having suffered.[29]

Eckhart will later shift his emphasis on present as opposed to past suffering, as he will have his followers dwell neither on the past nor the future, especially in anticipation of suffering, but only in the present moment, in which suffering mediates the very presence of God.

The Book of Divine Comfort

The Book of Divine Comfort is the only work by Eckhart which directly addresses pain and suffering, particularly grief. It is generally thought to have been composed in 1308 for Agnes, the Queen of Hungary. Already widowed by the death of her husband, Andrew III, in 1301, she was now mourning the death of her father, King Albert of Hapsburg, who was assassinated by his nephew that year. At the time, Eckhart was in Bohemia as Vicar-General of the Master of the Dominican Order, Aymeric of Piacenza.[30]

By twentieth-century standards, a grieving adult daughter reading a work like *The Book of Divine Comfort* might be tempted to sue the author for emotional abuse, so challenging is it as a work of spiritual theology, much less consolation. But the treatise is far from an offer of cold comfort. Agnes was not only very intelligent, but spiritually mature and evidently well versed in theology. And the little book has come down to us as a masterwork of spiritual literature. It contains a general introduction

and 30 points of reflection on detachment. Although thirteen propositions abstracted from it were objected to by Eckhart's Cologne prosecutors, only one remark found its way into the list of propositions
condemned in Avignon in 1329. As Professor Duclow has said, 'It is a
work of pastoral care and consolation which aims to transform the experience of suffering from within.'[31]

Eckhart first sets out the purpose and plan of his treatise:

> I propose in this book to impart some teachings whereby a man may
> find consolation in all adversity, unhappiness and suffering. [. . .] The
> first is misfortune occurring to outward goods; the second, to our rela-
> tives and dearest friends; the third, to ourselves: dishonour, hardship,
> pain of body and heart's distress.[32]

It is all one to Eckhart, although he will on occasion specify one or
another source of particular discomfort. He begins by setting out three
main principles, which he illustrates by argument and examples. This is
the brief theological or theoretical preface to his book, which serves as a
kind of abstract.

Eckhart's first principle and its corollary are familiar from earlier works:
'. . . in God there is no sorrow or suffering or distress. If you would be free
from all adversity and pain, turn and cleave entirely to God . . .'[33] The
second is also familiar. It is in fact the palimpsest of Eckhart's teaching
concerning the transcendence of suffering inasmuch as God becomes our
suffering. Here he describes the effect or consequence of conformity with
God: 'When outward ills befall the good and just man, if he remains in
equanimity with the peace of his heart unmoved, then it is true, as I have
said, that nothing that happens to him can disturb the just.'[34]

Consistent with his earlier teaching, in the third principle Eckhart
locates the source of suffering and sorrow:

> . . . all sorrow comes from love of that which loss has deprived me of. If
> I mind the loss of outward things, it is a sure sign that I am fond of
> outward things, and really love sorrow and discomfort! [. . .] My heart
> and inclination ascribe to creatures what belongs to God. I turn to crea-
> tures, whence by nature discomfort comes, and turn away from God,
> from whom all comfort flows.[35]

The second, largest part of *The Book of Divine Comfort* consists of 30 maxims or examples. Some are simple, even to the point of platitude. Perhaps Eckhart is here dealing with the obvious in order to lead up to what is not at all obvious although surprisingly simple. In his second counsel, he remarks, 'If you would be comforted, forget those who are better off and just remember those who are worse off than you.' Again, this is not especially profound. But Eckhart follows it with a statement of what is in fact the heart of his teaching, one not far removed from the fundamental insight of Buddhist teaching: 'All suffering comes from love and attachment. So if I suffer on account of transitory things, then I and my heart have love and attachment for temporal things, I do not love God with all my heart and do not yet love that which God wishes me to love with Him.'[36]

Anticipating an obvious objection, the third maxim draws us closer to the heart of Eckhart's teaching:

A good man should trust in God, believe and be assured that God is so good that it is impossible for God, His goodness and love to endure that any pain or suffering befall a man unless either to save that man from further suffering, or else to give him greater consolation on earth, or to make thereby and therefrom something better which should redound more largely and fully to God's glory.[37]

This appears to be a restatement of the general Christian philosophy of evil, that God could allow harm to befall only if it ultimately leads to a greater good. Eckhart continues, however:

Yet be that as it may: by the mere fact of its being God's will that it should occur, the good man's will should be so much at one and united with God's will, that that man would will the same as God, even though it were to his own harm or indeed his damnation. [Further,] ... the truly perfected man should be wont to be so dead to self, so lost in God to his own form and so transformed in God's will, that his entire blessedness consists in unknowing of himself and all things, and knowing only God, willing nothing and knowing no will but God's will, willing to know God, as St Paul says, 'as God knows me' (cf. 1 Cor. 13:12).[38]

Eckhart has moved almost imperceptibly to the notion of spiritual poverty, a theme that pervades the beguine literature of the time and is already suggestive of the doctrine of the notorious sermon No. 52, *Beati*

Pauperes Spiritu. (Not surprisingly, the sole passage from this treatise with which the judges found fault at Avignon comes from this section.) Eckhart continues, paraphrasing St Thomas Aquinas, a qualification overlooked by his judges. Here he unobtrusively introduces his vision of God's suffering, portrayed as grief:

> In this way one wills to do without God for God's sake, to be sundered from God for God's sake, and that alone is true repentance for my sins: then I grieve for sin without grief, as God grieves for all evil without grief. I have grief, the greatest grief, for my sins, for I would not sin for everything that is created or creaturely, even though there were a thousand worlds existing to all eternity – and yet without grief; and I accept and take the suffering in God's will and from God's will. Such suffering alone is perfect suffering, for it arises and springs from pure love of God's sheer goodness and joy.[39]

For Eckhart, discomfort and comfort both come from God and therefore both give us God. But discomfort more so, as he indicates in a move unusually similar to the attitude of voluntary suffering favoured by the beguines:

> If God wills to give me what I want, then I have it and have the pleasure of it; if God does not will to give it to me, then I get it by doing without, in God's same will, and thus I take by doing without and not taking. So what do I lose? Really and truly, one receives God in a truer sense by doing without than by getting, for when a man gets something, it is the gift itself which is the cause of his being happy and comforted. But if he receives nothing, he has, finds and knows nothing to rejoice at but God, and God's will alone.[40]

Active renunciation or voluntary detachment figures just as prominently in Eckhart's teaching as the acceptance of physical suffering, and both to the expense of pursuing of such suffering.

> . . . no vessel can hold two separate kinds of drink. If it is to contain wine, we must pour out the water; the vessel must be bare and empty. And so, if you would receive divine joy and God, you must pour away creatures. St Augustine says: 'Pour out, that you may be filled. Learn not to love that you may learn to love. Turn away that you may be turned towards.' In short, to take in, to be receptive, a thing must be empty.[41]

Becoming 'empty', devoid of concepts and 'whys', is one of Eckhart's characteristic counsels, similar to the Zen doctrine of *sunyatta*. Here Eckhart has in mind what became the linch-pin of beguine spirituality: poverty of spirit rather than material deprivation, although without ruling out the latter. Here, too, is a hint of the teaching that would appear later in the sermon *Beati Pauperes Spiritu*:

> He is poor who has nothing. 'Poor in spirit' means: as the eye is 'poor' and bare of colour yet receptive of all colours, so is he poor in spirit who is receptive of all spirit, and the spirit of all spirits is God. The fruit of the spirit is love, joy and peace . . .
>
> So, if you would seek and find perfect joy and comfort in God, see to it that you are free of all creatures and of all comfort from creatures; for assuredly, as long as you are or can be comforted by creatures, you will never find true comfort. But when nothing can comfort you but God, then God will comfort you, and with Him and in Him all that is bliss.[42]

'God is my Suffering': Eckhart's Doctrine of Co-suffering

The culmination of the second part of *The Book of Divine Comfort* is based on Eckhart's reading of Psalm 34 and leads to his distinctive teaching:

> Again, one should reflect, if a man had a friend who was in sorrow, pain and distress on his account, surely it would be proper to be with him and comfort him with his presence and with such consolation as he could give. Therefore our Lord says in the Psalms that He is with him in his sorrow (Ps. 34:18).[43]

In his third point under this heading, Eckhart begins a long explanation of how God is not only with us in our suffering, but suffers with us and in us:

> . . . I say that God's being with us in suffering means that He suffers with me Himself. Truly, he who knows the truth knows that I speak truth. God suffers with man, indeed, He suffers in His fashion before, and far more than that man who suffers for His sake. So I declare, if God Himself wills to suffer, then it is only right that I should suffer, for if it is well with me, then I want what God wants. I pray every day, and God

bids me pray: 'Lord, thy will be done', and yet, when God wants suffering, I complain at the suffering, which is quite wrong. I also declare of
a surety that God is so fond of suffering with us and for us if *we* suffer
purely for God's sake, that He suffers without suffering. To suffer is such
joy to Him that suffering for Him is no suffering. And so, if we were in
a right state, our suffering would be no suffering but a joy and a
comfort.[44]

Here again is the transformation thematic introduced in the *Talks of
Instruction*, the reconfiguration of suffering as joy, which Eckhart now
articulates with a directness and emphatic tone far beyond earlier descrip-
tions:

The seventh point about the saying that God is with us in suffering and
suffers with us is: we should be profoundly comforted by the fact of
God's being purely One without any adventitious quantity of difference
even in thought, so that everything that is in Him is God Himself. And
since this is true, I say: Whatever a good man suffers for God's sake, he
suffers in God, and God is with him in his suffering. If my suffering is
in God and God suffers with me, how then can my suffering be painful
when suffering loses its pain, and my pain is in God and my pain *is*
God?[45]

Eckhart's conclusion comes not so much as a surprise than as a challenge.
He does not counsel us to seek suffering, but to accept it, not with resignation as inescapable, but as a gift of God's presence and companionship.
In concluding, he glances once again at the obvious objection, dismissing
it perhaps too quickly for modern sensibilities: Why does God not just
prevent or simply remove suffering? He responds with a parable:

Once a sick man was asked why he did not pray to God to make him
well. He said he was unwilling to do this for three reasons. One was that
he felt sure a loving God would never tolerate his being sick unless it
were for his good. The *second* was that if a man is good he wants whatever God wants, and not that God should want what man wants: that
would not be right. And therefore, if He wants me to be ill – and if He
did not, I should not be – then I ought not to wish to be well. For
without doubt, if it were possible for God to make me well against His
will, I would not want to care that He had made me well. Willing comes

from loving, not-willing from not-loving. It is far preferable, better and more profitable for me that God loves me and I am sick, than if I were well in body and God did not love me.[46]

For Catholic Christians, one of the most unusual and challenging aspects of Eckhart's teaching is his rejection of petitioning divine intervention as a response to suffering.

The third reason why I scorn and dislike to ask God to make me well is that I will not and ought not to pray to the mighty, loving and generous God for such a small thing. Suppose I came to the Pope a hundred or two hundred miles, and when I came into his presence I were to say: 'My Lord, Holy Father, I have travelled about two hundred miles with great difficulty and expense, and I beg you – and this is what I came for – to give me a bean', truly, he and whoever heard it would say, and rightly, that I was a great fool. But it is a certain truth, I declare, that all goods, indeed all creatures, are less compared with God than a bean compared with the entire physical world. And so, if I were a good and wise man, I should rightly scorn to pray that I might be made well.[47]

Without disparaging either faith or the power or will of God that we be whole and well, this final point is consistent with Eckhart's previous teaching. He teaches us that suffering is a gift, just as life is a gift, and health is a gift. Had God not willed that we suffer, we would not suffer; and, therefore, to pray, much less to strive to avoid suffering, is to attempt to avoid God. For God is not merely there *in* our suffering. Our suffering *is* God.

What Can Eckhart Teach Us about Pain, Suffering and Healing?

Far removed in time and spirit from the contemporary quest for the illusory medical panaceas Ivan Illich excoriated over 30 years ago, Eckhart's teaching may strike us today as fatalistic, if not simply bizarre. However, his concept of suffering as a gift, as a particular grace of God's presence, finds unsuspected support among contemporary practitioners. In his recent work *Spontaneous Healing*, Dr Andrew Weil writes,

. . . the most common correlation I observe between mind and healing in people with chronic illness is total acceptance of the circumstances of one's life, including illness. This change allows profound internal relaxation, so that people need no longer feel compelled to maintain a defensive stance toward life. Often, it occurs as part of a spiritual awakening and submission to a higher power.[48]

In this he sounds very much like Ursula Fleming! And, like Eckhart, he advises his patients to accept illness as a gift:

> Because illness can be such a powerful stimulus to change, perhaps the only thing that can force some people to resolve their deepest conflicts, successful patients often come to regard it as the greatest opportunity they have ever had for personal growth and development – truly a gift. Seeing illness as a misfortune, especially one that is undeserved, may obstruct the healing system. Coming to see illness as a gift that allows you to grow may unlock it.[49]

The Deeper Healing

For Eckhart, illness and suffering could be considered as an aspect or dimension of the spirituality of detachment that in fact disposes towards wellness. This seems in many respects to run counter to the common wisdom of 'fighting' disease and illness. But to reclaim one's health, and one's people's health from the health-care industries, from the insurance industry, from government and from the assumptions of a consumer society, requires courage, education and access to resources of physical, psychological and spiritual reintegration precisely opposite to the questionable but costly benefits offered by a technologically oriented, consumerist society. From my viewpoint, such resourcefulness is the contribution of authentic spiritual traditions, a groundedness in nature recognized and celebrated as Creation, and an unswerving belief in the dignity and ultimate value of the human person. Eckhart, as I read him, provides one such approach, a particularly powerful one.

In *Love, Medicine, and Miracles*, Dr Bernie Siegel tells us that

> In achieving peace of mind, cancer may be healed, sight may be restored, and paralysis may disappear. All of these things may occur through peace of mind, which creates a healing environment in the body.[50]

For that is therapy – the healing of the injuries, disease and disability that afflict our sisters and brothers throughout the world, beginning at our own doorstep. It also points to the healing of the wound of sin that infects the planet, the Galaxy, the cosmos itself, this great body of God groaning in travail, awaiting the revelation of the full glory of all God's children (Rom. 8:22–23). To that extent, therapy is also spirituality.[51]

Eckhart does not counsel anyone to *seek* suffering for its own sake, nor even as a special mode of God's presence. In this he differs considerably from most of his contemporaries, and even some of his own disciples. Eckhart's way is to seek God in *all* things, and all things in God, *even* suffering, not with fatalistic resignation as inescapable, but as a gift of God's presence and companionship:

> A master says he knows God aright, who is equally aware of Him in all things. I once said: to serve God in fear is good; to serve Him in love is better; but to be able to grasp the love in fear, that is best. For a man to have a peaceful life is good, but for a man to have a life of pain in patience is better; but that a man should have peace in a life of pain is best.[52]

Notes

1. Portions of this chapter have been adapted from lectures at Eckhart House, Dublin, Ireland, and the Eckhart Society Conference, 27 August 2004, Plater College, Oxford. See also Richard Woods, *Wellness: Life, Health and Spirituality* (Dublin: Veritas Publications, 2009), Chapter 6: 'Pain, Suffering, and Healing'.
2. Ursula Fleming, *Meister Eckhart: The Man from whom God Hid Nothing* (Leominster: Gracewing, 1995 ed.), p. 52.
3. Ivan Illich, *Medical Nemesis: The Expropriation of Health* (London: Calder and Boyars, 2001 ed.), p. 97.
4. Andrew Weil, M.D., *Spontaneous Healing* (New York: Alfred A. Knopf, 1995), p. 262.
5. For an overview of medical knowledge and practice in the Middle Ages, see N. G. Siraisi, *Medieval and Early Renaissance Medicine: An Introduction to Knowledge and Practice* (Chicago: University of Chicago Press, 1990); and P. Biller and J. Ziegler, eds, *Religion and Medicine in the Middle Ages*, York Studies in Medieval Theology Series, 3 (Rochester, NY: Boydell & Brewer, 2001).
6. See especially Elizabeth Robertson, 'The Corporeality of Female Sanctity in The Life of Saint Margaret', in R. Blumenfeld-Kosinski and T. Szell, eds, *Images of Sainthood in Medieval Europe* (Ithaca and London: Cornell University Press, 1991); and Marina Warner, *Alone of All her Sex: The Myth and Cult of the Virgin Mary* (New York: Random House, 1986). Caroline Walker Bynum points out that 'both men and women saw female saints as models of suffering and inner spiri-

tuality, male saints as models of action', Caroline Walker Bynum, *Holy Feast and Holy Fast: The Religious Significance of Food to Medieval Women* (Berkeley and Los Angeles: University of California Press, 1987), p. 29.

7. Jo Ann McNamara, 'The Need to Give: Suffering and Female Sanctity in the Middle Ages', in Blumenfeld-Kosinski and Szell, ed. cit., pp. 199–221.

8. Not only did noble women voluntarily join the ranks of the poor, but they more or less successfully transformed both the need of the indigent and their almsgiving into spiritual value. Not surprisingly, the doctrine of purgatory receives its fullest development at this time, and the practice of benefiting souls, rather than bodies, by vicarious atonement, becomes a spiritual *leitmotif*. This was especially true among the Dominicans. See McNamara, art. cit., pp. 212–21.

9. *Daz buoch der goetlichen troestunge, The Book of Divine Comfort*, Walshe, Vol. III, p. 64. See also Sermon 76, cited below. As with modern German, *troesten* can be rendered as both 'comfort' and 'consolation', and practice varies from translation to translation. Unless otherwise indicated, I have followed Walshe's practice..

10. *Talks of Instruction*, No. 11, Walshe, Vol. III, pp. 27–8.

11. Ibid., No. 11, p. 28. Walshe notes that the same teaching is found in Sermon 2 (DP 2, Walshe No. 8).

12. Ibid., No. 7, my translation. See Walshe, Vol. III, p. 20 and *The Essential Sermons, Commentaries, Treatises and Defense*, ed. and trans. by Bernard McGinn and Edmund Colledge (New York: Paulist Press, 1981), p. 255. The same teaching is found in his sermons: 'God is equally in all things and all places, and is equally ready to give Himself as far as in Him lies: and he knows God rightly who knows God equally (in all things).' Sermon 68 (Walshe No. 69, Vol. II, p. 167, DP 36).

13. Compare Sermon 51 (Walshe No. 83, Vol. II, p. 254): 'Our Lord said: "Your darkness – that is, your suffering – shall be changed into clear light" (cf. Isaiah 58:10). Yet I should not seek it or strive for it.'

14. *Talks of Instruction*, No. 16, *Of True Penance and Holy Living*, Walshe, Vol. III, pp. 33–4.

15. Ibid., No. 17, pp. 35–6.

16. Ibid., No. 18, pp. 37–8. Compare the 'Cautales' of St John of the Cross in this regard in *The Ascent of Mt. Carmel*, Book I, Ch. 13, Nos 10–11.

17. Ibid., No. 18, p. 38.

18. Ibid., No. 20, p. 43. Eckhart adds, 'Rather, the suffering of the senses and the lower powers are not your concern, nor this assault of the world: for the greater and fiercer the struggle, the greater and more glorious the victory and the honour of victory.'

19. Ibid., No. 23, p. 57.

20. Sermon 49 (Walshe No. 89, Vol. II, pp. 290–1).

21. Sermon 76 (Walshe No. 7, Vol. I, p. 68, DP 35).

22. Sermon 2 (Walshe No. 8, Vol. I, p. 75, DP 2).

23. Ibid.

24. Sermon 25 (Walshe No.10, Vol. I, pp. 92–3, DP 38).

25. Sermon 4 (Walshe No. 40, Vol. I, pp. 281–2, DP 4).

26. Sermon 12 (Walshe No. 57, Vol. II, p. 87, DP 13).

27. On the debate regarding the authenticity of the treatise, see McGinn, *The Mystical Thought of Meister Eckhart* (New York: Crossroad, 2001), p. 13, n. 83.

28. 'On Detachment', Walshe, Vol. III, p. 118.

29. Ibid., pp. 128–9.
30. Apparently, Eckhart was on close terms with the imperial family. In 1313, Agnes retired to the monastery founded by her mother at Königsfelden in the Aargau, where she died in 1364. Agnes' daughter, Elizabeth, was a Dominican nun at Töss in Switzerland, where she became a member of the circle influenced by Blessed Henry Suso, Eckhart's most faithful and ardent disciple.
31. Donald F. Duclow, '"My Suffering is God": Meister Eckhart's *Book of Divine Consolation*', *Theological Studies*, 44 (December 1983), p. 582.
32. *Book of Divine Comfort*, Walshe, Vol. III, Prologue, p. 61.
33. Ibid., p. 64.
34. Ibid., p. 65.
35. Ibid., pp. 65–6.
36. Ibid., p. 67.
37. Ibid., pp. 69–70.
38. Ibid., p. 70.
39. Ibid., p. 71.
40. Ibid., pp. 71–2.
41. Ibid., p. 75.
42. Ibid., pp. 75–6.
43. Ibid., p. 92.
44. Ibid., p. 93.
45. Ibid., pp. 95–6.
46. Ibid., pp. 98–9.
47. Ibid., p. 99.
48. Weil, op. cit., p. 100.
49. Ibid., p. 251.
50. Bernie Siegel, *Love, Medicine and Miracles* (New York: Harper and Row, 1986), p. 112.
51. 'Therapy' itself originally conveyed a religious rather than medical connotation: 'The word comes from the Greek noun *therapeia*, which meant "service", particularly temple service, and eventually "healing service". The verb *theapeuō*, a classical Greek term found in Hesiod, Aristotle, and other writers meaning to serve, or be a servant, particular of a divinity. It also came to mean "to care for, wait upon, or to treat medically", and eventually "to heal", mainly because the ancient practitioners of health care in both Egypt and Greece were priests in attendance at temples known to be healing sites. In biblical literature, the derivative noun *therapōn*, "servant", used by the Greeks for attendants at the temple of Dionysios and Askleipios, the god of healing, is used exclusively to describe Moses, as in Exodus 4:10, Numbers 12:7, Wisdom 10:16, and Hebrews 3:5.' Woods, *Wellness: Life, Health and Spirituality*, op. cit., p. 36.
52. Sermon 68 (Walshe No. 69, Vol. II, pp. 166–7, DP 36).

Chapter 12

Epilogue: Meister Eckhart's Wider Ecumenism[1]

Nineteenth-century and early twentieth-century commentators tended to minimize Eckhart's reliance on ancient and contemporary sources, especially when these seemed to compromise Eckhart's originality or his orthodoxy. More recent studies have shown that Eckhart incorporated elements from a very rich and extensive array of theological, philosophical and spiritual writers, often transforming them in the process, no doubt more than he realized. I also believe that, as Alain de Libera has argued, in both his pastoral works, notably his sermons as well as his scholarly treatises, Eckhart was deliberately continuing the approach of St Albert the Great, the founder of the Cologne Dominican school, who sought to create a grand theological and philosophical synthesis embracing pagan, Jewish, Christian and Muslim resources.[2] This tendency represents Eckhart's 'wider ecumenism', a term Dom Sylvester Houédard favoured in referring to the widespread interest shown today in Eckhart's works by a variety of religious, philosophical and spiritual seekers.[3]

As Bernard McGinn has reminded us, until the indices to the critical edition of Eckhart's German and Latin works are completed, such efforts must be regarded as provisional and preliminary.[4] Nevertheless, as Dr McGinn himself has recently shown, it is possible to glimpse the general contours of Eckhart's astonishingly wide array of sources. And, as Dom Sylvester shrewdly estimated, his resource list is richly, even surprisingly, ecumenical.[5]

Disputes concerning Eckhart's philosophical and theological resources date from the middle of the nineteenth century, when German scholars began sifting through mountains of manuscript material to unearth his authentic German and Latin works. While recognizing Eckhart's speculative brilliance as well as his spiritual gifts and eloquence, during the Thomistic revival of the late nineteenth and early twentieth centuries, Dominican commentators beginning with Heinrich Denifle and continuing with

Gabriel Théry and Gundolf Gieraths, among others, found the Meister's reliance on Neoplatonic themes philosophically and theologically disconcerting. As Bernard McGinn pointed out several years ago, 'The majority of the twenty-eight propositions from his works condemned by Pope John XXII in the bull "In Agro Dominico" of March 27, 1329, involve or imply aspects of his appropriation of Neoplatonism. Three of them (articles 23, 24 and 26) relate directly to his doctrine of God . . .'[6] Moved perhaps by defensive sentiment in the face of the charges of unorthodoxy laid against Eckhart's doctrine and its subsequent condemnation in 1329, some commentators have gone so far as to claim that Eckhart disavowed Neoplatonism. More careful scholars have recognized that Eckhart was not only a profound exponent of Christian Neoplatonism, but was also the outstanding representative of the Dominican School of Cologne, founded by his mentor, St Albert the Great.[7]

Eckhart scholars now tend to agree that these major themes formed the nucleus of a projected mystical, theological, philosophical and spiritual system similar to that of Thomas Aquinas's *Summa Theologiae*, but also daring in its departures and originality. It was intended to be not only an outline and model of God's progressive self-revelation, but also a map of the human spirit's itinerary from and back to its eternal Source – the Christian Neoplatonic schema that Eckhart inherited from St Albert the Great and Thomas Aquinas, and behind them Hugh and Richard of St Victor, Thomas Gallus, John Sarracenus, John Scottus Eriugena, Dionysius the Areopagite, the Cappadocian Fathers, Origen, Proclus, Plotinus, Philo and, at the source, 'the great priest', Plato himself.[8] What distinguishes Eckhart from virtually every other medieval figure is that a very large body of sermons and spiritual treatises embodying his theology exists alongside his more 'speculative' writings. Eckhart emphatically preached what he practised.

As noted earlier, Eckhart would undoubtedly have considered himself first and foremost a biblical theologian. Not surprisingly, his Latin scriptural commentaries on both the Hebrew Scriptures and the New Testament constitute the bulk of his writings, especially when the lost and missing works are added to the collection that has survived. In the 592 Latin excerpts made by Eckhart's brethren at Cologne and rediscovered by Thomas Kaepelli in 1960, 270 were from his commentary on John's Gospel alone – a work considered his theological masterpiece. Of the remainder, 97 were from the commentary on Wisdom, 74 were from the first commentary on Genesis, 69 from the commentary on Exodus, 46 from the second commentary on Genesis, 21 from the commentary on Sirach, and 15 from other sources.

But Eckhart's 'ecumenical' interests ranged as widely, or even more widely, than other students of Albert and Aquinas. As we have seen earlier, Eckhart's non-pagan sources included both Jewish and Islamic scholars, among them Isaac Israeli, Ibn Gabirol (Avicebron), Moses Maimonides, Al-Kindi, Avicenna, Averroes and the Islamic paraphrase of *The Book of Causes*.[9] As Rabbi Albert Friedlander and other Jewish scholars have shown,[10] Eckhart was not only remarkably open to the doctrines of Solomon Ibn Gabirol and Maimonides, but well versed in them, especially the latter, whom he cites more frequently than most of his Christian authorities. Maimonides was, of course, known to Aquinas as well, but there is a significant difference in the attitude towards the Rabbi's doctrine shown by Eckhart and Thomas. As Bernard McGinn observed, 'What is remarkable is Eckhart's positive attitude toward the Jewish philosopher – unlike Thomas and others, he never criticizes *Rabbi Moyses*.'[11] Rabbi Friedlander observed tellingly that

The Jewish roots of Christianity which are acknowledged today become visible in the Master's writings on Genesis and Exodus. Indeed, Rabbi Moyses – Maimonides – is often cited not only for his particular comments but also for his specific method. If, in the end, the final proof is sealed by a quote from Aquinas or Augustine, one can understand this without having to place it under the rubric of 'political correctness'. But other Jewish scholars are also cited, and I enjoyed a mention of Isaac Israeli (855–955).[12]

Later, Friedlander expands on Eckhart's reliance on Maimonides in his commentary on the creation of the stars and planets, concerning which neither scholar accepts the conventional notion that they were created 'for the sake of man'. God's purposes in Creation are far greater and more mysterious than a preoccupation with human pleasure or convenience, a theme expressed explicitly in the Book of Job. Friedlander comments,

Eckhart follows Maimonides here, who will not accept the meaning and purpose of these heavenly bodies to be their function of illuminating the earth: the lesser should not define the function of the greater! In the *Liber parabolarum* Eckhart also follows Maimonides in viewing

,acob's ladder as the symbol of the cosmos. Where angels pass one another on the same rung, Maimonides and Eckhart both view this as an image of the harmony of the spheres which thus, in their movement, maintain the heavenly constellations. Against existing theologies, they feel that it is not their function within the lower world which justifies their existence: the more perfect does not become defined through the less perfect; and the movement of the spheres is the harmony of the whole cosmos, not the maintenance of one of its parts. It is here that Maimonides argues against the notion that man is the ultimate and real purpose of the whole cosmos (a view rejected also by Aquinas). Maimonides here argues against the established Jewish tradition as well, taking a historical point of view which is unrelated to Creation-theology.[13]

Of his Muslim authorities, Eckhart gives special attention to Avicenna rather than Averroes, who was a more powerful influence on Thomas and other medieval theologians and philosophers such as Siger of Brabant. The Persian philosopher's doctrine of creation and his identification of angels with subsisting or separated intelligences, an Aristotelian theme, greatly fascinated Eckhart.[14] In recent years, increasing attention has been given to a number of areas of resonance between Eckhart's teaching and that of Ibn' Arabi and al-Farabi.[15]

What did Eckhart find in the Jewish and Muslim mystics that appealed to him? More than most of the spiritual thinkers of his time, he clearly sympathized with the resolute emphasis in their teaching that God remains utterly transcendent, beyond all human naming, but present in every minute detail of human existence, a living, caring, fount of love as well as a force for righteousness. Eckhart even distanced himself from Thomas Aquinas in his teaching on predication, the attribution of positive qualities to God, adopting a position closer to that of Maimonides. Only Eckhart could have said, 'I pray God to rid me of God!'[16]

Eckhart's tendency towards ontological monism brings him close to Advaita Vedanta as well, although he maintained a critical distinction between God and Creation that avoids the net of pantheism by developing the theme of 'indistinct distinction'. Spiritually and ontologically, Eckhart is here very close to the insight of St Catherine of Siena, to whom God confides, 'Do you know, daughter, who you are and who I am? If you know these two things you have beatitude in your grasp. You are she who is not, and I AM THE ONE WHO IS. Let your soul be penetrated with this truth, and the Enemy can never lead you astray.'[17] Our existence is wholly rooted in God's creative mind and preserved by God's power and love. It is borrowed, not owned.

The confluence of themes in Eckhart, Maimonides, the Sufi mystics, even Hindu and Buddhist thought, also raises the intriguing question, What do spiritual teachers in these traditions find so appealing in Eckhart today?[18] The widespread interest in his thought by scholars of classical Jewish, Muslim, Hindu and Buddhist teaching is at first somewhat hard to fathom. Despite the culminating disaster of the papal condemnation of fifteen propositions taken from his works, Eckhart had been valued by the members of the Order of Preachers and other church leaders as an orthodox Christian and a highly capable administrator, often charged with the reform of religious houses and even whole districts entrusted to his care. Today, even his suspect teachings are recognized by Christian scholars and even the late Pope, as part of the doctrine of 'a reliable guide'. And surely that is also at least part of the reason for his importance today in interfaith discussion. Eckhart represents the greater tradition. He was not some kind of renegade Christian whose thought easily lends itself to a wide variety of applications. The genius of his thought is that it is so profoundly reflective of the deepest spiritual aspirations of human beings everywhere that the more Christian he is, the more universal he appears. Eckhart does not need to be rehabilitated.

Eckhart's Ecumenical Appeal: East and West

Eckhart's 'wider ecumenism' embraced not only biblical works, classical pagan, Christian, Jewish and Islamic authors, but also more contemporary figures who remain anonymous in his works in keeping with medieval custom, and whose influence is now recognized as of immense importance in understanding Eckhart's ecumenical agenda. The most important of these figures are the beguines, Mechthild of Magdeburg and Marguerite Porete. While direct influence of the Dutch poet, Hadewijch of Antwerp, is unlikely, Eckhart would probably have known something of the works of Hildegard of Bingen in one form or another. It should be recalled, however, that despite the existence of similar themes in the great German women's writings, such as the 'greenness' and desert or wilderness themes in Hildegard, Eckhart's interpretation is usually distinctive and, in these instances, significantly different. For Hildegard, the desert is a place of dryness and spiritual desolation, the very opposite of the greenness she associates with God; for Eckhart, the desert is the privileged ground of divine–human encounter.

It is hardly surprising that in recent times, as philosophical, theological and mystical currents intermingle across continents and oceans, including a recovery of women's voices in scholarship and spiritual teaching, Eckhart has found an ever wider and appreciative audience. Elsewhere I have written about the interest in Eckhart studies on the part of Jews, Muslims, Buddhists and Hindus – an attraction that has, if anything, continued to increase exponentially. Such interest in a figure whose Christian faith was never in question, and even whose most controverted statements have now been shown to be deeply rooted in the mystical theology of the ancient Church (despite their often startling mode of expression), cannot be explained simply because he came to possess a certain exotic cachet as a rebel, a proto-Reformer, and so forth. The case appears to be just the opposite. Eckhart remains 'a man for all seasons' not because he rejected the deepest sources of spiritual wisdom in the Christian tradition, but because he embodied them.

And what did Eckhart say?

Eckhart's Mystical Way[19]

Two interrelated strands pervade Eckhart's spiritual doctrine as a whole and can be regarded as foundational: first, the necessity of developing the interior life of prayer and contemplation; and second, appropriately ordering the exterior life of the senses and action. Although such spatial metaphors can be misleading, ancient Christian authority sanctions their use. Thus for Eckhart, *interiority* is essentially Augustinian illuminism – human self-awareness in which dwells the inner light or spark of the soul that betokens the hidden presence of God.[20] The Middle High German term he coined to point to this conscious or interior world was *Innerkeit*: 'innerness' or 'inwardness'. By *exteriority*, he generally meant our sense of and entanglement in the natural and social world of daily experience – a realm where we risk losing both the sense of God's presence and our own deepest identity.

Clearly, for Eckhart the first and essential focus of the spiritual life thus lies in the revelation or discovery within the depths of consciousness of the presence of God, not as an object of thought, but as what he would famously describe as 'the ground of being' – a ground, moreover, of indistinct union of the self and God. In Sermon 68, Eckhart cites his favourite quotation from St Augustine in defence of his position on inwardness: 'God is nearer to the soul than she is to herself.'[21] He continues,

> I am as certain as that I am a man, that nothing is so close to me as God. God is closer to me than I am to myself: my being depends on God's being near me and present to me. So He is also in a stone or a log of wood, only they do not know it. If the wood knew God and realised how close He is to it as the highest angel does, it would be as blessed as the highest angel. And so man is more blessed than a stone or a piece of wood because he is aware of God and knows how close God is to him. And I am the more blessed, the more I realise this, and I am the less blessed, the less I know this. I am not blessed because God is in me and is near me and because I possess Him, but because I am aware of how close He is to me, and that I know God.[22]

The same teaching is found in his treatise, *The Nobleman*:

> I say that there is no blessedness without a man's being aware and well knowing that he knows God . . . For man must be one in himself and must seek it in himself and in one – that is, to see God alone; and 'returning' is being aware and knowing that one knows God and is aware of it.[23]

Eckhart frequently refers to this recognition of God's presence in the core of one's being as the 'birth of the Word in the soul', a theme that has been extensively studied by Hugo Rahner,[24] Shizuteru Ueda[25] and others. This self-disclosure and recognition of God's presence is not an automatic process, however. It requires spiritual discipline, particularly the 'negative' (apophatic) way of 'unknowing' (Middle High German: *unwizzen*) which includes the process of 'stripping away' (*aphairesis*), by which images and concepts of God are progressively dismissed so that the imageless, transcendent sense of God can become manifest. Such a revelation is not simply 'given', however. It requires a deep and difficult introversion, a retreat first of all from the clamour of the sense and the external world. As Eckhart says in one sermon, 'A man cannot attain to this birth except by withdrawing his senses from all things. And that requires a mighty effort to drive back the powers of the soul and inhibit their functioning.'[26]

For it is in the 'depths' of human interiority that God's hidden presence is first met:

For whoever would enter God's ground, His inmost part, must first enter his own ground, his inmost part, for none can know God who does not first know himself. He must enter into his lowest and into God's inmost part, and must enter into his first and his highest, for there everything comes together that God can perform.[27]

Such self-awareness, devoid of images and concepts, is not simply reflexive knowledge. This would intrude the element of self-referential subjectivity that apophatic mystics in particular find repellent, as brilliantly described in *The Cloud of Unknowing*.[28] Eckhart seems to be pointing to concomitant, congruent, or indirect self-awareness that does not deflect attention from the object of its gaze. In his treatise on *The Nobleman*, Eckhart writes,

I say that when a man, the soul, the spirit, sees God, he realises and knows himself as knowing. That is, he knows that he sees and knows God. Now some people have thought, and it seems credible, that the flower and kernel of bliss lies in that knowledge, when the spirit knows that it knows God; for if I had all joy and did not know it, what good would that be to me, and what joy would that be? But I definitely deny that that is so. Though it is true that the soul cannot be happy *without* that, yet felicity does not depend on it; for the *first* condition of felicity is that the soul sees God naked [i.e., free from images and concepts]. From that she derives all her being and her life, and draws all that she is, from the ground of God, knowing nothing of knowledge, nor of love, nor of anything at all. She is utterly calm in God's being, knowing nothing but being there and God. But when she is aware and *knows* that she sees, knows and loves God, that is a turning away and a reversion to the former stage according to the natural order . . .[29]

Hence the necessity of a double divestiture of both self and God, the refusal to divert our gaze to our own self-image from the 'naked' presence of God, which is to say, the One behind and beneath all concepts and images of 'God'. Self-forgetfulness and conceptual 'stripping' (*aphairesis*) constitute the necessary precondition of God's 'coming to birth' in the soul. The disclosure of God in the depths of the human spirit does not leave the mystic seeker immobilized in the depths of introversion, however, but returns her, active, to the world.

The Man from Whom God Hid Nothing

Eckhart von Hochheim was an immensely gifted thinker whose scholarly ambitions ultimately exceeded his ability to complete not because he failed to integrate his wide-ranging interests, but because he practised what he preached. He was more than a gifted thinker. Eckhart is remembered today primarily as a spiritual guide, not a scholastic theologian. The years following his crowning achievement of obtaining the coveted degree of Master of Sacred Theology from the University of Paris were devoted not to academic writing and lecturing, but to administration and preaching. And while he never used the term 'mystical' for what he preached, he has been known ever since as one of the greatest mystics of all time, the 'peak of the range', as Rufus Jones had it.[30]

For Eckhart, and for those who follow him, the 'wayless way' of attentive inwardness leads inevitably to the realization of God's presence everywhere – in all things, as he would say. The God within is identical to the God beyond. There is a double reciprocity at work here – the mutual knowledge and indwelling of God and the soul, and the identity of the divine presence intuited within and in the world beyond.

Eckhart said,

> You must know that this is in reality one and the same thing to know God and to be known by God, to see God and to be seen by God. In knowing and seeing God we know and see that He makes us know and see. And just as the luminous air is not different from the fact of illuminating, for it illumines because it is luminous, so do we know by being known, and because He makes us know.[31]

Again, he says notoriously in a different sermon,

> The eye with which I see God is the same eye with which God sees me: my eye and God's eye are one eye, one seeing, one knowing and one love.[32]

Summarily, Eckhart's full spirituality can be described in surprisingly pre-Ignatian terms as the discovery of God in all things and all things in God. He said, for example,

A man may go out into the fields and say his prayers and know God, or he may go to church and know God: but if he is more aware of God because he is in a quiet place, as is usual, that comes from his imperfection and not from God: for God is equally in all things and all places, and is equally ready to give Himself as far as in Him lies: and he knows God rightly who knows God equally (in all things).[33]

His teaching is here, as in many places, based on his profound appropriation of the thought of St Augustine: '. . . God is unseparated from all things, for God is in all things and is more inwardly in them than they are in themselves.'[34]

Thus, as he told his young Dominican students,

Now if a man truly has God with him, God is with him everywhere, in the street or among people just as much as in church or in the desert or in a cell. If he possesses God truly and solely, such a man cannot be disturbed by anybody. Why? He has only God, thinks only of God, and all things are for him nothing but God. Such a man bears God in all his works and everywhere, and all that man's works are wrought purely by God . . .[35]

Again, he reminded them, 'We shall find God in everything alike, and find God always alike in everything. . . [T]hose who manage this are in a right state: taking God equally in all things, they find God in equal measure in all.'[36]

One of the finest tributes to Eckhart's Way is found, I think, in a letter by Fr Alfred Delp, a Jesuit priest executed in Berlin by the Nazis toward the end of the Second World War. In his last days he found Eckhart an abiding help:

During the daytime I read a little Eckhart, the only one of my books I have managed to retain. The whole Eckhart question would be simpler if people remembered that he was a mystic and his mind and soul and spirit were always soaring into higher spheres. He did his best to follow their flight in word and expression – but how can any ordinary mortal succeed in an undertaking that defied even St Paul? Eckhart failed as, in his own way, every person must fail when it is a matter of analyzing and passing on an intimate personal experience: *individuum ist ineffabile* [individuality is inexpressible]. Once we have got back to the point where the ordinary person can have inexpressible secrets, then a favored few will emerge and God will find them sufficiently advanced to draw them into the creative dialogue as he drew Eckhart. With this in mind, reading him becomes more rewarding and more comforting. It gives the reader a glimpse of the divine secret in every human heart.[37]

A few weeks later, on the feast of the Purification of the Blessed Virgin Mary, Delp was hanged at Ploetzensee Prison.

Let Eckhart's farewell here be that at the conclusion of one of his finest sermons:

May God help us thus to ascend from one love to another and to be united in God, to abide there in bliss eternally. Amen.[38]

Notes

1. Eckhart Society Conference, 16 March 2002, St Bartholomew-the-Great, London, England.
2. See *Introduction à la Mystique Rhénane d'Albert le Grand à Maitre Eckhart* (Paris: O.E.I.L., 1984).
3. Dom Sylvester (1924–92), a monk of Prinknash Abbey in Gloucestershire, was a renowned poet, scholar, patron of the Eckhart Society, and my good friend. He was very active in bridging apparent chasms between the Christian faith and world religions. Dom Sylvester died of a sudden heart attack as he left for a meeting of the Trustees of the Eckhart Society on 15 January 1992.
4. See Bernard McGinn, *The Mystical Thought of Meister Eckhart* (New York: Crossroad, 2001), p. 163.
5. The following reflections on Eckhart's sources are based in part on my article, 'Meister Eckhart and the Neoplatonic Heritage: The Thinker's Way to God', *The Thomist* 54:4 (October 1990): 609–39. See above, Chapter 3.
6. Bernard McGinn, 'Meister Eckhart on God as Absolute Unity', *Neoplatonism and Christian Thought*, ed. by Dominic J. O'Meara (Albany: State University of New York Press, 1982), p. 129 (hereafter: 'God as Absolute Unity').
7. On Eckhart as a Christian Neoplatonist, see Chapter 2 above and (among other sources) Edmund Colledge and Bernard McGinn, trans. and eds, *Meister Eckhart: The Essential Sermons, Commentaries, Treatises and Defense* (New York: Paulist Press, 1981), pp. 27, 34, 40–4; de Libera, op. cit., pp. 242–50, 256, 265, 278–9, 290–2; Vladimir Lossky, *Théologie négative et connaissance de Dieu chez Maître Eckhart* (Paris: Vrin, 1960), pp. 22–6 et passim; Andrew Louth, *The Origins of the Christian Mystical Tradition from Plato to Denys* (Oxford: Clarendon Press, 1981), pp. 110f.; Josef Koch, 'Meister Eckhart: Versuch eines Gesamtbildes', *Kleine Schriften* (Roma: Edizioni di Storia a Letteratura, 1973), 1:214; *Pseudo-Dionysius: The Complete Works*, trans. by Colm Luibheid and Paul Rorem (New York: Paulist Press, 1987), p. 30; Bernard McGinn, 'God as Absolute Unity', pp. 137–9; Kurt

Ruh, *Meister Eckhart: Theologe, Prediger, Mystiker* (München: Beck, 1985), pp. 55–8, 87–9; Hugo Rahner, 'Die Gottesgeburt: Die Lehre der Kirchenväter von der Geburt Christi im Herzen der Glaübigen', *Zeitschrift für katholische Theologie* 59 (1935): 412ff; Reiner Schürmann, *Meister Eckhart, Mystic and Philosopher* (Bloomington, Ind.: Indiana University Press, 1978), pp. 140–3 and passim; and Frank Tobin, *Meister Eckhart: Thought and Language* (Philadelphia: University of Pennsylvania Press, 1986), p. 62, 210, n. 81. Cf. also Evelyn Underhill, *The Mystics of the Church* (London: James Clarke, n.d.), p. 134.

8. See German Sermon 28 (Walshe 17, p. 145: 'Now Plato, that great priest [*der grôze pfaffe*], begins to speak and would discourse on weighty matters.')

9. See above, Chapter 2, p. X.

10. See especially Albert H. Friedlander, 'Meister Eckhart, Maimonides, and Paul Celan', *Eckhart Review* 3 (Spring 1994): 14–30, originally delivered at the Sixth Conference of the Eckhart Society held at Plater College, Oxford, England, 27–9 August 1993.

11. McGinn, *The Mystical Thought of Meister Eckhart*, op. cit., p. 172.

12. Friedlander, art. cit., p. 16. In a note, Rabbi Friedlander supplies the reference: 'In *V[on] e[deln] M[enchen]*: 'Man sol ze dem ersten wizzen und ist ouch wol offenbar, daz der mensche hat in im zweierhande nature: lip und geiSt Dar umbe sprechet ein *geschrift*: (Isaac Israeli: *Liber de diffinitionibus*: . . . "philosophia est cognicio hominis sui ipsius . . . homo enim cum scit seipsum vera cognicione sui cum spiritualite et corpocitate sua, tun iam comprehendit scienciam totius, scil. scienciam substanciae spiritualis et substancie corporeae; etc. . . ."' (*Anmerkungen zu VeM*; 3, p. 120).

13. Ibid., p. 21.

14. See especially McGinn in this respect, ibid., pp. 173–4.

15. On Ibn'Arabi and Eckhart, see Dom Sylvester Houédard, O.S.B., *Commentaries on Meister Eckhart Sermons* (Oxford: Beshara Publications, 2000); Michael Sells, 'Meister Eckhart and Ibn'Arabi on Time and Mystical Union, *Eckhart Review* 9 (1999): 2–19; and Reza Shah-Kazemi, 'Transcendence and Immanence: Common Themes in Eckhart, Ibn' Arabi and Shankara', *Eckhart Review* 6 (1997): 13–25. On Eckhart and al-Farabi, see Atif Khalil, 'Some Tensions in Farabi's Metaphysics of the One and the Emanative Descent', *Transcendent Philosophy* 1: 83–108, esp. n. 8. http://www.iranianstudies.org/Journal/v6n1/v6n1a5.pdf.

16. See Sermon 52 (Walshe No. 87, Vol. II, p. 271).

17. Raymond of Capua, *The Life of Catherine of Siena*, I, x, 93, p. 86. Cited by Suzanne Noffke, O.P., *Catherine of Siena: Vision through a Distant Eye* (Collegeville, MN: Liturgical Press, 1996).

18. For additional references, see the appended list of recommended readings at the end of this book.

19. Adapted from 'Meister Eckhart: Preacher and Teacher', *God in Multicultural Society: Religion, Politics, and Globalization*, ed. by Edward Alam (Louaize, Lebanon: Notre Dame University Press, 2006), pp. 99–110.

20. Evelyn Underhill's synopsis of Augustinian mysticism admirably describes Eckhart's approach: 'Augustinian psychology operates on the premise that human nature cannot contemplate God at all until the internal image has been "reformed by grace". Augustine teaches that it is the divine image within man that impels him toward contemplative union with God. The logical conclusion

of such thinking is that man's true identity is found in his identification with God, arrived at by the complete spiritual life, which actualizes the soul's potentialities and ultimately leads to transformation in God and "deification". Augustine proclaims that he who feeds on the Divine will have had his substance transformed into His.' Evelyn Underhill, *Mysticism* (New York: World Pub. Co., 1955 ed.), p. 419.

21. From Augustine's *Ennaratio in Psalmum* LXXIV.
22. Sermon 68 (Walshe No. 69, Vol. II, pp. 165–6).
23. *The Nobleman*, Walshe, Vol. III, p. 114. (Compare Josef Quint's modern German version: 'So also sage ich, daß es zwar Seligkeit nicht gibt, ohne daß der Mensch sich bewußt werde und wohl wisse, daß er Gott schaut und erkennt ... Denn der Mensch muß in sich selber Eins sein und muß dies suchen in sich und in Einen und empfangen in Einen, das heißt: Gott lediglich schauen; und <zurückkommen>, das heißt: wissen und erkennen, daß Man Gott erkennt und weiß. (*Von Edeln Menschen*, Josef Quint, ed. and trans. *Meister Eckehart: Deutsche Predigten und Traktate* (Munich: Carl Hanser, 1955), p. 148.
24. Hugo Rahner, art. cit., pp. 333–418.
25. Shizuteru Ueda, *Die Gottesgeburt in der Seele und der Durchbruch zur Gottheit. Die mystische Anthropologie Meister Eckharts und ihre Konfrontation mit der Mystik des Zen Buddhismus* (Gütersloh: Mohn, 1965). See Especailoyl, Bernard McGinn, *Mystical Thought*, op. cit., pp. 56–60.
26. Sermon 104 (Walshe No. 3, p. 25). He adds, significantly, 'This must be done with force, without force it cannot be done.' Similarly, in Sermon 102, we find Eckhart reaffirming that a master (most likely himself) says, 'To achieve an interior act, a man must collect all his powers as if into a corner of his soul where, hiding away from all images and forms, he can get to work.' Here he must come to a forgetting and an unknowing [*unwizzen*]. There must be a stillness and a silence . . . (Walshe No. 2, Vol. I, p. 20). Compare, 'For you to know God in God's way, your knowing must become a pure unknowing, and a forgetting of yourself and all creatures.' (Sermon 103 [Walshe No. 4, p. 40f., DP 59.]) As noted before, these sermons are now generally accepted as authentic and are numbered in the critical edition edited by Georg Steer, DW IV.
27. Sermon 54b (Walshe No. 46, Vol. II, p. 21).
28. See especially Chapter 44.
29. *The Nobleman* (*Von Edeln Menschen*), Walshe trans., III, p. 112. Eckhart continues (p. 113), 'How could a man know that he knows God, if he does not know himself? For indeed a man knows himself and other things not at all, but only God, when he gains felicity, in the root and ground of blessedness. But when the soul knows that she knows God, then she has knowledge of both God and herself.'
30. See Rufus Jones, 'Meister Eckhart: The Peak of the Range', *The Flowering of Mysticism in the Fourteenth Century* (New York: Hafner Publishing Co., 1971 [1939]), pp. 61–85.
31. Sermon 76 (Walshe No. 7, Vol. I, p. 65, DP 35). He continues, 'God makes us knowing Him, and His being is His knowing, and His making me know is the same as my knowing; so His knowing is mine just as in the master, what he teaches is one and the same as, in the pupil, what he is taught.'
32. Sermon 12 (Walshe No., 57, Vol. II, p. 87, DP 13). Objected to by Cologne

censors. Eckhart replied by citing Augustine, *De Trinitate* ix, 2 (Quint). For explanation of conjoint action, see Walshe, Vol. II, p. 100.

33. Sermon 68 (Walshe No. 69, Vol. II, p. 167, DP 36).
34. Sermon 77 (Walshe No. 49, Vol. II, p. 39).
35. *Talks of Instruction* No. 6, Walshe, Vol. III, p. 16.
36. Ibid., No. 7, Walshe, Vol. III, p. 20.
37. Mary Frances Coady, *With Bound Hands: A Jesuit in Nazi German – The Life and Selected Prison Letters of Alfred Delp* (Chicago: Loyola Press, 2003). I am indebted to Mrs Caroline Cracraft for this reference.
38. Sermon 75 (Walshe No. 88, Vol. II, pp. 282–3).

Bibliography

Among recent and enduringly relevant works (mainly in English) on the inter-faith significance of Eckhart's thought, I would especially include the following:

John Caputo, 'Heidegger, Eckhart and Zen Buddhism', *The Thomist* 42 (April 1978): 203–17.

Donald Goergen, O.P., 'Atman, Grunt, and Spirit: An Unfinished Reflection', *Eckhart Review* 15 (2006): 17–33.

Rudolf Otto, *Mysticism East and West*, Bertha Bracey and Richenda Payne, trans. (New York: Macmillan, 1960 (1933)).

Brian Pierce, O.P., 'Empty Fullness in the Eternal Now Eckhart and the Buddhists', *Eckhart Review* 15 (2005): 4–16.

Brian J. Pierce, O.P., *We Walk the Path Together: Learning from Thich Nhat Hanh and Meister Eckhart* (New York: Orbis Books, 2007).

Ajahn Santacitto, 'Eckhart from a Theravada Buddhist Viewpoint', *Eckhart Review* 2 (1993): 44–62.

Reiner Schürmann, 'Meister Eckhart and Zen Buddhism', in *Wandering Joy: Meister Eckhart's Mystical Philosophy* (Barrington, MA: Lindisfarne Books, 2001) (republication of *Meister Eckhart: Mystic and Philosopher*, Bloomington: Indiana University Press, 1978), appendix, pp. 221–6.

Reiner Schürmann, 'The Loss of Origin in Soto Zen and Meister Eckhart', *The Thomist* 42 (April 1978): 281–312.

Reiner Schürmann, 'Trois penseurs du relaissement, Maître Eckhart, Heidegger, Suzuki', *J. HiSt Phil.*, 12, 4 (October 1974): 455–78 and 13, 1 (January 1975): 43–60.

Michael Sells, 'Meister Eckhart and Ibn'Arabi on Time and Mystical Union', *Eckhart Review* 9 (1999): 2–19.

Reza Shah-Kazemi, 'Transcendence and Immanence: Common Themes in Eckhart, Ibn' Arabi and Shankara', *Eckhart Review* 6 (1997): 13–25.

D. T. Suzuki, 'Meister Eckhart and Buddhism', in *Mysticism Christian and Buddhist* (New York: Harper and Row, 1971).

Shizuteru Ueda, '"Nothingness" in Meister Eckhart and Zen Buddhism', James W. Heisig, trans., *The Buddha Eye: An Anthology of the Kyoto School*, Frederick Franck, ed. (New York: Crossroad, 1982) (repr. from *Tranzendenz und Immanenz: Philosophie und Theologie in der veränderten Welt*, ed. D. Papenfuss und J. Söring (Berlin: 1977)).

Shizuteru Ueda, *Die Gottesgeburt in der Seele und der Durchbruch zur Gottheit. Die mystische Anthropologie Meister Eckharts und ihre Konfrontation mit der Mystik des Zen Buddhismus* (Gütersloh: Mohn, 1965).

Bibliography

I. SOURCE DOCUMENTS

Meister Eckhart: Die deutschen und lateinischen Werke. Herausgegeben im Auftrage der Deutschen Forschungsgemeinschaft (Stuttgart and Berlin: Verlag W. Kohlhammer, 11 Vols, 1936–).

Josef Quint, ed. and trans., *Meister Eckehart: Deutsche Predigten und Traktate* (Munich: Carl Hanser, 1955).

Augustine Daniels, O.S.B., ed., 'Eine lateinische Rechtfertigungsschrift des Meister Eckharts', *Beiträge zur Geschichte der Philosophie des Mittelalters*, 23, 5 (Münster, 1923): 1, 4, 12, 13, 34–35, 65–66.

Franz Jostes, ed., *Meister Eckhart und seine Jünger: Ungedruckte zur Geschichte der deutschen Mystik* (De Gruyter, 1972) (Series: Deutsche Neudrucke Texte des Mittelalters).

Thomas Kaepelli, O.P., 'Kurz Mitteilungen über mittelalterliche Dominikanerschriftsteller', *Archivum Fratrum Praedicatorum* 10, (1940): 293–94. [Letter fragment of John XXII to Archbishop Henry II of Virneburg.]

Thomas Kaepelli, O.P., *Scriptores ordinis Praedicatorum medii aevi.* Vol. I (A–F) (Rome, 1970).

M. H. Laurent, 'Autour du procés de Maître Eckhart. Les documents des Archives Vaticanes', *Divus Thomas* (Piacenza) 39 (1936): 331–48, 430–47. Records of Eckhart's trials at Cologne and Avignon with related documents.

Franz Pelster, S.J., ed., Articuli contra Fratrem Aychardum Alamannum, Vat. lat. 3899, f. 123^r 130^v, in 'Ein Gutachten aus dem Eckehart Prozess in Avignon', *Aus der Geistewelt des Mittelalters, Festgabe Martin Grabmann*, Beiträge Supplement 3 (Munster, 1935), pp. 1099–1124. [Opinion of Avignon Commission against Eckhart.]

Gabriel Théry, O.P., 'Édition critique des piéces relatives au procés d'Eckhart continues dans le manuscrit 33b de la Bibliotheque de Soest', *Archives d'histoire littéraire et doctrinal du moyen âge*, 1 (1926): 129–268. [Eckhart's Defense at Cologne.]

II. TRANSLATIONS AND COMMENTARIES

The Complete Mystical Works of Meister Eckhart, M. O'C. Walshe, trans. and ed., revised with Foreword by Bernard McGinn (New York and London: Crossroad Publishing, 2009) (Revised edition of M. O'C. Walshe translation of 1987.)

Meister Eckhart, *Sermons and Treatises*, M. O'C. Walshe, trans., 3 vols (Longmead, Shaftesbury, Dorset: Element Books, 1987).

Meister Eckhart, *The Essential Sermons, Commentaries, Treatises and Defense*, Bernard McGinn and Edmund Colledge, ed. and trans. (New York: Paulist Press, 1981).

Ursula Fleming, ed., *Meister Eckhart: The Man from Whom God Hid Nothing* (Leominster: Gracewing, 1995).

Meister Eckhart: Teacher and Preacher, Bernard McGinn and Frank Tobin, eds (London: SPCK, 1987).

James Midgely Clark, *Meister Eckhart: An Introduction to the Study of His Works with an Anthology of His Sermons* (Edinburgh: Nelson, 1957).

James M. Clark and John V. Skinner, eds and trans., *Treatises and Sermons of Meister Eckhart* (New York: Octagon Books, 1983) (Reprint of Harper and Row edn, 1958).

Meister Eckhart: Selected Writings, Oliver Davies, ed. and trans. (London: Penguin, 1994).

III. BOOKS ON ECKHART (A SELECTION)

Jeanne Ancelet-Hustache, *Master Eckhart and the Rhineland Mystics* (New York and London: Harper and Row/Longmans, 1957).

Oliver Davies, *Meister Eckhart: Mystical Theologian* (London: SPCK, 1991).

Michael Demkovich, *Introducing Meister Eckhart* (Ottawa/Ligouri, MO: Novalis/Fides, 2005/6).

Robert K. Forman, *Meister Eckhart: Mystic as Theologian* (Rockport, Mass./Shaftesbury, Dorset: Element Books, 1991).

Amy Hollywood, *The Soul as Virgin Wife: Mechthild of Magdeburg, Marguerite Porete, and Meister Eckhart* (Notre Dame and London: University of Notre Dame Press, 1996).

C. F. Kelley, *Meister Eckhart on Divine Knowledge* (New Haven, CT: Yale University Press, 1977). Reprinted with a foreword by William Stranger (DharmaCafé Books (Random House), New York, 2009).

Bernard McGinn, *The Harvest of Mysticism in Medieval Germany* (Volume 4 of *The Presence of God*) (New York: Crossroad, 2005).

Bernard McGinn, ed., *Meister Eckhart and the Beguine Mystics Hadewijch of Brabant, Mechthild of Magdeburg, and Marguerite Porete* (New York: Continuum, 1994).

Bernard McGinn, *The Mystical Thought of Meister Eckhart: The Man from Whom God Hid Nothing* (New York: Crossroad, 2001).

Bruce Milem, *The Unspoken Word, Negative Theology in the German Sermons of Meister Eckhart* (Washington: Catholic University of America Press, 2002).

Cyprian Smith, *The Way of Paradox: Spiritual Life as Taught by Meister Eckhart* (London/New York: Darton, Longman and Todd/Paulist Press, 2004 edn (1987)).

P. H. Stirnimann and Rudi Imbach, eds, *Eckardus Theutonicus, homo doctus et sanctus* (University of Fribourg, 1993).

Frank Tobin, *Meister Eckhart: Thought and Language* (Philadelphia: University of Pennsylvania Press, 1986).

Richard Woods, O.P., *Eckhart's Way* (Dublin: Veritas Publications, rev. edn, 2009).

IV. ARTICLES

Benedict Ashley, O.P., 'Three Strands in the Thought of Eckhart, the Scholastic Theologian', *The Thomist* 42 (1978): 227, n.3.

John Caputo, 'The Nothingness of the Intellect in Meister Eckhart's Parisian Questions', *The Thomist* 39 (1975): 85–115.

Edmund Colledge, O.S.A., 'Meister Eckhart: His Times and His Writings', *The Thomist* 42 (April 1978) 2: 240–58.

Oliver Davies, 'Why Were Eckhart's Propositions Condemned?', *New Blackfriars* 71 (1990): 433–44.

Donald F. Duclow, '"My Suffering is God": Meister Eckhart's *Book of Divine Consolation*', *Theological Studies* 44 (December 1983): 570–86.

Henry L. Finch, 'A Note on Two Traditions in Western Mysticism: Meister Eckhart and Jacob Boehme', *Centerpoint* 3 (1978) 1: 41–50.

Margaret B. Guenther, 'The Spirituality of Eckhart's German Sermons', *Studies in Spirituality* 9 (1999): 93–108.

Alois M. Haas, 'The Nothingness of God and its Explosive Metaphors', *Eckhart Review* 8 (1999): 6–17.

Mark James, 'Individuation and Mystical Union: Jung and Eckhart', *Studies in Spirituality* 15 (2005): 91–108

Grace Jantzen, 'Eckhart and Women', *Eckhart Review* 3 (Spring 1994): 31–47.

Karl Kertz, 'Meister Eckhart's Teaching on the Birth of the Divine Word in the Soul', *Traditio* 15 (1959): 327–63.

Richard Kieckhefer, 'Meister Eckhart's Conception of Union with God', *Harvard Theological Review* 71 (1978): 203–25.

Dom David Knowles, O.S.B., 'Denifle and Ehrle', *History* 54 (1969), 1–12.

Niklaus Largier, 'Recent Work on Meister Eckhart. Positions, Problems, New Perspectives, 1990–1997', *Recherches de théologie et philosophie médiévales* 65 (1998) 1: 147–67.

Frans Maas, 'Meister Eckhart: Man's Divine Life', *Studies in Spirituality* 16 (2006): 71–109.

Bernard McGinn, 'Meister Eckhart: An Introduction', *An Introduction to the Medieval Mystics of Europe*, Paul E. Szarmach, ed. (Albany: State University of New York Press, 1984), pp. 237–57.

——— 'Meister Eckhart on God as Absolute Unity', *Neoplatonism and Christian Thought*, Dominic J. O'Meara, ed. (Albany: State University of New York Press, 1982), pp. 128–39.

——— 'The God beyond God', *Journal of Religion* 61 (1981): 1–19.

——— 'Meister Eckhart's Condemnation Reconsidered', *The Thomist* 44 (1980): 390–414.

——— 'St Bernard and Meister Eckhart', *Citeaux* 31 (1980): 373–86.

Bruce Milem, 'Meister Eckhart and the Image: Sermon 16b', *Eckhart Review* 8 (Spring 1999): 47–59.

Sr Margaret R. Miles, 'The Mystical Method of Meister Eckhart', *Studia Mystica* 4 (Winter 1981) 4: 57–71.

Steven Ozment, 'Eckhart and Luther: German Mysticism and Protestantism', *The Thomist* 42 (April 1978) 2: 259–80.

Reiner Schürmann, 'Meister Eckhart's 'Verbal' Understanding of Being as a Ground for Destruction of Practical Teleology', *Sprache und Erkenntnis im Mittelalter*, Jan P. Beckmann *et al.*, eds (Berlin and New York: Walter de Gruyter, 1981), pp. 803–9.

Walter Senner, 'Meister Eckhart in Köln', in Klaus Jacobi, ed., *Meister Eckhart. Lebensstationen – Redesituationen* (Quellen und Forschungen zur Geschichte des Dominikanerordens, Neue Folge, Bd. 7) (Berlin: Akademie-Verlag, 1997), pp. 207–37.

Ernst H. Soudek, 'Eckhart, Meister', in *Dictionary of the Middle Ages*, Vol. 4 (New York: Charles Scribner's, 1984).

Loris Sturlese, 'Mysticism and Theology in Meister Eckhart's Theory of the Image', *Eckhart Review* 2 (Spring 1993): 18–31.

———— 'A Portrait of Meister Eckhart', *Eckhart Review* 5 (Spring 1996): 7–12.

Frank Tobin, 'The Mystic as Poet: Meister Eckhart's German Sermon 69', *Studia Mystica* 2 (1979) 4: 61–75.

Shizuteru Ueda, '"Nothingness" in Meister Eckhart and Zen Buddhism', *The Buddha Eye: An Anthology of the Kyoto School*, Frederick Franck, ed. (New York: Crossroad, 1982) (repr. from *Tranzendenz und Immanenz: Philosophie und Theologie in der veränderten Welt*, D. Papenfuss und J. Söring, eds (Berlin: 1977. Trans. by James W. Heisig)).

Felix Vernet, 'The Dominicans', *Mediaeval Spirituality*, Benedictines of Talacre, trans. (St Louis, MO: B. Herder Book Co., 1930), pp. 53–65.

Wolfgang Wackernagel, 'Establishing the Being of Images: Master Eckhart and the Concept of Disimagination', Thomas Epstein, trans., *Diogenes* 162 (1993): 77–98.

———— 'Some Legendary Aspects of Meister Eckhart: The Aphorisms of the Twelve Masters', *Eckhart Review* 7 (Spring 1998): 30–41.

Richard Woods, 'The Condemnation of Meister Eckhart', *Spirituality* 33, 6 (November–December 2000): 342–7.

———— 'Eckhart's Imageless Image: Art, Spirituality, and the Apophatic Way', *Eckhart Review* 12 (Spring 2003): 5–20.

———— 'Eckhart's "Wayless Way"', paper and discussion, Ibn Arabi Society, 23 May 1992, Chisholme House, Roberton, Hawick, Roxburghshire, Scotland.

———— 'Ecology, Spirituality, and Eckhart: On Loving the World', *Eckhart Review* 11 (Spring 2002): 36–47.

———— 'I am the Son of God: Eckhart and Aquinas on the Incarnation', *Eckhart Review* (June 1992): 27–46.

———— 'Meister Eckhart and Contemplation', *Eckhart Review* 6 (Spring 1997): 3–12. Paper read at the Eckhart Society Conference, Plater College, Oxford, 1 September 1996.

———— 'Meister Eckhart: Mystic under Fire', *Priests and People* 8, 11 (November 1994): 433–8. ('Ekharto Reabilitacijos Belaukiant', Lithuanian trans. by Mantas Adoménas, *Naujasis Zidinys*, No. 5 (Vilnius, 1993): 72–5.)

———— 'Meister Eckhart and the Neoplatonic Heritage: The Thinker's Way to God', *The Thomist* (October 1990): 609–39.

———— 'Meister Eckhart on Pain, Suffering, and Healing', *Eckhart Review* 14 (Spring 2005): 5–29. Paper read at the Eckhart Society Conference, Plater College, Oxford, 27 August 2004.

———— 'Meister Eckhart: Preacher and Teacher', *God in Multicultural Society: Religion, Politics, and Globalization*, Edward Alam, ed. (Louaize, Lebanon: Notre Dame University Press, 2006), pp. 99–110:

———— 'Meister Eckhart's Wayless Way and the Nothingness of God', *Mysticism and Prophecy: The Dominican Tradition* (London and New York: Darton, Longman and Todd/Orbis Books, 1998), pp. 77–91.

———— 'Meister Eckhart's Wider Ecumenism', the Eckhart Society Conference, 16 March 2002, St Bartholomew-the-Great, London, England.

———— 'The Spiritual Doctrine of Meister Eckhart: Detachment for Commitment',

Alister Hardy Research Centre, Maria Assunta Centre, London, 21 April 1993
——— 'Women and Men in the Development of Late Medieval Mysticism', in Bernard McGinn, ed., *Meister Eckhart and the Beguine Mystics* (1994): 147–64.

ADDITIONAL REFERENCES

Frances Beer, *Women and Religious Experience in the Middle Ages* (Woodbridge, Suffolk and Rochester, NY: The Boydell Press, 1992).

Fiona Bowie and Oliver Davies, eds, *Hildegard of Bingen: An Anthology*, Robert Carver, trans. (London: SPCK, 1990).

Caroline Walker Bynum, *Fragmentation and Redemption: Essays on Gender and the Human Body in Medieval Religion* (Brooklyn: Zone Books, 1992).

Herbert Grundmann, *Religious Movements in the Middle Ages*, Steven Rowan, trans., intro. by Robert E. Lerner (Notre Dame and London: University of Notre Dame Press, 1995).

Maria Shrady, ed. and trans., *Johannes Tauler: Sermons* (New York: Paulist Press, 1987).

Frank Tobin, trans., ed. and commentary, *Henry Suso: The Exemplar with Two German Sermons*, preface by Bernard McGinn (New York: Paulist Press, 1989).

Index